Complete Catalan

Anna Poch Gasau and
Alan Yates

For UK order enquiries: please contact Bookpoint Ltd,
130 Milton Park, Abingdon, Oxon OX14 4SB.
Telephone: +44 (0) 1235 827720. *Fax:* +44 (0) 1235 400454.
Lines are open 09.00–17.00, Monday to Saturday, with a 24-hour
message answering service. Details about our titles and how to
order are available at www.teachyourself.com

For USA order enquiries: please contact McGraw-Hill
Customer Services, PO Box 545, Blacklick, OH 43004-0545, USA.
Telephone: 1-800-722-4726. *Fax:* 1-614-755-5645.

For Canada order enquiries: please contact McGraw-Hill
Ryerson Ltd, 300 Water St, Whitby, Ontario L1N 9B6, Canada.
Telephone: 905 430 5000. *Fax:* 905 430 5020.

Long renowned as the authoritative source for self-guided
learning – with more than 50 million copies sold worldwide –
the *Teach Yourself* series includes over 500 titles in the fields of
languages, crafts, hobbies, business, computing and education.

British Library Cataloguing in Publication Data: a catalogue record
for this title is available from the British Library.

Library of Congress Catalog Card Number: on file.

First published in UK 2004 as *Teach Yourself Catalan* by
Hodder Education, part of Hachette UK, 338 Euston Road,
London NW1 3BH.

This edition published 2010.

The *Teach Yourself* name is a registered trade mark of Hachette UK.

Typeset by MPS, a Macmillan Company.

Printed in Great Britain for Hodder Education, an Hachette UK
Company, 338 Euston Road, London NW1 3BH.

The publisher has used its best endeavours to ensure that the URLs
for external websites referred to in this book are correct and active
at the time of going to press. However, the publisher and the
author have no responsibility for the websites and can make no
guarantee that a site will remain live or that the content will remain
relevant, decent or appropriate.

Hachette UK's policy is to use papers that are natural, renewable
and recyclable products and made from wood grown in sustainable
forests. The logging and manufacturing processes are expected to
conform to the environmental regulations of the country of origin.

Impression number   10 9 8 7 6 5 4 3 2 1

Year   2014 2013 2012 2011 2010

Contents

Credits

Front cover: © Mark ZYLBER/Alamy

Back cover and pack: © Jakub Semeniuk/iStockphoto.com,
© Royalty-Free/Corbis, © agencyby/iStockphoto.com, © Andy
Cook/iStockphoto.com, © Christopher Ewing/iStockphoto.com,
© zebicho – Fotolia.com, © Geoffrey Holman/iStockphoto.com,
© Photodisc/Getty Images, © James C. Pruitt/iStockphoto.com,
© Mohamed Saber – Fotolia.com

Pack: © Stockbyte/Getty Images

Meet the authors

Anna Poch Gasau

I come from Cornellà del Terri, a village situated in central Catalonia between the Mediterranean to the East, the Pyrenees to the North and Barcelona to the South. I was born in 1972, when Franco's dictatorship was in its death throes, and I grew up speaking, reading and hearing only Catalan, except for cartoons on TV and school textbooks.

With a first degree in Catalan and Spanish language and literature, and after a short period working in a secondary school, I went travelling in Europe. I started in France, where I taught Catalan as a *lectora* at the Universities of Grenoble and Rennes. At the same time I obtained a master's degree in Romance Languages and undertook training in the teaching of French as a second language. Moving to England, I taught Spanish to adults and worked on a research project on sport in Catalan literature from the early twentieth century.

I am now living in France again, where I am a project manager in the languages department of a Chamber of Commerce training service unit. As well as providing foreign-language courses for private companies my work involves keeping up to date with language-teaching materials. My post also offers me opportunities to 'fly the Catalan flag'.

Alan Yates

I was born in Northampton at the end of the War and then spent my childhood in Sheffield where all of my schooling was done. In 1963 I won a scholarship to read Modern Languages (French and Spanish) at Cambridge, where I was introduced to Catalan. After graduation I began doctoral research on modern Catalan literature, moving to a lectureship at Sheffield University (1968) which enabled me to develop fully my interests in Catalan language and culture. The original version of Complete Catalan (1975) was a product of these circumstances, as were my early publications on the literature of Catalonia. I was made Professor of Catalan Studies in 1990.

From the beginning of my academic career I occupied various positions in the Anglo-Catalan Society. I have received several awards and prizes for contributions to Catalan linguistic and literary studies. In 2005 I was made a corresponding member of the Philological Section of the Institut d'Estudis Catalans.

Since official retirement in 1998 I have kept up my activities on both the linguistic and the literary fronts, and I have also been able to cultivate more actively my interest in translation. Regular 'working' visits to Catalonia and walking holidays in the Pyrenees keep me in touch with the region and with the many Catalan friends I have made over the years.

Only got a minute?

Catalan is the national language of Andorra and is co-official with Spanish in the autonomous Spanish communities of Catalonia, the Balearic Islands and Valencia. These make up by far the greatest part of the approximately 68,000 square kilometres of territory where Catalan is spoken, and of the total population of over 13 million. Of these, more than 9 million declare themselves to be Catalan-speakers, and a further 2 million register as 'understanding' the language. These totals also include the narrow fringe of eastern Aragon, where Catalan, without official status, shows continuing vitality; and then a more vestigial presence on the French side of the eastern Pyrenees and in the Sardinian town of L'Alguer/Alghero. (This present-day geographical distribution of the language reflects both its origins and its subsequent expansion from the early Middle Ages onwards.) The statistics for Catalan are interesting when compared with figures for *national languages* in a good number of established *nation states* within Europe. In terms of area, the Catalan domain ranks 27th out of over 50 European countries or dependencies, and in terms of numbers of speakers the language comes 22nd out of the 36 recognized 'mother tongues' of Europe. The figures demonstrate Catalan's status as by far the most widely spoken of Europe's 'minority' languages. This leads in turn to the concept of 'stateless nation' and the associated political issues. However, the main motivation for wanting to learn Catalan is likely to stem from considerations of a different order: that the Catalan-speaking parts of the Mediterranean world are much-favoured destinations for foreign visitors, and that the Catalans, through their language, enjoy an extraordinarily rich cultural inheritance of which many larger nations would be proud to boast.

Since the 1980s Catalan has occupied a prominent place in public life in the three autonomous Spanish communities where it enjoys co-official status. There are differences in language policy between Catalonia, the Balearics and Valencia, but social and official use of their 'own' language is a normal part of life for all the citizens of these regions, in local and regional government, in education, in culture and in the media.

5 Only got five minutes?

Catalan is a member of the Romance group of languages, a close relative then of French, Spanish, Italian, Portuguese, etc. This represents one of Catalan's strengths, in terms of adaptability, compared with the situation of other 'minority' languages, Basque for example in relation to Spanish, or Welsh up against world-wide English. But there is a down-side, too, in Catalan's proximity to Spanish: the subordinating influence, on many levels, of the politically dominant language.

From the perspective of the foreign learner, however, the family resemblances with its close relatives make Catalan a comfortably accessible language. French and Spanish, because of their geographical proximity and because of historical connections going back for many centuries, present the most substantial points of comparison. Those with some knowledge of the other two languages will encounter many features of Catalan vocabulary and grammar that are obviously similar and familiar. Indeed, because of its geographical position and its history, Catalan can usefully be looked on as a sort of 'bridge' between French and Spanish. Sometimes it is distinctly closer to one or the other, but there are many areas where Catalan appears to straddle the divide between its two neighbours.

We can consider first some examples where clear similarities with French are recognizable. Many individual Catalan words look (although they do not sound) identical to their French counterparts: **pont** (= *bridge*), **vent** (= *wind*), **fort** (= *strong*), **cas** (= *case*), **qui** (= *who*), etc., or very close indeed **faç**/*face* (= *face*), **llet**/*lait* (= *milk*), **perill**/*péril* (= *danger*), **llac**/*lac* (= *lake*), **lentament**/*lentement* (= *slowly*), **portar**/*porter* (with silent final -r in each case: = *to carry*), **fer**/*faire* (= *to do, make*), etc. Catalan too has its adverbial pronouns (**en** and **hi**) which behave very much like the corresponding French ones, *en* and *y*.

On the other hand there are numerous cases of identical forms in Catalan and Spanish vocabulary: **sí** (= *yes*), **pagar** (= *to pay*), **enviar** (= *to send*), **encantador** (= *charming*), etc. Or we can recognize the presence of the same root in both Catalan and Spanish words: **ceba**/*cebolla* (= *onion*), **manar**/*mandar*, (= *to order, command*), **comptar**/*contar* (= *to count*), **avinguda**/*avenida* (= *avenue*), **passejar**/*pasear* (= *to walk, stroll*), **meravellós**/*maravilloso* (= *marvellous*), **plàtan**/*plátano* (= *banana*) etc., etc. And just as Spanish has two verbs, *ser* and *estar*, which express different aspects of English *to be*, so too Catalan has both **ser** and **estar**, although their use and range are different.

Interestingly, certain features of Catalan combine similarities with both French and Spanish. We can take three instances. Negation in Catalan is generally expressed by **no** placed before the verb (as in Spanish), but there is a specialized, emphatic negative construction **no... pas** which is reminiscent of French *ne... pas*. The singular definite article in Catalan, as in Spanish, is **el** (masculine) or **la** (feminine): however, before a noun beginning with a vowel (or **h** + vowel) these Catalan articles take the apostrophized form, **l'**, just like French *le* and *la* becoming *l'* in this situation. Finally, variations in how the three languages express 'uncle' and 'aunt' present a curious lexical detail that perfectly illustrates the point being made here:

French	*l'oncle*	*la tante*
Spanish	*el tío*	*la tía*
Catalan	*l'oncle*	*la tia*

So far we have been looking at Catalan's similarities with two closely related languages. Brief mention should now be made of a few of the many features which are unique to it, especially in relation to Spanish. In its historical evolution Catalan showed a strong inclination to eliminate the final syllable of many Latin words, resulting in a consonantal ending. This, together with the tendency to retain the stressed vowel of the Latin root-word, has given the sound system of Catalan a distinctive staccato and consonantal effect, emphasized by the relatively high frequency of one-syllable words: **un poc de vi** (Spanish: *un poco de vino* = *a little wine*), **fa molts anys** (Spanish: *hace muchos años* = *many years ago*).

Catalan, like French, has the **ç** cedilla (often where Spanish has *z*: **plaça**/*plaza* = *square*), but is distinctive in using this letter in a final position: **capaç** (= *able*), **feliç** (= *happy*). The sound represented by ñ in Spanish (resembling *-ni-* in English *onion*) is shown in Catalan by the combination **ny**, which can also be a final consonant: **Catalunya** (= *Catalonia*), **lluny** (= *far*). Such two-letter combinations representing a single sound are known as digraphs, and Catalan has a pair of them, **-ig** and **-tx**, preceded by a vowel, which are used to write the sound of *ch-* as in English *chips* or *-tch* as in *fetch*: **faig** (= *beech tree*), **despatx** (= *office*). While Catalan coincides with Spanish in representing with double **ll** the sound similar to *-lli-* in English *million*, it is distinctive in having this digraph as the initial consonant of many words (where other languages have just the single l): **llibre** (Sp. *libro*, Fr. *livre*: = *book*), **llet** (Sp. *leche*, Fr. *lait*: = *milk*), **llac** (Sp. *lago*, Fr. *lac*: = *lake*). Unique to Catalan is use of the raised dot in the digraph **l·l**, representing a geminate (prolonged) *l* sound: **novel·la** (= *novel*), **intel·ligent** (= *intelligent*, *clever*).

The vowel system of Catalan is more complex than that of Spanish, as is described in the section on Pronunciation, with the five vowel letters representing a range of eight distinct sounds. A characteristic of the language is the frequency of the 'relaxed', neutral vowel (represented by either **a** or **e** in an unstressed position), sounding similar to the ending of English words like *sugar* and *butter*. Both **e** and **o**, when in the stressed position, can show an 'open' or a 'close' sound (see Pronunciation). When unstressed, **o** represents the same sound as **u**. The function of written accents in Catalan reflects the features of pronunciation outlined above. Where Spanish uses only the acute (´) accent to indicate stress, Catalan uses both this and the grave accent (`) according to whether the stressed vowel (**e** or **o**) is open or close. The 'French connection' comes into view once again.

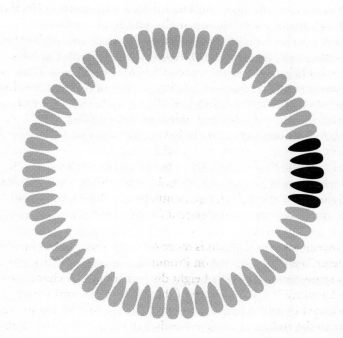

10 Only got ten minutes?

Standard Catalan is centred on the language of the Barcelona area (reaching northwards to Girona and southwards to Tarragona), referred to as the Eastern Central dialect. The dominance of this particular variety is due to historical and demographic factors as well as being a reflection of the importance and vitality of Barcelona itself as a major European metropolis which has performed and continues to perform all the functions of an authentic capital city. Barcelona's pre-eminent social, civic and cultural role has been enhanced in recent years by various factors: its influence as an economic hub and prominence in the politics of regional-government after the end of the Franco regime, the legacy of the 1992 Olympic Games, the successes and high international standing of FC Barcelona whose slogan proclaims it to be 'more than a club'...

To regard Catalan exclusively as the language of Barcelona, however, would be quite a false perspective. Such a view would misrepresent both the strength and relevance of the language throughout the region of Catalonia itself (with its other major 'provincial' centres like Girona, Lleida, Tarragona, etc.) and also the important contribution of the other main dialects of Catalan, including the Valencian and Balearic varieties, to the total complexion of the language.

The major dialect division is between Eastern and Western Catalan. The eastern group includes the variety spoken in French Catalonia and in the Pyrenean zone to the east of Andorra. To this group also belong Central Catalan (in the eastern part of Catalonia), the Balearic varieties and *alguerès* (in Sardinia). Western Catalan covers western and southern Catalonia, eastern Aragon and the Valencian territory. The map on page 1 illustrates this distribution.

The dialect differences of Catalan are comparable to those of other important languages, and all the dialects of Catalan are to a very high degree mutually intelligible. Divergences between them can be likened to those between British and American English, for example, or between the English heard in Northumberland and that heard in Cornwall. There are some very marked regional 'accents' and some particular variations of vocabulary and word-formation. Suffice it to say, though, that the spoken modality of standard Catalan is universally acceptable and that the written language is, to all intents and purposes, uniform. One may easily read a page of text in Catalan before coming on a feature which marks it as belonging to one regional standard variety rather than another.

We shall now look at some general points of comparison and contrast with English, as guidance for the interested learner about to embark on teaching her/himself Catalan. We begin with the similarities, which make access to Catalan relatively easy for the English speaker and provide encouragement to persevere. (This is in line with references to coincidences with French and Spanish which have been made already in the 5-minute summary.)

Vocabulary

Even as an outright beginner as soon as you hear (and even more so if you see in writing) a couple of sentences in Catalan you will almost certainly pick up the meaning of a good number of words. These may be identical to their English equivalents, or certainly very easy to recognize. This is particularly true of those words which in both languages derive from Latin or Greek roots: (Latin) **divisió** – *division*, **contemplar** – *to contemplate*, **perspectiva** – *perspective*, **possible** – *possible*, etc.; (Greek) **programa** – *programme*, **sistema** – *system*, **escola** – *school*, **gimnàs** – *gymnasium*, etc. You will be able also to deduce the meanings of many Catalan words from the similarity or correspondence between certain forms (especially word endings), for example Catalan **-ció** /English *-tion* (**acció** – *action*, **situació** – *situation*), **-at/-ty** (**llibertat** – *liberty*, **universitat** – *university*), **-ment/-ly** (**especialment** – *especially*, **exactament** – *exactly*), **-ic/-al** (**idèntic** – *identical*, **pràctic** – *practical*), **-ista/-ist** (**artista** – *artist*, **dentista** – *dentist*). But you must watch out for 'false friends', certain words which look the same but which have different meanings in Catalan and English: **actual** means *current, present* (not *actual*), **assistir** means *to attend, to be present* (not *to assist*), **carpeta** means *folder* or *file*, not *carpet*, etc. One more tip in this area: watch out for initial **es-** before certain consonants. This reflects a characteristic of Catalan pronunciation which might be a distraction from deducing the meaning of a particular word: **estació** – *station*, **escàndol** – *scandal*, **esperit** – *spirit*, **esquadra** – *squadron*, etc.

Grammar

To begin with, it is worth remarking that the standard sentence pattern of subject + verb + object is almost as frequent in Catalan as it is in English: **la cambrera no parla català** (= *the waitress does not speak Catalan*). This said, in sign-posting some key features of Catalan grammar it is worth focusing on certain significant contrasts rather than on similarities.

a) Nouns and gender.

All Catalan nouns (whether they signify persons, things or ideas) are either masculine or feminine. The neuter category of English for things and ideas is alien to Catalan. For many nouns gender might be indicated by certain particular word-ending: **-a**, for example, is predominantly a female ending, and the majority of words that end in **-ió** will be feminine too. This feature also affects articles (*the, a*) and adjectives, both of which reflect the number and the gender of the noun to which they apply, as in the following scheme:

el noi xinès = *the Chinese boy*
la noia xinesa = *the Chinese girl*
un fet curiós = *a curious fact*

una idea curiosa = *a curious idea*

els nois xinesos = *the Chinese boys*
les noies xineses = *the Chinese girls*
uns fets curiosos = *some curious facts*

unes idees curioses = *some curious ideas*

As seen above, adding final **-s** is the usual way of indicating the plural in Catalan, but this may entail certain (minor) changes in word-structure and spelling.

b) Adjectives.

In English, words which describe or qualify someone or something almost invariably stand before the noun(s) to which they apply. Catalan does place certain classes of adjectives before the noun, but the general pattern is for the qualifying word, the adjective, to come second:

el meu amic català = *my Catalan friend*

moltes flors boniques = *many pretty flowers*

c) Verbs.

The Catalan infinitive (English '*to…*') is always a single word: **parlar** = *to speak*, **venir** = *to come*, **saber** = *to know*. A major contrast with English is that the words for *I, you, he, she*, etc., are usually omitted in Catalan, as the verb ending itself is in most cases sufficient to indicate the person, as in **parlo francès** = *I speak French*, where the final **-o** indicates that the subject is *I*, and similarly for **parlem/parlen…** (= *we/they speak…*). Tense (*when* the action of the verb is presented as taking place: in the present, in the past or in the future) is also expressed by various modifications in verb-endings: from the infinitive **viure** we thus have **visc** (= *I live*), **vivia** (= *I used to live*), **viuré** = (*I shall live*).

The majority of Catalan verbs follow fixed patterns of change for the various tenses and these are called regular verbs. The largest class of these are the ones whose infinitive ends in **-ar**. Then there are two other sets of regular verbs: groups ending in either **-er/-re** or in **-ir**. Once the forms for a particular tense have been learnt the model can be applied to all the verbs in the same classification. Different tenses of the numerous first-conjugation verbs in **-ar**, for example, can be formed by studying and assimilating the behaviour of the model **parlar** (= to speak): **parlo**, I speak; **parlava**, I used to speak; **parlaré**, I shall speak; etc. The same is true to an extent for the other two classes of regular verbs, but these are less numerous and they can be affected by certain variations. For example, many regular verbs which end in **-ir**, take the increment **-eix-** before the ending in some parts of the present tense: thus **conduir** meaning to drive has **condueixo** for the first-person present (= I drive), etc. Features such as this will become familiar with study and practice.

The same can be said of the large family of verbs in Catalan, verbs which do not show the same uniformity as regular ones like **parlar**. These irregular verbs tend to be among the most frequently used ones (**ser**, to be; **tenir**, to have; **anar** to go, etc.), and there are no short-cuts to accuracy and fluency here.

Also under the heading of verbs, we can draw attention to the ways that Catalan has for addressing another person/other people. The Catalan for you has different forms indicating number (singular or plural) and also whether the speaker is adopting an informal/ familiar or formal/polite attitude. Generally, the informal **tu** (one person) and **vosaltres** (more than one person) are used to address friends, family members, equals, such as colleagues, and younger people, even if you have not met them before. Put another way, these are the forms applied in speaking to people with whom you are on first-name terms. Of course, as already mentioned, the corresponding form of the verb itself is usually sufficient, without the explicit presence of the pronoun: **parles/parleu català?** (= do you speak Catalan?). In more formal contexts, the polite forms **vostè** (singular) and **vostès** (plural) are used. These (just like Spanish **usted/ustedes**) go with the third-person of the verb, because the pronouns derive from the expression equivalent to 'your grace': **vostè viu a París?** (= do you live in Paris?). Since a degree of deference is entailed, the pronoun **vostè(s)** is less frequently suppressed than in the case of **tu/vosaltres**.

d) Questions and negative sentences.

Both of these aspects of Catalan are generally more straightforward than their counterparts in English. The commonest and simplest way of formulating a question in Catalan is by using the same words as in an affirmative statement but pronounced with a rising intonation: **ja no treballen aquí** (= *they don't work here any longer*), **ja no treballen aquí?** 'Tag questions', which are quite complicated in English, are very easily expressed in Catalan by use of the single word **oi?: no és tan difícil, oi?** (= *it isn't so difficult, is it?*).

To make a simple negative statement in Catalan all that is necessary is to place **no** before the verb: **puc fer-ho** (= *I can do it*), **no puc fer-ho** (= *I can't do it*). There are more subtle and complex aspects of negation in Catalan, but this basic pattern is very easy to assimilate.

Written accents

The relationship between pronunciation and spelling in Catalan determines the importance of written accents in this language. Both the acute (´) and the grave (`) accent are used, to indicate where the stress falls in certain words (reflecting the sound of the word as pronounced) and also to differentiate between pairs of words with different meanings but otherwise identical spellings. The letter **a** can carry (when required) only a grave accent **à**; **e** may appear with either an acute **é** or a grave **è** accent, according to its pronunciation; when an accent is required over **i**, this will be acute **í**; like **é/è**, the letter **o** may be written with either an acute **ó** or a grave **ò** accent, according to pronunciation; the letter **u** can be written (when required) only with an acute **ú** accent. The dieresis (¨) occurs in **ï**, indicating that in speech the **i** sound is pronounced separately and not merged into a diphthong with a preceding vowel. It is also appears in **ü** coming after **q** or **g**, to indicate the pronunciation of the **u** in the combinations **qü/gü**. So **qü** in **qüestió** sounds like English *qu* as in *quick*: otherwise Catalan **qu/gu** has the hard **k/g** sound of English. Other conventions of written Catalan are use of the cedilla **ç** and the raised dot in **l·l** indicating that the **l** sound is prolonged.

Capital letters

The use of capital letters in Catalan is less extensive than in English. The following words do not require capital letters in Catalan: nouns and adjectives corresponding to place names, including nationality (**menorquí, britànic, francès**); days of the week (**dilluns, dimarts**, etc.) and months of the year (**gener, febrer**, etc.); words denoting political groups and religions (**el partit comunista** – the Communist party, **la fe catòlica** – the Catholic faith), official titles (**el rei Enric IV** – King Henry IV, **el papa Climent I** – Pope Clement I), book and film titles, except for the first letter (**Diccionari de termes literaris** – Dictionary of Literary Terms, **L'altra cara de la lluna** – The Other Face of the Moon).

And now...

If you have read this far, the chances are that you have more than just a passing curiosity about the Catalan language. The title of this book (and the collection to which this book belongs) speaks for itself and we are confident that the contents live up to the claim expressed there. The written material, of course, goes hand in hand with the audio contents of the CDs. Before setting to work on these study materials, be sure to read very carefully the Introduction to the course, which gives advice on how to work with it and how to organize your study. The preliminary pages on Pronunciation and Spelling are not intended to be read once and not looked at again. You will derive much benefit by returning regularly to this section as your study of Catalan proceeds and as your competence in the language develops.

Whatever your motives in wanting to learn Catalan (personal, academic, cultural, commercial or professional) and whatever your communication needs, there are certain basic language activities which you will have to engage in and handle efficiently. The primary communication situations are covered in this book, from simple ones such as giving information about yourself, introducing yourself and others, asking for directions, shopping or ordering food, asking for travel information, etc, to more complex ones like talking about your work or your daily routine, using the phone, giving biographical information, talking about the past or the future, etc. Being able to deal with these adequately will in turn allow you to transfer what you have learnt to new situations thus expanding your capacity to communicate. When you finish this course you will, moreover, be in a strong position to develop further your competence in both spoken and written Catalan, having gained the right of access to a rich and proud culture at the very heart of Europe.

Acknowledgements

The authors are grateful to Virginia Catmur, Managing Editor of the Languages series in the Teach Yourself collection of Hodder Education, for her encouragement and sound advice throughout all the stages of preparation of this book. Thanks are also due to Rosemary Morlin for her scrupulous preparation of the text for the printers; and to the voices on the recording – Elisenda Marcer i Cortés, Carles Punsí Ribugent and Carme Rodríguez i Arenas, Sarah Sherborne, Jordi Vilaró i Berdusan Montserrat Estañol Xargay.

The authors and publishers wish to thank the following for permission to reproduce their copyright material: Avui newspaper; Vilaweb; the Departament de Sanitat i Seguretat Social of the Generalitat de Catalunya, and Sergi Pàmies through Editorial Quaderns Crema. Thanks also to Joan Nadal who kindly and sympathetically produced various pieces of artwork for this project; to various other friends who responded to enquiries and requests for material; and to Nita, Joan and Aleix.

Finally, we are indebted to Oier Bikondoa, without whose magnanimous support the project might have foundered and thanks to whom this book can be dedicated to Ibai: Katalana gure arteko hizkuntza izatea aukeratzeagatik, eskerrik asko.

Where Catalan is spoken

Eastern dialects

Western dialects

State frontier

Regional boundary

Language boundary

Introduction

Welcome to **Complete Catalan**

The fact that you are planning to use this book most probably
means that you already have an interest in or curiosity about
Catalan. You may already know something about where the
language is spoken, about its history and its status in the wider
family of European language communities. Space is not available
here to go into these matters, and for essential background
information of this kind you are referred to the titles listed in our
section **Taking it further**. Initially, though, a glance at the map on
page 1 will give a picture of where Catalan is spoken.

Of a population of over 13 million people some 9 million declare
themselves to be Catalan-speakers, and a further 2 million register
as 'understanding' the language. The geographical distribution
and the statistics are relevant to the status of Catalan as one of
the most prominent of Europe's 'minority' languages, and also to
the condition of the Catalan-speaking community as a 'stateless
nation'. These are not political abstractions. The more you are
able to enjoy communicating directly with Catalan-speakers the
more you will become aware of the *fet diferencial* – the 'differential
factor' founded in a commitment to their *own* language – and how
large this looms in their sense of identity and collective outlook.

You will be reassured to be told, at this point, that **Complete
Catalan** starts 'from scratch' and that the method you will be
following presupposes no previous knowledge of this language
and little or no previous experience of formal language study.

About this course

Using printed material alone to 'teach yourself' a new language
can be quite an uphill struggle. Success can be achieved, of course,
and this book has been designed so that it can be used by those
who choose to or have to study in such a way. Some people may
be lucky and be able to count on having contact with the living
language through native speakers among their acquaintances
who are prepared to give them help, or they may be studying in a
'total immersion' situation, residing, in this case, in a place where
Catalan is spoken. Such conditions may also be enjoyed, perhaps,
and be a bonus for the student who is using both the book and the
recorded material. We should also say here that no opportunity
should be lost to attend classes in the language if these are
available. This course has been planned so that it can work either
as a self-study complement to organized tuition or even as a course
book for use by a class. The idea of 'teaching yourself', though, is
our basic philosophy and method.

The importance of the recordings as the starting point for each unit
of the course has been alluded to in the 10 minute summary (clear
reference to the recorded materials are supplied giving CD and track
numbers throughout the book). Here you have the opportunity
to listen to native speakers talking naturally in real-life situations.
The type of language you are introduced to reproduces the features
of 'standard' or 'general' Catalan, which is based, mainly, on the
Central dialect of Barcelona and its region. The confines of this
course do not allow coverage of the variations of dialect and accent
which Catalan, like all languages, displays. Our map gives an initial
picture of the principal dialect divisions and some items in **Taking it
further** will guide those who wish to pursue the matter. Suffice it to
say, though, that the language you learn from this course will enable
you to communicate freely with Catalan-speakers from whichever
region, and that the written language is completely uniform.

The printed material of the course supplies transcriptions as
required, vocabulary, explanations of grammatical points and

cultural information necessary for you to understand fully the exchanges you can listen to in the recording. The complementary exercises then reinforce what you have studied in the dialogues, with additional vocabulary being introduced. This enables you to 'speak for yourself', communicating what you want to say, in the subject areas defined for each unit. The subject areas themselves reproduce real-life circumstances, combining situations familiar to foreign visitors with others where the perspective is that of the 'insider'. The various components of the course are integrated so that your competence is steadily developed in the four basic skills of listening and reading comprehension, speaking and writing.

How to work with the course and organize your study

Progression and other general features

The early units are carefully pitched at 'absolute beginner's' level. From Unit 5 onwards, with the gentle guidance still continuing, the pace begins to accelerate and you are encouraged to use the framework of the course to assimilate basic structures and extend your own capacity. Rather as for an athlete, it is expected that by now you will have established quite a rigorous training schedule, the benefits of which are evident in ever improving performance. In the last six units you reach what is known as intermediate or 'threshold' level, where it is assumed that material from earlier stages has been fully assimilated and that you are now capable of stretching yourself further and further.

The course units

The general plan of the course and the structure of individual units are as follows:

Pronunciation and spelling
This preliminary section describes the main phonetic features of spoken Catalan and how the sounds of the language are

reproduced in writing. The explanations given here will only make full sense when they are related to live examples, principally in the dialogues, as emphasized below. You are advised to keep referring back to this section as you practise 'speaking for yourself'. Most units contain an individual exercise which focuses on a particular feature of pronunciation. The symbol ◄» indicates that the recording is to be used for the section it refers to.

Dialogues

These are the backbone of the course. In the first place they present you with the sounds of Catalan in live contexts. You should study them carefully from this point of view, referring to the introductory section **Pronunciation and spelling**. Working with a partner or in a group will obviously make it easier for you to 'act out' the dialogues, as is suggested in each unit. If working alone, however, you will still be able to get your ear attuned to spoken Catalan and have ample practice in pronunciation following a reliable model.

The dialogues provide vocabulary and expressions at work in the topic area upon which each unit is built. New vocabulary introduced in the dialogues is given in **Quick vocab** where translation of individual entries is 'slanted' towards their meaning in the particular context. An asterisk before an entry here means that this item is covered in the **Grammar** section of the unit.

Author insight boxes

Each unit contains a number of these, clearly marked, which are intended to support the learning progress. They contain condensed information, clarification, cross-references and guidance on particular features of language use. They are based on the authors' varied experience as teachers, incorporating the perspectives of a native- and a non-native speaker of Catalan. The insights focus on elements that may at first be difficult to grasp or are essential cogs in the machinery of the language. They refer principally to aspects of grammar (and reinforce the relevant Grammar sections) but they also cover features of pronunciation, idiomatic usage, etc.

Exercises

True or false (*Veritat o fals*), or a similar comprehension exercise, is a straightforward initial test of whether you have understood the main contents of the dialogues. More Catalan is gradually introduced in this exercise, in step with your developing competence in the language. To reinforce and extend the content of the dialogues, there are several ensuing **Exercises**, varied in format, where the practical objectives defined for each unit are further worked upon. Before tackling the exercises you should be sure that you fully understand the dialogues themselves and feel confident about moving on to working with related materials that test your own powers of response and ability to communicate.

These activities are designed not as simple 'brain teasers' but rather to encourage you to use Catalan in a range of practical situations. Unlike the dialogues (where guidance is essential for assimilating the material), the exercises are not accompanied by lists translating the new vocabulary they may introduce. This is done deliberately so that your powers of interpretation or deduction of meaning are fully stretched. You will probably be surprised at how much sense you can make of utterances or exchanges even when you have not 'learned' some of the words they contain. In this way you come to acquire new vocabulary in the most active and productive way. When you do decide that you need to check on the meaning of a particular word you can then refer to the final Catalan–English wordlist, which provides full coverage of all the vocabulary used in the exercises.

Interspersed between the exercises of each unit are various other sections which are integrated into the total method of study.

Key words and sentences

This section is prominent in the early units, after which its function is subsumed into other components of the course, notably the end-of-unit résumés. The main objective is to supply you with essential vocabulary and expressions to serve as a kind of springboard into communication on topics closely tied to the stated objective of each unit. From Unit 10 onwards it is assumed that you have acquired both the habit of working in this way and the ability to build up your own repertoire of key words and sentences, taking your guidelines from the final résumé of each unit and using the word-lists at the end of the book.

Grammar

Here you are given straightforward explanations of the principal features of Catalan grammar as they are encountered in the dialogues (and further illustrated in the exercises). Specialized terminology is kept to a minimum, and where it is used, for economy of presentation, it is accompanied by clear illustration through examples. You will notice a steady progression as the description is gradually built up and as some of the issues involved become more demanding. The pace is deliberately restrained in the early units, to develop your ability to think about the language you are using in terms of its grammatical structures. After this point you are gently stretched further and grammatical explanations are made more complete. By the end of the course, for example, you will have been introduced to all the main tenses of Catalan verbs, will have seen the passive voice in action and will even have had a first introduction to use the subjunctive mood. You will also have acquired confidence in using object pronouns and even working with sentences in which two such pronouns are combined with a verb. This component of grammatical theory and explanation, though, is neither the starting point nor an end in itself of the method you are following. Rather it is integrated into the course, linked to the themes and expressive skills focused on in each unit, so that you acquire a secure formal basis for interpreting what you hear and read, and for being able to generate your own authentic Catalan.

Cultural information

As we are aiming at linguistic competence in real-life situations, most units contain a brief explanation of a salient aspect of life, behaviour or culture in the Catalan-speaking areas. This information is designed to help you 'feel at home' when using the language.

Reading

From Unit 5 onwards a specific reading exercise is incorporated in some units, to reinforce this aspect of comprehension.

End-of-unit summaries

You are given ten key points highlighting material that has been introduced in the unit in question. The main component comprises vocabulary, structures and idioms relating to the topic of the unit. Then there are succinct pointers to the main grammatical structures that have been presented in the unit. This item is not intended simply as a checklist to be referred to passively. It is meant to help you reflect on what you have been studying, and to provide a basis on which to actively extend your own communicative proficiency. A simple way to apply this is to create for yourself a number of varied sentences or exchanges based on the samples provided. The summary also offers a diagnostic tool relating to your own progress. Before proceeding to work on the following unit, you should be confident that you can respond to and use the range of vocabulary and the key expressions indicated in the sample sentences given. Likewise you should have a clear idea of the main grammatical structures referred to and of how they function. Any necessary revision will thus be sign-posted by constructive use of the summaries.

Key to the exercises

You will find this answer section is basically for self-correction as you are working through the course.

Reference tables

As the main grammar contents of the course are integrated progressively into the units, this section provides only a summary, in tabular form, of information about gender and number of nouns / adjectives, about weak pronouns in relation to the verb they accompany and about the conjugation of irregular verbs.

Vocabulary

The Catalan–English list brings together, for reference, all the main vocabulary that appears both in the dialogues and in the various exercises. Note again what is said above about words introduced in the exercises. Also provided is a short Catalan–English wordlist which should be useful as a reference tool of first resort in communicating what you want to say.

Taking it further
This section provides information about supplementary tools for study of the language, and sources for 'background' on the history of the language, Catalan society, culture and politics.

Index
This provides easy reference to information about grammatical features.

Pronunciation and spelling

This section is designed to accompany the recorded materials of the course (see the Introduction). (If you do not have the recording you will still benefit from studying the guidelines given below.) All the examples given here can be heard and practised in the first part of the recording.

Syllables and stress

◄) **CD1, TR 1**

Most Catalan words of one syllable are stressed (**gros, set, vuit**), but **que** and **i**, articles (**el, la**, etc.), weak pronouns (**em, ens**, etc.) and some prepositions (**a, de, en, amb, per**) are pronounced without stress. You will notice how Catalan words of more than one syllable are stressed on one of the syllables: **cog-nOm, san-dA-li-es**. Also you will notice how certain vowels carry written accents. The two features are related. To understand it, you have to know that a Catalan word, generally, has as many syllables as it has vowels. Exceptions to this are:

a **qu** and **gu** before e and i, representing a single consonant like the hard *c* and *g* in English *cat* and *gun*: **quina, guerra**.
b Certain groups of two vowels, known as diphthongs, forming a single syllable: **sisplau, riu, ous**. Diphthongs are formed with a vowel + i (except i + i) and vowel + u. Other examples are: **espai, avui, teu**. Be careful because other two-vowel combinations, like **ia** or **ue** are not diphthongs, so they are pronounced as two syllables: **ve-ni-es, his-tò-ri-a, du-es**.

Without a written accent a word of more than one syllable will have the stress on the next-to-last syllable if the word ends with a vowel (excluding diphthongs), a vowel + -s, -en or -in: **parlo**, **parles, parlen**. Otherwise stress will be on the final syllable: **parlem**, **parleu**. A written accent on a vowel indicates that these two principles do not apply, and that stress falls on the vowel carrying the accent: **màquina, església, acció, gimnàs**.

The diaeresis on **ü** or **ï** indicates that there is no diphthong involving the preceding vowel (**veí/veïna, país/països**) or (in the case of **gü** and **qü**) that the **u** is pronounced (like English *w*) before the following vowel (**qüestió, següent**).

Vowels

🔊 **CD1, TR 2**

Stressed vowels

a When stressed, Catalan **a** shows a sound between the *a* of standard English in *cat* and *father*: **pa, anys**. As this is always an open sound, letter **a** can take only a grave accent (**català, germà**) when stress has to be indicated in writing.

i and u The sounds represented by **i** and **u** in stressed positions are always 'close' (pronounced with the lips slightly extended), and both can thus take only the acute accent (**matí, menú**). These vowels are pronounced, respectively, like *ee* in English *feet* and *oo* in English *hoot*: **mida, alguna**.

e and o In the stressed position each of these vowels can represent either an open or a close sound. This is why these vowels can carry either a grave or an acute accent.

▶ Open **e** like the sound represented by *e* in English *get*, *bet*: **vostè, guerra**.
▶ Close **e** involves making a more 'forward' **e** sound, with the mouth becoming half-closed and the lips slightly extended: **bé, adéu, gens**.

- ▶ Open o like the sound represented by *o* in English *hot coffee*: **bona, però, història**.
- ▶ Close o involves a more 'backward' sound, with the mouth more closed, like the *o* in English *note* (without the final 'glide'): **fons, meló, estació**.

Unstressed vowels

The full range of Catalan vowel sounds is completed by a 'relaxed' vowel, always unstressed. This is the neutral sound represented by the *a* and *e* in the endings of English *sugar* and *butter*. In Catalan this sound is also represented by **a** or **e**, when either is in an unstressed position. If we show this unstressed sound as ə, observe in the first dialogue of Unit 1 the pronunciation, for example, of:

Perdoni, senyor, el punt de trobada?
pərdoni sənyor əl punt də trobadə

In an unstressed position o represents the same sound as **u**, Showing it as μ, observe on the recording the pronunciation, for example, of:

Ho sento, no ho entenc.
hμ sentμ no hμ entenc

While regional variations occur in pronunciation, the conventions of the written language (spelling, written accents, etc.) are uniform throughout.

Consonants

◀) **CD1, TR 3**

The sounds of Catalan consonants are, in general, very similar to their English counterparts. Here your attention is drawn to some differences.

b and v	Mostly like *b* in English *bat*, but sometimes (notably between vowels) having a 'softer' sound, with only very slight contact between the lips: **dèbil, hivern.**
ç	Sounding like *c* in English *acid*, ç appears only before **a**, **o** and **u** or at the end of the word: **adreça, cançó, feliç**, and has the same sound as the **c** before **e** and **i** (cf. **cèntim, ciutat, acceptar**).
d	Generally more 'dental' than English *d* (pronounced with the tip of the tongue on the teeth), notice how it sounds like English *th* in *they* when appearing between vowels (and in certain other contexts): **dedicar, cada, perdona.**
g	Followed by **e** or **i**, shows a sound like *s* in English *measure*: **germà, Girona.**
h	Always silent, as in **hora, hivern.**
j	In any position shows the same sound as **ge** and **gi** (see above): **jardí, juliol, mitja.**
l	Pronounced generally from further back in the mouth than usual English *l* (closer to *ll* in *all*). This effect is even stronger with **l** in final position: **lavabo, abril, total.**
r	Pronounced in most positions with the single 'trill', more rolled than English *r* (closer to Scottish pronunciation), as in **ara, Carme.** The trill is double, strongly rolled (see **rr**, below), at the beginning of a word or after **l, m, n, s**: **roba, riure, enraonar.**
s	Generally 'unvoiced', like *s* in English *say*, as in **sal, després, capses.** A 'voiced' sibilant sound (like *s* in *rose*) is represented by single **s** between vowels or before a 'voiced' consonant: **cosa, empreses, turisme.**
x	Represents three different sounds, according to position and to contiguous sounds: like *sh* in English *sherry*, **xai, xerrar**; like *x* in *tax*, **taxi, explicar**; like *gs* in *legs*, **èxit, exacte.**

Besides the individual consonants there are some pairs of consonants, or vowel and consonant, which represent a single sound. These are called digraphs and they play an important part in the Catalan pronunciation and spelling system:

-ix	After a vowel **-ix** is pronounced like the *sh* in English *shellfish* and like initial Catalan **x**: compare **mateix, caixa** with **xai**, that you have just heard.

ny	Shows a sound rather like *ni* in English *onion*: **juny, Catalunya.**
ll	Shows a sound rather like *lli* in English *million*: **lluny, bacallà, mirall.**
rr	Represents a strongly rolled **r** (more Scottish than English: see **r** above): **carretera, arribar.**
ss	Represents, between vowels, the 'unvoiced' **s** sound (like in English classic: cf. **ç** and **s**, above): **dissabte, espessa.**
l.l	Corresponds to a reinforced **l** sound, as in **pel·lícula, intel·ligent.**
qu, gu	See above.
-ig, -tx	Represent the sound *tch* in English *catch*: **maig, passeig, mig, cotxe.**
tz	Sounds like *ds* in English *beds*: **dotze, tretze.**
-tg, -tj	(**tg** + **e/i** and **tj** + **a/o/u**) sound like *dge* in English *edge*, as in **metge, mitjó.**

The behaviour of some 'silent' consonants is described in the section on 'word liaison'.

Written representation (spelling, accents) of sounds

◀) CD1, TR 4

The sets of words listed below illustrate the principles described in the preceding pages. As you listen, pay close attention to how the words are written. You will observe how spelling modifications and accentuation frequently reflect consistency of pronunciation. Again, the gap provides space for you to imitate what you hear, and then to check this against the recorded model.

València/valencià/valenciana   Puigcerdà/La Seu d'Urgell
Arenys de Mar/Ripoll   coixí/coixins
Eugeni/Eugènia   any/anys

autobús/autobusos
oli/oliós
difícil/dificilíssim
quedar/qüestió
taronja/taronges
truco/truques
plaça/places
placa/plaques
únic/unir

veí/veïns/veïnes
català/catalans/catalanes
escocès/escocesa/escocesos
aigua/aigües
mig/mitja/mitjà
porro/porró
origen/orígens
patata/patates
campus/campió/campions

Word liaison

In natural speech, in accordance with meaning and spontaneous
patterns of utterance, two or more words are often 'run together'.
Such groupings become the basic unit of pronunciation, rather than
individual words which are conventions of the written language.
Word liaison, as this phenomenon is called, is something which
'comes naturally' in the sense that it corresponds to how the speech
organs behave when uttering sounds in sequence. In seeking fluency
in Catalan, your main attention should be upon careful listening to
and imitation of this aspect of native speech. Good general advice
is to observe especially:

a) vowels in contact,
b) final/initial consonants of words which may be affected by
pronunciation of the immediately contiguous sounds,
c) instances (with exceptions) of: final -r, silent in most cases;
silent t, in the endings vowel + lt, vowel + nt, pronounced before a
following vowel; silent b of amb, pronounced before a following
vowel.

Practising word liaison

The recording illustrates the features just described (and some additional details). It is designed to prepare you for subsequent work in this important part of the 'teach yourself' process. The sets of words listed here contain instances of how particular sounds are affected by contact with their neighbours. Before listening, and then repeating the examples for yourself, look carefully at each set of words and try to anticipate how word liaison will operate.

els	els altres
dues peces	dues noies
feliç	feliçment
mig	migdia
maig	maig i abril
vint	vint-i-dos
parlar	parlar-ne
dormir	dormir-hi
nord	nord-est
anar	anar al cine/anar-hi
hi arribava	no arribava
és inútil	serà inútil
fred	freda i humida
pa amb tomàquet	pa amb oli
cap home	cap dona
peix fresc	peix gros
vaig cantar	vaig venir
un fill	un marit
fil negre	fil groc
la sang	sang i aigua
cinc filles	cinc obres
porta tancada	porta oberta
vols callar?	vols venir amb mi?
carrer ample	carrer estret

Benvingut!
Welcome!

In this unit you will learn
- *How to greet someone*
- *How to introduce yourself*
- *How to attract someone's attention*
- *How to say and ask where someone is from*

1 Com va això? *How are things?*

Tim, a young Englishman, arrives at Barcelona Sants train station where some Catalan friends are waiting for him at **el punt de trobada** *the meeting point*. Before they meet he asks for help in the Information Office.

Tim	Perdoni, senyor, el punt de trobada?
Informació	És aquí mateix.
Tim	Moltes gràcies.
Informació	De res.
Tim	Ei, Montse, Carles! Sóc aquí!
Montse	Hola Tim. Com va això?
Tim	Molt bé, i vosaltres?
Carles	Bé, també.

CD1, TR 6, 00:02

perdoni, senyor/-a *excuse me, sir/madam*
*és *it is*
aquí (mateix) *(right) here*
(moltes) gràcies *(many) thanks/thank you (very much)*
de res *you are welcome*
ei! *hey!*
*sóc *I am*
hola *hello*
(molt) bé *(very) well*
i *and*
vosaltres *you* (plural)
també *also*

*Throughout the course an asterisk in the vocabulary box means that the entry thus marked is referred to in the **Grammar** section.

Insight

De res means literally *for nothing*, but is obviously not translated as such. In Catalan it is customary to reply thus (or with an equivalent formula) whenever someone thanks you. Not to do so would appear impolite.

Insight

Hola! is the commonest way of greeting someone. We also hear in this dialogue **ei!** with the same meaning. As well as expressing *hello!* **ei!** is also used to draw attention to something, to make an objection or to point out a mistake, as, for example, in a statement like **Ei, això no és correcte!** *Hey! this is not correct.*

---

2 Com et dius? *What's your name?*

With Carles and Montse there is another girl, Isabel, who doesn't know Tim.

Tim	Bon dia, com et dius?
Isabel	Em dic Isabel, sóc una amiga d'en Carles. I tu ets en Tim, oi?
Tim	Sí, exacte.
Isabel	Molt de gust.
Tim	Igualment. I de cognom, com et dius?
Isabel	Freixa.
Tim	Com s'escriu això? Ho pots lletrejar?
Isabel	F de Figueres, R de Rosa, E d'Eva, I d'Isabel, X de Xavi i A d'Anna.

QUICK VOCAB

bon dia *good morning*
*em dic *my name is*
un amic/una amiga *a friend (male/female)*
*en + masculine name *personal article*
*tu ets *you are*
oi? *is/isn't that so?*
sí, exacte *yes, that's right*
molt de gust *nice to meet you*
igualment *likewise*
de *from, of*
el cognom *family name*
com s'escriu això? *how do you write it?*
ho pots lletrejar? *can you spell it/that?*

Insight

com et dius? – em dic... are formed from what is known as the 'reflexive' form of the verb **dir** (*to say, tell*). You can study how it is used for persons other than *I* and *you* in Grammar section B. Another instance of a verb used 'reflexively' is present in this dialogue (**com s'escriu això?**) and further ones will appear in the next two units. In Unit 5 you will be given a basic explanation of this construction. For the time being, though, it is best to concentrate on assimilating examples as they occur, taking them as set phrases or vocabulary items.

3 Sóc de Tarragona *I am from Tarragona*

A lady at the station talks to Tim thinking he is someone she has come to meet.

◀ CD1, TR 6, 02:22

Senyora Vicens	Hola, bon dia, vostè és en Bill Wright?
Tim	No, senyora.
Senyora Vicens	Ostres, ho sento! Jo sóc la Núria Vicens i espero un senyor de Londres, en Bill.
Tim	Doncs jo també sóc anglès, però em dic Tim i sóc de Bristol. I vostè d'on és?
Senyora Vicens	Jo sóc catalana, de Montroig.
Tim	Bé, adéu.
Senyora Vicens	Adéu, que vagi bé!

QUICK VOCAB

*vostè és *you are*
ostres! *gosh!*
ho sento *I am sorry*
espero *I'm waiting for*
Londres *London*
doncs *well*
*anglès/-esa *English*
però *but*
on *where*
adéu *good-bye*
que vagi bé! *all the best!*

Insight

The use of capital letters in Catalan is less extensive than in English. The following words do not require capital letters in Catalan: nouns and adjectives corresponding to place names, including nationality (**menorquí, britànic**), days of the week (**dilluns, dimarts**, etc.) and months of the year (**gener, febrer**, etc.), words denoting political groups and religion (**el partit comunista** – the Communist party, **la fe**

catòlica – the Catholic faith), official titles (**el rei Enric IV** – King Henry IV, **el papa Climent I** – Pope Clement I).

Exercise 1
Listen to the dialogues again and make sure you understand everything. Try to repeat them from the written text, imitating the Catalan pronunciation as closely as possible.

Exercise 2
◄) **CD1, TR 7, 00:02**

Now listen to the letters of the alphabet in Catalan and repeat them:

a, b, c, ç, d, e, f, g, h, i, j, k, l, m, n, o, p, q, r, s, t, u, v, w, x, y, z

Insight
The only unfamiliar letter here will be **ç** (**ce trencada**) which appears in words like **feliç** *happy*, **caça** *hunting*. Not included in the alphabet as presented is **l·l** (**ela geminada**), which is peculiar to Catalan and is found in words like **col·legi** *school*. A double letter is presented as **doble** or **dues** except **ll**, which is always referred to as **ella**.

Exercise 3
◄) **CD1, TR 7, 01:48**

Listen to someone spelling out six words, and write them down.

Useful expressions

◄) **CD1, TR 7, 02:51**

Listen to some expressions you need to know to ask for help or explanation. These are written out for you below.

Què vol dir ...?	What does ... mean?
Com es diu en català...?	How do you say ... in Catalan?
Ho pot repetir, sisplau?	Can you say it again, please?
Parli més a poc a poc, sisplau.	Please, speak more slowly.
Ho sento, no ho entenc.	I'm sorry, but I don't understand (it).

Numbers 0–10

◄)) **CD1, TR 7, 03:35**

0 zero	4 quatre	8 vuit
1 u	5 cinc	9 nou
2 dos	6 sis	10 deu
3 tres	7 set	

Cultural information
Polite mode of address (*vostè* vs. *tu*)

Addressing a person for whom 'first name terms' are appropiate (children, relatives, friends, close acquaintances or colleagues, etc.) the **tu** you (singular) form of the verb is used. The **vosaltres** you (second-person plural) form is used for addressing more than one person in these categories.

| **Ets (tu) anglesa?** | *Are you English?* |
| **Com us dieu (vosaltres)?** | *What are your names?* |

When one addresses someone who does not fall into these categories of familiarity or someone to whom particular respect is due, a special polite form is used. This involves use of **vostè** (plural **vostès**). It is always followed by a verb in the third person:

És (vostè) anglesa?
Com es diuen (vostès)?

Exercise 4

Change **tu** in this conversation into vostè:

Pere	Hola, ets el senyor Reig?
Sr. Reig	Sí, i tu com et dius?
Pere	Jo sóc en Pere Marquès, de Lleida. I tu, d'on ets?
Sr. Reig	Sóc de Lleida també, com tu!

Key words and sentences

Greeting someone

Hola, com va això?	*Hello, how are things?*
Com estàs? Com està?	*How are you? (informal/formal)*
(Molt) bé/malament.	*(Very) well/bad.*
I tu?	*And (how are) you?*
Bon dia./Bona tarda./	*Good morning./Good afternoon./*
Bona nit.	*Good night.*

Saying who you are

Com et dius? Com es diu?	*What's your name? (informal/formal)*
Em dic Natàlia.	*My name is Natalia.*
Ets la Natàlia?	*Are you Natalia?*
Molt de gust, encantat/-da.	*Nice to meet you.*
Igualment.	*Likewise.*

Attracting someone's attention

Perdona/Perdoni!	*Excuse me (informal/formal).*
Ei, hola!	*Hey, hello!*

Questions and statements about place of origin

D'on ets?/D'on és?	*Where are you from?* *(informal/formal)*
Sóc de París.	*I am from Paris.*
Sóc francès. / Sóc francesa.	*I am French* (m/f).

Exercise 5

Match each sentence on the left with one on the right:

1 Bon dia, Pere!
2 Com va això?
3 Et dius Anna?
4 Jo em dic Mireia.

a Doncs jo sóc l'Aleix.
b Hola!
c Bé, i tu?
d Sí, i tu?

Grammar

A The verb *ser* and personal pronouns

(jo) sóc	*I am*
(tu) ets	*you are*
(ell) és	*he is*
(ella) és	*she is*
(vostè) és	*you* (formal) *are*
(nosaltres) som	*we are*
(vosaltres) sou	*you are*
(ells) són	*they are*
(elles) són	*they are*
(vostès) són	*you* (formal) *are*

The personal or subject pronoun in Catalan is very frequently omitted, even when no other subject of the verb is expressed. This is possible because the verb itself conveys which person is indicated. **Són** means *they are*, **som** means *we are*, and so on.

When the pronoun is used it is to give emphasis or to avoid ambiguity.

Insight

What is explained above about subject pronouns is well illustrated in Dialogues 2 and 3: study them again, paying particular attention to where the pronoun is present and where it does not appear. The polite forms **vostè/vostès** (see the Information section at the beginning of the book) are omitted less often than the other subject pronouns, because of the deference implied.

B The verb *dir-se* 'to be called'

(jo) em dic	*my name is*
(tu) et dius	*your name is*
(ell) es diu	*his name is*
(ella) es diu	*her name is*
(nosaltres) ens diem	*our names are*
(vosaltres) us dieu	*your names are*
(ells) es diuen	*their names are*
(elles) es diuen	*their names are*

C An introduction to nouns and articles

Nouns denote persons (**noi** *boy*), things (**cadira** *chair*) or abstractions (**amor** *love*). All Catalan nouns are either masculine or feminine, whether personal/animate or non-personal/ inanimate. The definite article *the* is **el** or **l'** for masculine singular nouns and **la** or **l'** for feminine ones. The shortened form **l'** appears before masculine and feminine singular nouns begining with a vowel or **h**+ vowel: **el cafè** but **l'home; la sortida** but **l'amiga**.

The word for *a* (the indefinite article) is **un** for the masculine singular and **una** for feminine singular: **un noi** *a boy*, **una noia** *a girl*. We look at plural articles in Unit 2.

D The personal article

As in Dialogue 2 (**en Carles**) and Dialogue 3 (**la Núria Vicens**), before personal names or surnames the definite article is often used with little or no change of emphasis: **el** and **en** are used before masculine names begining with a consonant, **en Joan, el Miquel;** **la** before feminine names begining with a consonant, **la Marta, la Carla; l'** is used before masculine or feminine names begining with a vowel or **h** + vowel: **l'Arnau, l'Helena.** Note that this article is not used when the person is addressed directly (**escolta, Maria** *listen, Maria*). Note also that it appears with **ser** but not with **dir-se: sóc en Pere,** but **em dic Pere.**

Exercise 6
Put a personal article before these names:

1	Imma	**4**	Jordi
2	Tomàs	**5**	Carme
3	Hortènsia	**6**	Enric

Exercise 7
Complete the sentences with the correct form of the verb **dir-se** or **ser**:

1 Ella _____ Maria.
2 Vostè _____ en Pere Pujol?
3 Tu _____ l'Arnau.
4 Jo _____ la Lídia.
5 Ells _____ en Miquel i en Santi.
6 Nosaltres _____ Carme i Eva.

Grammar

E Descriptive or qualifying words (adjectives)

The foreigner (**estranger/estrangera**) is often in the position of explaining where he/she is from or his/her nationality. Feminine identity is regularly indicated in Catalan by the ending **-a**, as in **senyor/senyora, estranger/estrangera**. Where Tim says here **sóc anglès**, an English girl or woman would say **sóc anglesa**, while the masculine equivalent of Sra. Vicens's **sóc catalana** would be **sóc català**.

This regular indication of feminine identity is both for personal and non-personal nouns, as seen in this basic scheme:

Masculine	*Feminine*
bon dia *good day*	bona nit *good night*
en Nils és suec *Nils is Swedish*	la May és sueca *May is Swedish*
molt pa *a lot of bread*	molta farina *a lot of flour*

To be observed for later practice is the fact that the usual position for descriptive or qualifying adjectives in Catalan is after the noun: **un llibre danès** *a Danish book*, **una pel·lícula danesa** *a Danish film*; **un llibre bo** *a good book*, **una pel·lícula bona** *a good film*.

In the expression **moltes gràcies** we have met the distinctive feminine plural ending **-es**. So we would say **la Núria i l'Amèlia són catalanes** *Nuria and Amelia are Catalans*. More attention to these questions will be paid at several points in future units.

Exercise 8
Look at the country or town the people below come from and then supply the appropriate adjective (from the box below) for their origin or nationality. You will in some cases have to make the appropriate agreement for gender.

Example: L'Antònia Ferriol és de Mallorca. És mallorquina.

1 En Sean Connery és d'Escòcia. És _____.
2 En Cormac O'Callaghan és de Dublín. És _____.
3 La Mary Shelley és d'Anglaterra. És _____.
4 La Sofia Loren és d'Itàlia. És _____.
5 L'Antonio Banderas és d'Andalusia. És _____.
6 La Carmen Robles és d'Espanya. És _____.

7 El Gérard Depardieu és de França. És _____.

8 La Yaki Takamoto és del Japó. És _____.

---

italià, espanyol, irlandès, andalús, anglès,
escocès, francès, japonès

Exercise 9

Someone stops you in the airport. Complete the following conversation.

Turista	Bon dia. Que ets en Marcel?
(You)	1 _____.
Turista	Ho sento. 2 _____?
(You)	Sóc del Canadà.
Turista	Molt de gust. Adéu!
(You)	3 _____!

Insight

At the end of this first unit you may perhaps feel rather overwhelmed by the amount of challenging material that has been presented here. This is understandable. When you first set about learning an unfamiliar language, there are so many features that are new to you, demanding a big mental effort to take them on board. Even the simplest utterance in the language you have begun to study opens directly onto its particular structures and complexities. Gradually becoming familiar with these is essential to gaining confidence and fluency. Do not be discouraged. We aim to help you through the challenges of getting started. A good way to appreciate this is to sit back now and reflect on all the things you have already learnt as means of communicating in Catalan. Using the final section as a guide, think of situations in which you would be able to understand and to make yourself understood. You might be surprised at how sound the footing you are now on is, with all the possibilities for development this stage offers.

Points to remember

1 (moltes) gràcies *thank you (very much)*, de res *don't mention it*

2 com et dius? *what's your name?* em dic ... *my name is...*

3 bon dia, com va això? *good morning, how are things?*

4 ho sento *I am sorry*

5 d'on és (vostè)? and d'on ets? (formal and informal) *where are you from?* sóc de.... *I am from...*

6 adéu *goodbye*

7 Masculine and feminine gender of nouns and adjectives: three definite articles el, la, l' and two indefinite un, una.

8 Articles with names: en Carles, la Núria, l'Anna.

9 Feminine identity regularly indicated by the ending -a.

10 The verbs ser *to be* and dir-se *to be called*: use and omission of subject pronouns.

2

On vius?
Where do you live?

In this unit you will learn
- *How to introduce other people*
- *How to exchange personal details (age, address ...)*
- *How to talk about your family*
- *How to ask and say where places are (1)*

> **Insight**
> The main subject matter of this unit naturally entails use of possessives (*my*, *your*, etc). Before proceeding, you may wish to look at the explanation of this topic provided in Grammar section B. Alternatively you may prefer to work first through all four dialogues, thus beginning to get familiar with how possession is expressed in Catalan.

1 Et presento els meus pares *Meet my parents*

Montse is going to introduce Tim to her parents. They live in a flat in the Gràcia neighbourhood in Barcelona.

Montse	Tim, et presento els meus pares, en Roger i l'Anna.
Anna	Molt de gust de coneixe't.
Roger	Encantat

Tim	Igualment. Així només viviu vosaltres tres en aquest pis tan gran?
Roger	No! També hi ha la meva mare, l'àvia de la Montse. I els caps de setmana hi ha en Lluís, el nostre fill i germà gran de la Montse.
Tim	On viu normalment?
Anna	S'està a Lleida.

2 Quants anys tens? *How old are you?*

Montse and Tim are looking at a family photo.

Tim	Qui és aquest senyor?
Montse	Aquest home és el pare de la meva mare, l'avi Sebastià.
Tim	I aquesta noia?
Montse	També és de la família. És la meva cosina: es diu Sandra i ara viu a l'estranger.
Tim	I viu sola?
Montse	No, està casada i té una filla, la Raquel. El seu marit és aquell de l'esquerra.
Tim	I el teu germà, que està casat?
Montse	No, és solter.
Tim	Els meus oncles i els meus cosins viuen a Londres.
Montse	I quants anys tenen els teus cosins?
Tim	Vint-i-un anys té el meu cosí i trenta-tres la meva cosina.
Montse	I tu, quants anys tens?
Tim	Tinc vint-i-quatre anys.

QUICK VOCAB

*tenir ... anys to be (years old)
qui who
l'home (m.) man
l'avi (m.) grandfather
el cosí/la cosina cousin
ara now
a l'estranger abroad
sol/-a alone
està casada she is married
*té (s/he) has
*el seu his/her
el marit husband
*aquell/-a that, that one
esquerre/-a left
*el teu your
solter/-a single, unmarried
l'oncle (m.) uncle (plural, uncle and aunt)

Insight

In Catalan to be ... (years old) is expressed as to have ...
(years): **l'Eloi té vuit anys.** So, when talking about a person's

32

age, you need to adjust to the idea of *having* (years) rather than of *being* (a certain age, so many years old). We shall meet the same feature again when we talk about moods and physical feelings: **tenir fred/son/por**, etc. translating as *to be (or feel) cold/sleepy/frightened*, etc.

Insight

Masculine plurals forms like **pares, cosins, oncles, germans**, etc. often refer to both sexes. Thus **els meus pares** means *my parents*, **els seus germans** *his/her/their brother(s) (and sister(s))*.

---

3 On és el lavabo? *Where is the toilet?*

Montse explains to her friend where the rooms in the house are situated.

Montse	Aquesta és la teva habitació. És al costat de la meva.
Tim	I on és el bany?
Montse	Al fons del passadís, a mà dreta.
Tim	I la cuina, on és?
Montse	Just a davant del menjador, entre l'entrada i la teva habitació. I la sala d'estar és a l'esquerra del rebedor.

● CD1, TR 8, 03:03

QUICK VOCAB

l'habitació (f.) *room, bedroom*
al costat de *next to*
el bany *bathroom, toilet*
al fons *at the end*
*del *of the*
el passadís *corridor*
a mà dreta *on the right-hand side*
la cuina *kitchen*
davant *in front*
el menjador *dining room*
entre *between*
l'entrada (f.) *entrance*

la sala d'estar *living room*
el rebedor *entrance hall*

---

4 Quina adreça té? *What's his address?*

Tim wants to catch up with Esteve, an old friend.

◉ CD1, TR 8, 03:46

Tim	L'Esteve encara viu a Sitges?
Montse	No, ja no hi viu. Ara s'està a Barcelona amb un amic.
Tim	I quina adreça té?
Montse	Viu al Carrer

> *Isabel Carbó i Just*
> *Carles Mas i Garcia*
>
> Carrer de baix, 23, 3r A
> 46700 Gandia (La Safor)

Montse Diputació número dinou, al cinquè pis. L'edifici on viu és just davant d'un cinema i molt a prop d'un centre comercial. A més, al costat de casa seva hi ha una farmàcia.

QUICK VOCAB

encara *still*
ja no *no longer*
hi *there*
amb *with*
***al** see Grammar D
cinquè/-ena *fifth*
el pis *floor*
l'edifici (m.) *building*
(molt) a prop de *(very) close to*
el centre comercial *shopping centre*
a més *also*
casa seva *(his, her) house/home*
la farmàcia *chemist's shop*

Insight

In the dialogue we have heard l'**Esteve encara viu a Sitges?** and **ara s'està a Barcelona**. Pay attention because **viure** means *to live* (in general), *to be alive*, while **estar-se** means *to live* only in the sense of *to reside*, *to stay*. Did you pick this up in the last exchange of Dialogue 1?

Exercise 1

True or false?

1 Only four people live in Roger and Anna's flat.
2 Raquel is Montse's sister.
3 Montse's brother is not married.
4 Esteve lives in a flat near a shopping centre.

Exercise 2

Listen again to the dialogues and make sure you understand everything. Act out the situations, with a partner if possible.

Insight

By now your ear will be getting atuned to the 'relaxed', neutral sound (like the *e* in English *the*) represented in Catalan by either **a** or **e** in an unstressed position. (This feature is typical of the eastern dialects, whereas the western ones tend to differentiate between the **e** and the **a** sounds, even when unstressed.) You can compare how the two vowels are pronounced, for example, in **encantat** or **esquerra**. Note also that **afecte** *affection* and **efecte** *effect* sound the same in standard Catalan. For more information refer back to the Pronunciation and spelling section. It will be a good idea to focus on this feature as you revise the dialogues in preparation for doing Exercise 3.

Exercise 3

Say whether the underlined letters in these words from Dialogues 1 and 2 sound stressed or unstressed.

1 p**a**res **2** **a**quest **3** h**a** **4** mev**a** **5** germ**à** **6** gr**a**n **7** noi**a** **8** estr**a**nger

Notice also how **e** represents different sounds according to whether it is stressed or unstressed.

Ordinals and numbers 11–99

Before starting with more numbers, listen again to 1–10 from Unit 1 and then the corresponding ordinals:

🔊 **CD1, TR 9, 00:01**

1st	**primer, primera**	6th	**sisè, sisena**
2nd	**segon, segona**	7th	**setè, setena**
3rd	**tercer, tercera**	8th	**vuitè, vuitena**
4th	**quart, quarta**	9th	**novè, novena**
5th	**cinquè, cinquena**	10th	**desè, desena**

Now look at and listen to the numbers between 11 and 99. Pay careful attention to the spelling, mainly with the twenties.

11 **onze** 12 **dotze** 13 **tretze** 14 **catorze** 15 **quinze** 16 **setze**
17 **disset** 18 **divuit** 19 **dinou**
20 **vint** 21 **vint-i-u** 22 **vint-i-dos** 23 **vint-i-tres** 24 **vint-i-quatre**
25 **vint-i-cinc** 26 **vint-i-sis** ...
30 **trenta** 31 **trenta-u** 32 **trenta-dos** 33 **trenta-tres**
34 **trenta-quatre** 35 **trenta-cinc** ...
40 **quaranta** 41 **quaranta-u** 42 **quaranta-dos** ...
50 **cinquanta** 51 **cinquanta-u** 52 **cinquanta-dos** ...
60 **seixanta** 61 **seixanta-u** 62 **seixanta-dos** ...
70 **setanta** 71 **setanta-u** 72 **setanta-dos** ...
80 **vuitanta** 81 **vuitanta-u** ...
90 **noranta** 91 **noranta-u** ...

....

Insight

The form **u** is used when number one is on its own, such as when saying a telephone number. Just as **un/-a**, both as a numeral and as an indefinite article, agrees with the noun that it introduces, there is a distinctive feminine form **dues: dos llits** *two beds* but **dues cadires** *two chairs*, **trenta-un billets** *thirty-one banknotes* but **trenta-dues entrades** *thirty-two admission tickets*.

Insight

Note how the numbers from 21 to 29 are formed in combinations involving **vint** and the following number joined by **-i-**. (Observe, too, how the final **-t** of **vint-i-un** and **vint-i-quatre**, etc. is clearly heard.) From 31 onwards a hyphen alone is what joins the two numbers.

Cultural information
Addresses

Addresses in Catalan start with the name of the street **carrer**, *square* **plaça**, *avenue* **avinguda**, *main road* **carretera**, *promenade* **passeig**, *track* **camí** and so on, followed by the number and finally, if appropriate, the floor and the flat number. At the end we usually write the postcode **codi postal** before the name of the *city* **ciutat** or *town/village* **poble**. **El barri** is the word used for *district/neighbourhood* within a town or a city.

Cultural information
Family names

Catalans generally use two family names **cognoms**, usually but not always linked by **i** (the first one being the father's and the second one the mother's, although this order can be changed and many people use just the single surname). Examples: **Lluïsa Canals i Franch, Nicolau Dols Sala**. In all official papers both surnames must be given. Remember that the Catalan word for first or given name is **nom**.

Exercise 4
🔊 **CD1, TR 10, 00:01**

Listen to the recording and write out in the correct place all the information requested:

```
                        Fitxa personal
1 Nom: ...................    5 Població: ...............

2 Cognoms: .............     6 N. Passaport: ..........

3 Adreça: ..............     7 Edat: .....................

4 Codi postal: ........      8 Estat civil: ...........
```

Key words and sentences

Introducing other people

Et presento el senyor Soler.	*Let me introduce* (to you) *Mr Soler* (informal).
Li presento la Mireia Molas.	*Let me introduce (to you) Mireia Molas* (formal).

Asking people where they live and how old they are

On vius? On viu?	*Where do you live?* (informal/formal)
Quina adreça tens?	*What's your address?*
Quina adreça té?	(informal/formal)
Visc a ...	*I live in ....*
La meva adreça és ...	*My address is ...*
Quants anys tens?/	*How old are you?*
Quants anys té?	(informal and formal)
Tinc ... anys.	*I am ... (years old).*

Asking and saying where places are (1)

On és ...?	*Where is ...?*
És a ...	*It is ...*
la dreta/l'esquerra	*right/left (hand side)*
a mà dreta/a mà esquerra	*on the right-/left-hand side*
davant/darrere	*in front (of)/behind*
al fons	*at the end/at the bottom*
al costat (de)	*next (to)*
a prop (de)	*near (to)*
entre	*between*

Exercise 5

Look at this plan of an apartment and write down the name of each room.

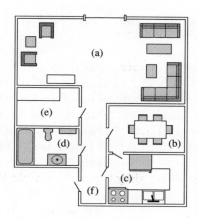

Grammar

A Demonstratives ('this', 'that', etc.)

Singular	*Plural*
aquest/-a *this (that)*	**aquests/-es** *these (those)*
aquell/-a *that*	**aquells/-es** *those*

The demonstrative can be used both as adjective and pronoun:

Aquesta és la meva habitació;   *This is my room; that one*
   aquella és la teva.   *(over there) is yours.*

Aquest/-a means *that* when it refers to something close to the person addressed.

On vas amb aquesta maleta?   *Where are you going with that*
                                    suitcase?

Note pronunciation of **aquest**: the **s** is silent except when the adjective precedes a noun which begins with a vowel or **h** + vowel. (Listen again to Dialogues 1 and 2 and pay attention to the pronunciation of **aquest**.)

B Possessives ('my', 'your', 'his', etc.)

	Singular	
	Masculine	*Feminine*
my	el meu	la meva
your	el teu	la teva
his, her, its, your (vostè)	el seu	la seva
our	el nostre	la nostra
your	el vostre	la vostra
their, your (vostès)	el seu	la seva

	Plural	
	Masculine	*Feminine*
my	els meus	les meves
your	els teus	les teves
his, her, its, your (vostè)	els seus	les seves
our	els nostres	les nostres
your	els vostres	les vostres
their, your (vostès)	els seus	les seves

Catalan possessives are generally preceded by the relevant definite article. There is agreement with the object of possession. Like the demonstratives, the possessives can function as adjectives and pronouns.

El nostre tramvia és el número tres (adjective).	*Our tram is the number three.*
Aquest tramvia no és el nostre (pronoun).	*This tram isn't ours.*

Exercise 6

Change the following sentences to indicate possession into:

a your (sg./pl.) **b** his/her **c** your (polite, sg./pl.) **d** our **e** their

1 Aquests papers són **meus**.
2 Les **meves** cosines viuen a Manresa.

Grammar

C Prepositions *a*, *de* and *per* (contractions)

The prepositions **a** (*to*, *at*, *in*, *on*), **de** (*of*, *from*, *about*) and **per** (*by*, *for*, *through*, *along*) are contracted when they join the masculine definite article – **el**, **els**, but not **l'** – to produce **al**, **als**; **del**, **dels**; **pel**, **pels**.

Viu a + el costat de + el cinema > Viu al costat del cinema.
S/he lives next to the cinema.

Partit per + el mig > Partit pel mig. *Split down the middle.*

D Question words

Què?	*What?*
Qui?	*Who?*
Quin/-a, quins/-es?	*Which?* (referred to people and things), *what?*

Quant/-a?	*How much?*
Quants/-es?	*How many?*
Quina senyora és aquesta?	*Which lady is this one?*
Quins llibres tens?	*Which books do you have?*
Quants germans té?	*How many brothers does s/he have?*

E *Viure* and *estar-se* 'to live'

(jo) visc	*I live*	(nosaltres) vivim	*we live*
(tu) vius	*you live*	(vosaltres) viviu	*you live*
(ell/ella) viu	*he/she lives*	(ells/elles) viuen	*they live*

(jo) m'estic	*I live*	(nosaltres) ens estem	*we live*
(tu) t'estàs	*you live*	(vosaltres) us esteu	*you live*
(ell/ella) s'està	*he/she lives*	(ells/elles) s'estan	*they live*

(The pronouns **em**, **et** and **es** before vowel or **h** + vowel take the apostrophized form.)

F The verb *tenir* 'to have'

(jo) tinc	*I have*	(nosaltres) tenim	*we have*
(tu) tens	*you have*	(vosaltres) teniu	*you have*
(ell/ella) té	*he/she has*	(ells/elles) tenen	*they have*

Exercise 7

Look at this information and write down a description in the first person:

Name: *Cristina*	Status: *single*
Age: *19*	Brother: *Esteve, 23 years old*
Place of origin: *Sabadell*	Father: *from Andorra*
Place of residence: *Barcelona*	Mother: *from Italy*

Exercise 8

Look carefully at this family tree and then complete the sentences below:

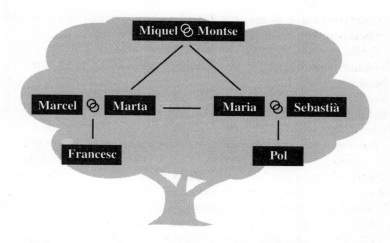

La Maria està _____ 1 amb en Sebastià i tenen un _____
2, en Pol. La Marta és la _____ 3 de la Maria i els seus _____
4 es diuen Miquel i Montse. El _____ 5 d'en Pol és en Francesc.
En Marcel està casat amb la _____ 6. En Sebastià és _____
7 d'en Pol, i l'_____ 8 d'en Pol es diu Marcel.

Grammar

G Plural nouns and articles

All plural nouns end in **-s**. Plural definite articles are **els** for the
masculine and **les** for the feminine (no shortened form with plurals);
plural indefinite articles are **uns** and **unes**, translating the idea of *some*.

In many cases the plural is formed quite simply by adding **-s** to the
singular form of the noun: **el meu fill** *my son* > **els meus fills** *my sons*.

In many other cases, however, the word undergoes some slight
change before taking the final **-s**. A major instance of this is with
words ending in unstressed **-a** which change the **-a** to **-e** before

taking the final -s: **la noia** *the girl* > **les noies** *the girls*; **una germana** *a sister* > **unes germanes** *some sisters*.

The information given in the **Reference tables** at the end of the book provides a fuller picture.

Exercise 9

Choose one word from each column to create the article + noun + adjective structure as in **unes noies menorquines**:

1 una	senyor	angleses
2 un	amic	alemanya
3 uns	cosina	espanyol
4 les	nois	catalans
5 l'	amigues	francès

Exercise 10

Choose the correct response:

1 Montse, et presento la meva àvia.
  a Hola, molt de gust.
  b Jo em dic Montse.
  c Igualment.

2 Quina és la teva adreça?
  a La meva adreça és aquella.
  b Plaça del Vi, número set.
  c Número set de la Plaça del Vi.

3 On viu la Cesca?
  a Vius a Terrassa.
  b Viu a Terrassa.
  c S'estan a Terrassa.

4 Qui és aquest noi?
  a És la meva germana.
  b És solter.
  c És el meu amic.

Points to remember

1 **et presento** ... *let me introduce you to* ... **encantat/-da** ... *nice to meet you* ...
2 **on és** ...? *where is* ...?

3 tinc ... anys, *I am ... years old* (conjugation and use of the irregular verb **tenir**)

4 visc a ... *I live in ...* (conjugation of the irregular verb **viure**)

5 dos germans, dues cosines *two brothers, two (female) cousins*

6 Possessives: **els meus pares, la nostra filla** ... *my parents, our daughter.*

7 Demonstratives: **aquest home, aquella dona** *this man, that woman.*

8 Position and location: **el lavabo és al fons, a l'esquerra** *the toilet is at the end, on the left...*

9 Spelling of numbers beyond 10.

10 Plural forms of nouns and adjectives: masculine -s and feminine -es.

3

Una cita
An appointment

In this unit you will learn
- *How to make an appointment*
- *How to ask and tell the time*
- *How to make a simple call*
- *How to ask and say where places are (2)*

Insight

Note the use of **que** in the heading of Dialogue 1. (Perhaps you spotted this in Dialogue 2 of Unit 2: **que està casat?**) Short, simple questions which are not introduced by an interrogative word like **on?** *where?*, **com?** *how?*, **quin/quina?** *which?*, etc. are invariably preceded in Catalan by **que**. It is not translated in English, but your Catalan will sound more authentic if you do use it.

---

1 Que hi és l'Esteve? *Is Esteve there?*

Tim has decided to call his old friend, Esteve.

Tim	Montse, que tens el número de telèfon de l'Esteve?
Montse	Sí, és el 932 34 27 58.
Dona	Digui?
Tim	Bon dia, que hi és l'Esteve?

Dona	Em sembla que s'equivoca. A quin número truca?
Tim	Al 932 34 27 58.
Dona	Aquí és el 932 34 28 58.
Tim	Perdoni, em sap greu.
Dona	No hi fa res, adéu.
Noia	Digui?
Tim	Que hi ha l'Esteve?
Noia	Sí, un moment, sisplau.
Esteve	Sí? Amb qui parlo?
Tim	Esteve, sóc en Tim! Sóc a Barcelona.
Esteve	Ei Tim, quant de temps! Com va això?

la dona *woman*
digui? *yes, hello?*
em sembla que *I think that*
s'equivoca (vostè) *you are wrong*
truca *you call*
em sap greu *I am sorry*
no hi fa res *don't worry about it, it doesn't matter*
el noi / la noia *boy / girl*
sisplau *please*
amb qui parlo? *who is speaking?*
quant de temps! *what a long time!*

Insight

sisplau *please* is a contraction of **si us plau** *if you please* (like French *s'il vous plaît*). Note that a request without *please* does not sound as impolite in Catalan as it might in English.

Insight

hi ha (*there is/there are*) is often used to ask if someone is in. But note that it is used only for asking the question and not the reply. When Tim asks **que hi és l'Esteve?** he could have said **que hi ha l'Esteve?**, but the answer could only be given as either **sí que hi és** or **no, no hi és**.

Esteve and Tim decide to get together.

CD1, TR 11, 01:50

Tim	Què et sembla de quedar aquesta tarda?
Esteve	A mi em va bé. Tinc tota la tarda lliure.
Tim	D'acord, a on?
Esteve	No ho sé. A veure ... et va bé al bar Mingo, al carrer Muntaner?
Tim	Sí. A quina hora?
Esteve	A les cinc?
Tim	Perfecte, fins després.
(in the bar)	
Cambrera	Què voleu prendre?
Esteve	Jo vull un cafè amb llet.
Tim	Per a mi un tallat i una pasta.
(later)	
Tim	Perdona, quina hora és?
Cambrera	Són dos quarts de vuit.
Tim	Ui, que tard! M'acompanyes a l'estació de trens?

QUICK VOCAB

què et sembla de quedar? *what (do you think) about meeting?*
la tarda *afternoon*
a mi em va bé *that's fine for me*
tot/-a *all*
lliure *free*
d'acord *fine, OK, agreed*
no ho sé *I don't know*
a veure ... *let's see*
a quina hora? *at what time?*
perfecte *all right*
fins després *see you later*
què voleu prendre? *what do you want to drink?*
*vull *I want*
el cafè amb llet *white coffee*
per a *for*

el tallat *coffee with a dash of milk*
la pasta *pastry*
*****són dos quarts de vuit** *it's half past seven*
ui, que tard! *oh! it's late!*
m'acompanyes? *can/will you come with me?*
l'estació (f.) *station*
el tren *train*

Insight

fins, meaning *until*, occurs in a lot of expressions used when saying goodbye. As well as **fins després** you can note some more examples: **fins demà** *see you tomorrow*, **fins aviat** *see you soon*, **fins ara** *see you shortly*, **fins dilluns** *see you on Monday*, **fins l'any que ve** *see you next year*.

---

3 És lluny? *Is it far?*

Tim and Esteve discuss how best to get to the station.

Tim	Agafem el metro o el bus?
Esteve	Hi ha una parada de bus en aquesta cantonada.
Tim	I l'estació de metro, és lluny?
Esteve	En aquest barri només n'hi ha una. És al final de tot d'aquesta avinguda.
Tim	Doncs millor el bus. Apa!

◗ CD1, TR 11, 03:14

agafar *to catch, to take*
el metro *underground*
l'(auto)bús (m.) *bus*
la parada *(bus / metro) stop*
la cantonada *corner*
el barri *neighbourhood*
*****n'hi ha una** *there is one*
al final (de tot) *(right) at the end*

QUICK VOCAB

millor *better, best*
apa! *let's go!*

---

4 A quina hora surt el tren?
What time does the train leave?

Tim asks about train times in the information office at the railway station.

CD1, TR 11, 03:56

Tim	Bona tarda. A quina hora surt el primer tren cap a Mataró demà?
Informació	Al matí el primer és a les set i cinc minuts.
Tim	I després?
Informació	A les vuit i deu minuts, i a un quart de deu.
Tim	I el viatge, quant dura?
Informació	Dura tres quarts, o sigui, quaranta-cinc minuts.

QUICK VOCAB

cap a *towards*
demà *tomorrow*
el matí *morning*
després *then, later*
*****un quart de deu** *a quarter past nine*
el viatge *journey*
quant dura? *how long does it take?*
o sigui *that is*

Exercise 1
True or false?

1 Esteve is not alone at home when Tim calls.
2 Esteve is not free in the afternoon.
3 The metro station is closer than the bus stop.
4 The third train to Mataró is at a quarter past ten.

Exercise 2

Study the dialogues carefully and repeat them. Then listen to the pronunciation of the words below (from Dialogues 1 and 2) and say whether the sound represented by the underlined letter is open, close or unstressed:

1 núm<u>e</u>ro **2** mom<u>e</u>nt **3** Barc<u>e</u>lona **4** qu<u>è</u> **5** b<u>é</u> **6** carr<u>e</u>r
7 Muntan<u>e</u>r **8, 9** d<u>e</u>sprés **10** tr<u>e</u>ns

Division of the day

🔊 **CD1, TR 12, 00:03**

la matinada	*early morning*	**el matí**	*morning*
el migdia	*noon*	**la tarda**	*afternoon*
el vespre	*evening*	**la nit**	*night*

The division of the day is made according to meal times and these, in Catalan-speaking society, differ slightly from north-European habits, with meals generally being taken later. **La tarda, el vespre** and even **la nit** do not correspond exactly to *afternoon, evening, night*. 6 pm will never be **les sis del vespre** but **les sis de la tarda**.

Numbers 100–1,000

🔊 **CD1, TR 12, 00:22**

Listen to the scheme of numbers from 100 to 1,000 and note where hyphens are written.

100 **cent** 101 **cent u** 102 **cent dos** 103 **cent tres** 104 **cent quatre** ...
110 **cent deu** 111 **cent onze** ...
120 **cent vint** 125 **cent vint-i-cinc** ...
232 **dos-cents trenta-dos** ...

356 tres-cents cinquanta-sis ...
567 cinc-cents seixanta-set ...
798 set-cents noranta-vuit ...
974 nou-cents setanta-quatre ...
1,000 **mil**

Insight

A hyphen is used to link tens and units (**setanta-vuit** *seventy eight*) and to link multiples of **cent** *hundred* (**nou-cents**, *nine hundred*). Like for **un/-a** and **dos/dues**, the compounds of **cent** agree in gender with the noun **nou-centes pàgines** *nine hundred pages*, **tres-centes vint-i-dues monedes** *three hundred and twenty-two coins*.

Exercise 3
◄) **CD1, TR 13, 00:01**

Listen to people giving some telephone numbers. Say whether they are correct or not. If not, correct them.

1 972 59 41 62
2 93 285 31 98
3 973 21 78 45

4 977 18 15 63
5 629 45 28 75
6 971 83 64 12

In the last exchange **aquí** does not mean *here* but refers rather to the place where the other person is talking from.

Cultural information
The time of day

In central Catalonia there is an alternative or complementary way of telling the time based upon quarters of an hour, as shown in the right-hand column below. (We use the hour from five to six o'clock as illustration.)

les cinc   **les cinc**

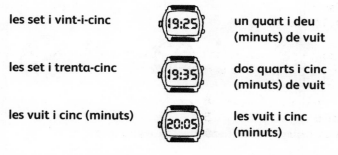

les cinc i quart — 17:15 — un quart de sis

les cinc i mitja — 17:30 — dos quarts de sis

les sis menys quart — 17:45 — tres quarts de sis

You might find the system shown in the right-hand column rather confusing at first. It is, in fact, very logical as it is based on the idea that the seventh hour, for example, begins at six o'clock. Look at some more cases:

les set i vint-i-cinc — 19:25 — un quart i deu (minuts) de vuit

les set i trenta-cinc — 19:35 — dos quarts i cinc (minuts) de vuit

les vuit i cinc (minuts) — 20:05 — les vuit i cinc (minuts)

Use of the 24-hour clock is becoming increasingly frequent, especially for timetables:

18:25 El meu tren surt a les divuit i vint-i-cinc minuts.
My train leaves at 18:25.

15:55 Aquest tren arriba a les quinze cinquanta-cinc.
This train arrives at 15:55.

Note that 'one o'clock' is singular and therefore takes **és**, while the other hours take **són**. (The same is also true of **quart/quarts: és un quart de deu/són tres quarts de dotze.**)

Exercise 4

Match the time shown on each clock with one of the expressions:

a Són tres quarts de vuit.
b Són les quatre i quart.
c És un quart i cinc de set.
d Són les quatre i vint-i-cinc minuts.
e Són tres quarts i cinc de quatre.
f Són les sis menys deu minuts.

Exercise 5

Write out, using both systems, the following times:

1 8.45 **2** 6.30 **3** 17.15 **4** 11.20 **5** 15.50

Insight

The Catalan tendency to use **un quart** *quarter of an hour* as a basic unit of time gives rise to some interesting refinements. The quarter itself can be divided, so that **un quart i mig de nou** means *(about)* 8.22 and **tres quarts i mig de dues** *(about)* 1.52. Then there is the idiom **a quarts de** which indicates somewhere between a quarter past one hour and a quarter to the next: **quedem per a quarts d'onze**, *let's meet around half-past ten*.

Key words and sentences

Asking and telling the time

Quina hora és?	*What time is it?*
(Que) tens hora? (Que) té hora?	*Have you got the time?*
És un quart de tres.	*It's quarter past two.*
Són les sis i cinc minuts.	*It's five past six.*
A les deu del matí.	*At ten in the morning.*
A un quart de sis de la tarde.	*At 5.15 in the afternoon.*

Asking about times

A quina hora comença la pel·lícula?	*What time does the film start?*
Quant dura el viatge?	*How long does the journey take?*

Asking and saying where places are (2)

Hi ha alguna parada de bus per aquí?	*Is there a bus stop near here?*
És lluny? / És a la vora?	*Is it far? / Is it nearby?*
en aquesta cantonada	*at this (street) corner*
al final del carrer	*at the end of the street*

Arranging an informal meeting

Et va bé a les set?	*Is seven o'clock all right for you?*

Talking on the telephone

Digui?	*Hello?*
Que hi ha/Que hi és ...?	*Is ... there?*
Sí que hi és.	*Yes, s/he is here.*
No, no hi és (ara).	*No, s/he isn't here (at the moment).*
Un moment sisplau.	*One moment, please.*
Amb qui parlo? / De part de qui?	*Who is speaking?*

Exercise 6

Complete the following telephone conversations:

1 **a** Que hi és la Marta?
   b _____.
   a D'acord, adéu.
2 **a** Que hi ha en Pere?
   b Sí _____.
   a Gràcies.
3 **a** Que hi ha l'Imma?
   b Em sembla que s'equivoca.
   a _____.

4 **a** Que hi és l'Arnau?
   b Un _____.
   a Gràcies.
5 **a** Que hi ha en Xavi?
   b No, _____.
   a Bé, adéu.
6 **a** Que hi és en Quim?
   b Sí, _____?
   a Sóc l'Oriol Martínez.

Grammar

> ### Insight
>
> We are beginning to work with an increasing number of
> Catalan verbs. Remember that, as a general rule, it is the
> conjugated form of the verb itself that indicates the subject:
> subject pronouns are expressed only in particular cases.
> There are two main classes of Catalan verbs, regular and
> irregular. In this unit we concentrate on the conjugation
> pattern of regular verbs with the infinitive in **-ar**, the first
> conjugation (**parlar, equivocar-se**: see Grammar section A).
> Once the six distinctive endings are memorized, you will be
> able to work with any verb whose infinitive ends in **-ar**, by
> far the largest of the three groups of regular verbs. The other
> two regular conjugations are presented in Units 4 and 5. The
> main irregular verbs are being introduced as we go along
> (**ser, tenir, dir-se**, etc., and, in this unit, **voler** and **sortir**).

A Regular verbs – present tense (1)

In this unit we have found some regular verbs in the simple present
tense like **s'equivoca, truca, parlo, m'acompanyes** and **dura**.

These are from the large group of regular verbs, referred to as the first conjugation, whose infinitive ends in -ar.

	parlar *(to speak, to talk)* stem-ending	equivocar-se *(to be wrong)* stem-ending
(jo)	parl-o	m'equivoc-o
(tu)	parl-es	t'equivoqu-es
(ell/-a, vostè)	parl-a	s'equivoc-a
(nosaltres)	parl-em	ens equivoqu-em
(vosaltres)	parl-eu	us equivoqu-eu
(ells/-es, vostès)	parl-en	s'equivoqu-en

Look at the stem of **equivocar-se** and see the changes made to the spelling, reflecting consistency of pronunciation. The same happens with **trucar: truco, truques,** etc. See **Pronunciation** and **Spelling** and also Unit 4, Grammar G.

B Irregular verbs *voler* 'to want' and *sortir* 'to leave'

(jo) vull	*I want*	(nosaltres) volem	*we want*
(tu) vols	*you want*	(vosaltres) voleu	*you want*
(ell/ella) vol	*he/she wants*	(ells/elles) volen	*they want*

(jo) surto	*I leave*	(nosaltres) sortim	*we leave*
(tu) surts	*you leave*	(vosaltres) sortiu	*you leave*
(ell/ella) surt	*he/she leaves*	(ells/elles) surten	*they leave*

C *hi ha – n'hi ha* 'there is'

Hi ha means *there is/are* and, as a question, *is/are there?*. After a question whatever is referred to is picked up by **n'** in any response.

Hi ha temps per a fer això? **Sí que n'hi ha.**	*Is there time to do this? There certainly is.*
Hi ha una adrogueria per aquí? **(Em sembla que) n'hi ha una després del semàfor.**	*Is there a grocery store round here? (I think that) there's one after the traffic lights.*

We look more closely at the behaviour of these two words, en (n')
and hi, in Units 4 and 5 respectively.

Exercise 7
Answer the following questions
using the information given in
the picture, as in the example:

Example: Hi ha alguna
farmàcia a prop
d'aquí?
Sí, n'hi ha una a la
segona cantonada a
mà dreta.

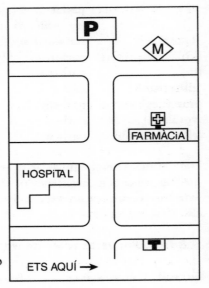

1 Hi ha algun pàrquing a
prop d'aquí?
2 Hi ha alguna parada de
taxis a prop d'aquí?
3 Hi ha algun hospital a prop
d'aquí?
4 Hi ha alguna estació de
metro a prop d'aquí?

Grammar

D *Que* and *què* in questions

Observe the difference, in both pronunciation and function,
between these two similar-looking words that introduce questions.
Que (not translated) frequently precedes a brief direct question
not headed by another interrogative word, as in **que hi és l'Esteve?**
Remember, **el teu germà, que està casat?** from Unit 2 Dialogue 2.

| Que vols un cafè? | *Do you want a coffee?* |
| Que és lluny l'estació? | *Is the station far away?* |

Què? is the exact equivalent of *what?*

| Què vols? | *What do you want?* |
| Què hi ha al final del carrer? | *What is there at the end of the street?* |

Exercise 8
Put this dialogue into the correct order:

1 Ui, que tard!
2 I quina hora és ara?
3 A les sis i vint minuts.
4 A quina hora surt l'autobús?
5 No, home, encara tens temps!
6 Són les sis i deu.

Exercise 9
Look at these bus times and write out in full the answers to the questions which follow.

Vic	→ Girona	Girona	→ Vic
10.10	11.35	09.15	10.40
12.20	13.45	11.25	12.50
14.05	15.30	13.05	14.30
15.45	17.10	14.45	16.10
17.10	18.35	16.10	17.35
19.20	20.45	18.25	19.50

1 A quina hora surt el primer autobús cap a Girona?
2 A quina hora surt el segon bus cap a Vic?
3 A quina hora surt el primer bus de la tarda cap a Girona?
4 A quina hora arriba el darrer autobús a Girona?
5 A quina hora arriba el cinquè bus a Vic?

Points to remember

1 quina hora és? *what time is it?* són les tres de la tarda *it's three o'clock in the afternoon* és un quart de deu *it's a quarter to ten*

2 a quina hora surt...? *what time does... leave?*

3 quant dura el viatge? *how long does the journey take?*

4 hi ha tres bars a prop d'aquí *there are three bars near here*

5 que hi és l'Alba? no, no hi és ara/sí que hi és *is Alba there? no, she isn't here (at the moment)/yes, she is here*

6 et va bé a les quatre? *is four o'clock alright for you?*

7 és lluny? és a la vora? *is it far? is it near?*

8 que introducing simple questions.

9 Numbers beyond 100.

10 The pattern for the present tense of regular verbs of the first conjugation (-ar).

4

Anem a comprar
Let's go shopping

In this unit you will learn
- *How to ask about prices and pay for purchases*
- *How to ask about opening and closing times*
- *How to describe quantity, size and weight*

---

1 A quina hora obren? *What time do they open?*

Tim asks Montse's father about opening times at the post office, **correus.**

Tim	Roger, saps quin horari fan a correus?
Roger	Em sembla que obren a un quart de nou del matí.
Tim	I tanquen al migdia?
Roger	No, fan horari intensiu, fins a les dues. A la tarda tenen tancat.
Tim	Vull enviar unes postals al meu país i necessito segells.
Roger	Si vols, pots anar a l'estanc a comprar-los. Allà també en venen i tenen obert a la tarda.
Tim	Quan obren?
Roger	Crec que obren a dos quarts de cinc i tanquen a dos quarts de nou del vespre.

CD1, TR 14, 00:08

*saps? *do you know*
quin horari fan? *what are the opening hours?*
obren *they open*
tanquen *they close*
*horari intensiu see 'Shops and opening times', this unit
fins a *until*
tancat/-da *closed*
obert/-a *open*
enviar *to send*
la postal *postcard*
el país *country*
necessito *I need*
el segell *(postage) stamp*
*pots anar *you can go*
l'estanc (m.) *newsagent-tobacconist's*
comprar *to buy*
allà *there*
*en see Grammar B
*venen *they sell*
quan *when*
crec *I believe*

Insight

You will almost certainly have deduced from the context of Dialogue 1 that **em sembla que...** means *I think that...*, literally *it seems to me that....* There is a verb, **pensar**, equivalent to *to think*, but the construction with **semblar** is very common indeed and you are encouraged to practise this usage. The point is discussed more fully in Unit 6, Grammar Section C.

Insight

In Dialogue 1 we introduced a small 'test' involving **semblar** to demonstrate how much language competence you will develop from your own instinctive responses in communication situations. And how did you interpret

comprar-los in this dialogue? The **-los** element obviously refers back to **segells**. This feature will be 'tested' in Dialogue 2 (watch out for **com els vols, els préssecs...?**), as a preliminary to the formal presentation of object pronouns in the Grammar section.

---

2 Quant en vols? *How much do you want?*

While Tim is at the newsagent's, Montse goes to the market. She first wants to buy some fruit.

Montse	Bona tarda, teniu peres?
Botiguera	Sí que en tenim. Aquestes són molt bones. Quantes en vols, noia?
Montse	A quin preu van?
Botiguera	A 1 euro i 60 cèntims el quilo.
Montse	Doncs dos quilos.
Botiguera	Alguna cosa més?
Montse	Sí, mig quilo de préssecs i sis taronges.
Botiguera	Com els vols, els préssecs, madurs o verds?
Montse	Més aviat verds.

CD1, TR 14, 01:15

la pera *pear*
el / la botiguer/-a *shop assistant*
bo/-na *good*
a quin preu van? *how much are they?*
el quilo *kilo*
alguna cosa més? *anything else?*
mig/mitja *half*
el préssec *peach*
la taronja *orange*
*els see Grammar A
madur/-a *ripe*
verd/-a *green, unripe*
més aviat *tending to be*

QUICK VOCAB

3 Quant val? *How much is it?*

Then Montse goes to a grocer's shop.

Pilar	A qui toca?
Montse	A mi. Hola Pilar, vull farina.
Pilar	Quanta en vols?
Montse	Dos paquets ... Tens melmelada de maduixes?
Pilar	Sí, cada pot val només 2 euros. Està d'oferta.
Montse	Vull també un litre d'oli d'oliva, una ampolla de vinagre, un parell de llaunes de tonyina i dos paquets de sucre.
Pilar	Les llaunes, les vols grosses o petites?
Montse	Petites.
Pilar	Res més?
Montse	Sí, voldria un tall de formatge.
Pilar	Aquest val 4 euros amb 35 el quilo. Així va bé?
Montse	Una mica menys, sisplau. I res més ... Quant és tot plegat?
Pilar	Són catorze euros amb vint-i-cinc cèntims. Gràcies.

a qui toca? *who's next?*
(em toca) a mi *it's my turn*
la farina *flour*
el paquet *bag*
la melmelada *jam*
la maduixa *strawberry*

cada *each*
el pot *can, tin, jar*
*****val** *(it) costs*
només *only*
està d'oferta *it's on offer*
el litre *litre*
l'oli d'oliva (m.) *olive oil*
l'ampolla (f.) *bottle*
el vinagre *vinegar*
el parell *couple*
la llauna *tin*
la tonyina *tuna*
el sucre *sugar*
*****les** *see Grammar A*
gros/-sa *big*
petit/-a *small*
res més? *anything else?*
voldria *I'd like*
el tall *piece, slice*
el formatge *cheese*
així va bé? *is that all right?*
una mica menys *a little bit less*
tot plegat *altogether*

Exercise 1

Read the dialogues again and try to repeat them, working with a partner if possible.

Insight

We know about the sound represented by **a** and **e** in an unstressed position. Something similar occurs with **o**, pronounced **u** when it stands in an unstressed position, as in **quilos** or **horari**. You can pay special attention to this detail when working on Exercise 2, while remembering that at this stage the main thing is to make yourself understood rather than to achieve a perfect accent.

Exercise 2

Look at the word groups below (all from Dialogues 1 and 2) and say whether the underlined letter **o** sounds open, close or unstressed. Notice also how the words in each group run together.

1 quin h<u>o</u>rari **2** unes p<u>o</u>stals **3** p<u>o</u>ts anar **4** crec que <u>o</u>bren
5, 6, 7 s<u>ó</u>n m<u>o</u>lt b<u>o</u>nes **8, 9, 10** d<u>o</u>ncs d<u>o</u>s quil<u>o</u>s

Exercise 3
Match the places with the opening hours:

1 estanc **2** ajuntament **3** restaurant **4** correus **5** hospital
6 supermercat

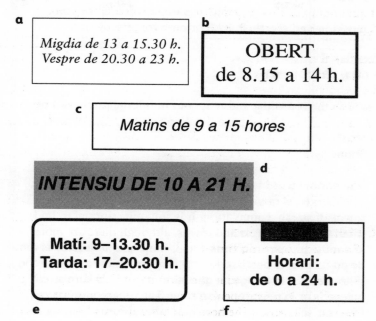

a

Migdia de 13 a 15.30 h.
Vespre de 20.30 a 23 h.

b

OBERT
de 8.15 a 14 h.

c

Matins de 9 a 15 hores

d

INTENSIU DE 10 A 21 H.

e

Matí: 9–13.30 h.
Tarda: 17–20.30 h.

f

Horari:
de 0 a 24 h.

Exercise 4
Now answer the following questions, using full sentences if you can:

1 A quina hora obre el restaurant?
2 Quin horari fan al supermercat?
3 A l'estanc, obren a la tarda?
4 Quan tenen obert a l'ajuntament?
5 A quina hora tanquen a correus?

Exercise 5
◀) **CD1, TR 15, 00:01**

Listen to the recording and write out in full the prices you hear.

> **Insight**
> Shops
>
> The normal word for *shop* is **la botiga** (plural, **les botigues**).
> The market, **el mercat**, is an important shopping place in
> towns of sizeable population. It is still quite normal to find
> small shops in villages and towns, although there are more
> and more big supermarkets. Small shops are **la fleca** or **el forn
> de pa** *baker's*, **la pastisseria** *cake shop*, **la fruiteria i verdureria**
> *greengrocer's*, **la botiga de queviures** *grocer's*, **la carnisseria**
> *butcher's* or **la peixateria** *fish shop*. The tobacconist's shop,
> **l'estanc**, sells postage stamps (and official forms bearing
> stamp duty) as well as the usual smokers' requisites.

Exercise 6
Match the products with the shop/store where they are sold, using
the vocabulary list at the end of the book to check any word of
which you are unsure.

1 els queviures
2 la carnisseria
3 la fleca/el forn de pa
4 la peixateria
5 la fruiteria/verdureria
6 l'estanc
7 la pastisseria

gamba porc coca mel galeta pernil lluç pa segell all vi
tabac tomàquet pastís de poma patata sucre

Insight

As you have seen, various words for shop end with -**eria**. This suffix relates either to what is on sale (**pastís** – **pastisseria**, **fruita** – **fruiteria**) or to the speciality of the shopkeeper (**peixater** – **peixateria**, **carnisser** – **carnisseria**).

Key words and sentences

Opening times

A quina hora obren? | *What time do they open?*
Tanquen al migdia. | *They close at lunchtime.*
Tenim obert fins a les ... | *We are open until ...*

Your turn

Vostè és l'últim-a? | *Are you the last one in the queue?*
Qui és ara? / A qui toca? | *Who is next? / Whose turn is it?*
(Em toca) a mi. / Toca a aquesta senyora. | *It's my turn. / It's this lady's turn.*

What do you want?

Què voldria? | *What would you like?*
Què li fa falta? | *What do you need?*
Què vols? | *What do you want?* (informal)

Asking for things

Voldria una barra de quart, sisplau. | *I would like a baguette, please.*
Vull un paquet de sucre, sisplau. | *I want a bag of sugar, please.*

Anything else?

Alguna cosa més? / Res més?	*(Do you need) something else? / Anything else?*
Res mes, gràcies.	*That's all, thank you.*

Paying

Quant val? / Quant et/li dec?	*How much is it? / How much do I owe you?*
Quant és tot plegat?	*How much is it altogether?*
Val 10£ i 35 cèntims. / Són 28£.	*It costs 10£ and 35 cents. / That's 28£.*

Grammar

A Some direct-object pronouns

Our introduction to direct-object pronouns is through the forms (**comprar**)-**los**, heard in Dialogue 1, **els** in Dialogue 2 and **les** in Dialogue 3. It is clear that these words, in the contexts here, refer to a masculine plural direct object, in the two first examples, and to a feminine plural in the last one: **segells** in the first, **préssecs** in the second and **llaunes** in the third.

Three main points you need to observe are that:

1 object pronouns can stand only in conjunction with a verb.
2 as well as indicating singular and plural (*it*, *them*), object pronouns also indicate gender.
3 The forms taken by these words may vary according to their position with the verb and according to the spelling of the verb.

The scheme, then, for *it / them* is as follows:

	Singular		Plural	
	m.	*f.*	*m.*	*f.*
Before verb				
Verb beginning with consonant	el	la	els	les
Verb beginning with vowel or **h** + *vowel*	l	l'	els	les
After verb				
Verb ending in consonant or **u**	-lo	-la	-los	-les
Verb ending in a, e, or i	'l	-la	'ls	-les

Normally, pronouns of this kind go before the verb, except with an infinitive, a command form or the gerund (English *-ing*). Further details are given in Units 9 and 10.

Note that after the verb the pronouns are always attached to it by a hyphen or an apostrophe:

El pastís, el vols gran o petit?	*Do you want a big cake or a small one?*
I la farina? On la tens?	*And the flour? Where do you keep it?*
Vull veure'ls ara.	*I want to see them now.*
Els mapes? Els tinc al cotxe.	*The maps? They're in my car.*
Mirant-la m'adono que és molt bonica.	*Looking at her I realize she is very pretty.*

B The pronoun *en*

More now on **en/n'** that we met in Unit 3. Basically **en** corresponds to **de** (*of, from*) and a noun already identified in the speaker's mind. It belongs to the family of object pronouns (always

appearing in conjunction with a verb) and it obeys the rules of
position and spelling described in the previous section.

Singular/plural

Before verb
Verb beginning with consonant **en**
Verb beginning with vowel or **n'**
  h *+ vowel*

After verb
Verb ending in consonant or **u** **-ne**
Verb ending in **a, e,** *or* **i** **'n**

In the context of shopping **en** has an important function in
indicating a quantity of something:

De tomates, quantes en vols? – **En** vull dos quilos.	*Tomatoes, how many (of them) do you want? – I want two kilos (of them).*
Teniu plàtans? – Ho sento, no **en** tenim.	*Do you have bananas? – I'm sorry, we don't have any.*

- -

Insight

You will have become aware that object pronouns are a
quite complex and demanding aspect of Catalan grammar.
Familiarity with other Romance languages can be helpful, but
there are no short-cuts for the foreign learner to acquire agile
and correct command of the Catalan pronoun system. As
you encounter more and more examples, paying attention to
pronoun functions and patterns of construction, you will gain
understanding of how the pronouns work and confidence in
using them yourself.

- -

Exercise 7
Complete this dialogue in a greengrocer's:

Botiguer	_____ 1?
(You)	A mi. _____ 2.
Botiguer	Com _____ 3, grosses o petites?

72

(You)	_____ 4 petites.
Botiguer	_____ 5?
(You)	Sí, també _____ 6.
Botiguer	Ho sento, però no _____ 7.
(You)	Doncs, res més. _____ 8?
Botiguer	_____ 9 quatre _____ 10 i seixanta-cinc _____ 11.

Exercise 8

Complete these sentences with an object pronoun:

1 No trobo els paquets de farina! On _____ deixes normalment?

2 Saps on és l'ampolla de vi? – No, no ho sé, però potser _____ té en Miquel.

3 Venen les entrades a l'ajuntament? – No, només _____ venen a les oficines de correus.

4 Venen bitllets d'autobús a l'ajuntament? – No, només _____ venen a l'estanc.

5 No sé on posar la fruita. – Pots posar _____ a la cuina.

6 El vi és molt bo. _____ vols provar?

7 Jo menjo molta fruita però vosaltres no _____ mengeu mai.

8 Pots agafar el llibre i portar _____ a la meva habitació.

Grammar

C Regular verbs (2)

Second conjugation

In this lesson we have found some verbs in the present tense that belong to the second conjugation (infinitive ending in **-er** and **-re**). Note that in this conjugation there are relatively few verbs which correspond to the regular model conjugation of **perdre**. **Voler** and **valer**, for example, have irregular first-person singular **vull** and **valc**.

Perdre (*to lose, to miss, to waste*)

(jo) perd-o	*I lose*	(nosaltres) perd-em	*we lose*
(tu) perd-s	*you lose*	(vosaltres) perd-eu	*you lose*
(ell/ella) perd	*he/she loses*	(ells/elles) perd-en	*they lose*

D Irregular verbs

In this unit several new irregular verbs are introduced: **fer** (*to do, to make*), **poder** (*can, to be able*), **saber** (*to know, to find out*), **valer** (*to be worth, to cost*) and **vendre** (*to sell*). Study the conjugations of **fer**, **poder** and **saber** which are very frequently used. See the Reference tables for **valer** and **vendre**.

fer	poder	saber
(jo) faig	(jo) puc	(jo) sé
(tu) fas	(tu) pots	(tu) saps
(ell/ella) fa	(ell/ella) pot	(ell/ella) sap
(nosaltres) fem	(nosaltres) podem	(nosaltres) sabem
(vosaltres) feu	(vosaltres) podeu	(vosaltres) sabeu
(ells/elles) fan	(ells/elles) poden	(ells/elles) saben

Exercise 9

Complete these sentences with the correct form of the present tense of the verbs in brackets:

1 _____ anar a la botiga i comprar dues barres de pa (tu)? Em sembla que (ells) les _____ a cinquanta cèntims. (poder, vendre)

2 No _____ quan _____ anar al banc (jo). _____ (tu) l'horari que _____ (ells)? (saber, poder, saber, fer)

3 _____ donar-me una poma (tu)? _____ gana i no _____ temps d'anar a comprar (jo). (poder, tenir, tenir)

4 Ells no _____ quant _____ les ampolles de vi. (saber, valer)

5 _____ (nosaltres) una visita a la Maria? (fer)

Grammar

E Questions

You have already met several words which introduce questions in Catalan, like **quant?** *how much*, **què?** *what?* and **quan?** *when?*, etc. Another kind of question is the simple yes/no type. In Catalan such questions do not entail change of word order (in English, *John is coming* but *Is John coming?*). You will have noticed (remember in Unit 2 Dialogue 2: **vint-i-un anys té el meu cosí i trenta-tres la meva cosina**) that the subject of a Catalan sentence can stand after the verb: **en Joan viu aquí = viu aquí en Joan**. The corresponding question (*Does Joan live here?*) can likewise be expressed as **en Joan viu aquí?** or **viu aquí en Joan?**. What gives a sentence an interrogative sense, then, making the difference between **l'estimo** *I love her / him* and **l'estimo?** *Do I love her / him?* is not word order but intonation. Your ear will detect this and you will quickly learn to reproduce the slight rise in final pitch that distinguishes the question from the statement:

◄) **CD1, TR 15, 01:30**

En Carles viu aquí. En Carles viu aquí?

> T'estimo. T'estimo?
> Viuen en aquest carrer. Viuen en aquest carrer?
> Obren aquesta tarda? Sí, senyora, obren aquesta tarda.

F Spelling changes (c > qu), (j > g), (g > gu)

The changes of the kind seen in the parts of **tancar** (see Grammar A in Unit 3) also affect many feminine plural forms. As well as **ca > ques** we also encounter **ja > ges** and **ga > gues**, in each case reflecting consistency of pronunciation.

So, **fleca > fleques, taronja > taronges, botiga > botigues**, etc.

Exercise 10

Match the words below with the correct pictures. Write both singular and plural forms.

| pera, maduixa, all, patata, raïm, taronja, pastanaga, tomata |

Insight

The words related to food in the last exercise are a reminder of how much Catalan vocabulary resembles other Romance languages and even, to a lesser extent, English: **pera, patata, tomata, taronja...**

Points to remember

1 **l'horari: obren a les nou i tanquen a les vuit** *opening hours: they open at nine and they close at eight.*
2 **voldria un quilo de pomes** *I'd like a kilo of apples.*
3 **teniu taronges? sí que en tenim** *have you got oranges? yes, we have.*
4 **les vull grosses** *I want big ones.*
5 **quant val? quant és?** *how much is it/will that be?*
6 **val...euros, són...euros** *it costs/that is/it will be ...euros.*
7 **un paquet de sucre, una llauna de tonyina, una barra de pa, un quilo de fruita, un tall de formatge, un litre de llet,** *a bag of*

sugar, a tin of tuna, a loaf of bread (baguette), a kilo of fruit, a piece of cheese, a litre of milk.

8 The pattern for the present tense of regular verbs of second-conjugation in **-er/-re**.

9 Direct-object pronouns.

10 The pronoun **en** corresponding to **de** (*of, from*) together with a noun already present in the speaker's mind.

5

Què fas?

What are you doing?

In this unit you will learn
- *How to talk about what you are doing now*
- *How to discuss your daily routine*
- *How to say how often you do something*

Before you start

The conjugated form of the verb in Catalan corresponds to three patterns in English: the first-person singular **parlo** (Unit 3) can mean *I speak*, *I do speak* and *I am speaking*. In addition, Catalan 'mirrors' the *am -ing* construction with its own combination of the irregular verb **estar** (*to be*) and a part of the verb called the gerund (see Grammar C), equivalent to the *-ing* form of the English verb. Catalan and English usage are not exactly the same, though, because use of the gerund in Catalan conveys always the idea of *(right) now*. Consider first: **Què fas? Escolto aquest disc/Estic escoltant aquest disc** (*I'm listening to this record*), where in English the *-ing* form is the only possibility.

Then compare: **Què fas aquesta tarda?** (*What are you doing this evening?*) – **Vaig al cine** (*I am going to the cinema*), where the Catalan construction **estar + gerund** cannot be used, as the idea is not *(right) now*.

In practice the common pattern in Catalan is for prompt questions to be made in the simple form, with the response often given with the continuous form: **Que dorms?** (*Are you sleeping?*) – **No, estic meditant** (or **medito**) (*No, I'm meditating*).

In this unit we complete our review of the three main types of regular verbs in Catalan. After this unit our vocabulary boxes will give just the infinitive of any verb introduced in the corresponding dialogues.

Also, from this point onwards, conjugated forms of irregular verbs will not be laid out in the Grammar sections of units where these verbs are introduced. Instead, a reference (irregular) will be given next to infinitives in the vocabulary boxes. You can then check the conjugation by consulting the **Reference tables** at the end of the book.

---

1 Estic llegint *I am reading*

Tim comes into the living room, where Lluís is watching the television. Then Tim goes into the kitchen.

Tim	Hola Lluís, què fas?
Lluís	Estic mirant un programa sobre animals salvatges a la tele. I tu?
Tim	Jo estic buscant el diari d'avui. No el trobo.
Lluís	El meu pare l'està llegint; és a la cuina ... Per cert, véns a la discoteca avui?
Tim	No, vaig al cine amb uns amics. Hi anem un cop per setmana i avui toca.
Tim	Hola Roger, què fas? Que no llegeixes el diari?
Roger	No, ja estic. Ara fregeixo els bolets per al sopar.

◆ CD1, TR 16, 00:09

mirar *to look at, to watch*
sobre *about*
salvatge *wild*

QV

buscar *to look for*
el diari *newspaper*
avui *today*
trobar *to find*
__*llegir__ *to read*
per cert *by the way*
venir (irregular) *to come*
anar (irregular) *to go*
__*hi__ *there*
un cop per setmana *once a week*
avui toca *today is the day*
ja estic *I've finished with it*
ara *now*
__*fregir__ *to fry*
el bolet *mushroom*
el sopar *dinner, evening meal*

Insight

Remember that the continuous tense (**estar** + gerund) is used only with the idea of *(right)* **now**. You can reinforce your understanding of this principle by observing how, in Dialogue 1, some verbs in the simple present tense could be converted into the continuous construction (**no estàs llegint el diari?** for **no llegeixes el diari?**, **ara estic fregint …** for **ara fregeixo …**), while others could not (e.g. **véns a la discoteca …?, vaig al cine …, hi anem …**).

2 El dissabte em llevo tard *On Saturday I get up late*

CD1, TR 16, 01:11

Pau and Montse try to find a day to go shopping.

Pau	Vols venir a comprar amb mi dimecres?
Montse	No puc. Cada dimecres vaig a la piscina.
Pau	És clar! Ah, i dijous?
Montse	Tampoc. Sortint de la feina tinc classe de francès.

Pau	Estàs molt ocupada, no?
Montse	Sí, el dilluns i el dimarts normalment plego tard del treball. Només tinc lliure el divendres.
Pau	Llàstima, justament aquest divendres no puc. Vaig a Manresa.
Montse	Doncs si vols hi anem dissabte.
Pau	D'acord, però jo el dissabte em llevo tard. Et va bé a les onze?
Montse	Perfecte. Jo també dormo moltes hores els dissabtes i a més no dino fins a les dues.

la piscina *swimming pool*
és clar! *of course!*
tampoc *neither*
sortint *(on) leaving*
la feina/el treball *work*
la classe de francès *French lesson*
ocupat/-da *busy*
plegar *to finish (work)*
la llàstima *pity*
justament *as it happens*
llevar-se *to get up*
*****dormir** *to sleep*
dinar *to have lunch*

Els dies de la setmana *The days of the week*
dilluns *Monday*, **dimarts** *Tuesday*, **dimecres** *Wednesday*, **dijous** *Thursday*, **divendres** *Friday*, **dissabte** *Saturday*, **diumenge** *Sunday*;
el cap de setmana *the weekend*

Insight

You will have noticed that Catalan has two verbs both covering senses of *to be*, **ser** and **estar**. For the time being you should keep an eye on the way these verbs are used in the dialogues. A pattern will begin to be established and you will find complementary explanations in Units 12 and 16.

Exercise 1
True or false?

1 Lluís and Tim go to the disco together.
2 Roger is preparing tomatoes for dinner.
3 Pau is going to Manresa on Friday.
4 Pau and Montse are going shopping on Saturday afternoon.

Exercise 2
Study the dialogues and make sure you understand everything.
If you can, act them out with a partner.

Exercise 3
Listen again to Dialogues 1 and 2 and say whether the letter c
sounds like English c in *cat* or c in *cent* in the following words.

1 cuina **2** discoteca **3** cine **4** cop **5** francès **6** ocupada

Notice also what happens in **estic mirant, estic buscant, tinc classe**
and **tinc lliure**.

Insight
Meals

els àpats principals	*main meals*
l'esmorzar (m.)	*breakfast*
el dinar	*lunch*
el berenar	*afternoon snack*
el sopar	*dinner*

All these words are also the corresponding verbs: e.g.
esmorzar *to have breakfast*. Times of meals are very flexible
but in general they are later than what we are used to.
El dinar can be between 1 and 2 p.m. (but can be as late
as 3–3.30 p.m., especially at the weekend). Some people,
principally children, have a snack (**berenar**) in the late
afternoon and, finally, **el sopar** can be taken any time
between 8 and 10.30 p.m., even later in summer.

Exercise 4
Look at senyora Frigolé's diary.

18 Dilluns agost *Dinar Montse* *Gimnàs*	**21** Dijous agost *5,15 dentista*

19 Dimarts
agost
     tren Mataró (8,35)
	22 Divendres
	agost *Dinar Montse*
	     concert Raimon a les 22H.

20 Dimecres
agost
     Dinar Montse
     Gimnàs amb la Rosa
	23 Dissabte
	agost
	Hospital
	tia Núria **24** Diumenge
	agost

Now say whether the following sentences are true or false:

1 La senyora Frigolé va al gimnàs un cop per setmana.
2 Cada dia dina amb la seva filla Montserrat.
3 Té visita al dentista dijous a la tarda.
4 Dimarts va a Mataró.
5 El cap de setmana es queda a casa.
6 Divendres al matí va a un concert.

Key words and sentences

Asking and saying what are you doing

Què fas (ara)?	*What are you doing (now)?*
Què estàs fent?	*What are you doing?*
M'estic pentinant. / Estic pentinant-me. / Em pentino.	*I am doing my hair.*

Asking and talking about daily routines

A quina hora et lleves?	*What time do you get up?*
Normalment em llevo a les set.	*I normally get up at seven.*
Quan plegues de treballar?	*When do you finish work?*
Plego tard.	*I finish late.*

Talking about pastimes (1)

Quan vas a classe d'italià?	*When do you go to your Italian lesson?*
Què fas els caps de setmana?	*What do you do at weekends?*

Saying how often you do certain things

sempre	*always*
cada dia	*every day*
sovint	*often*
normalment	*normally*
alguna vegada	*sometimes*
un cop/una vegada a la setmana/al mes/a l'any	*once a week/month/year*
poc sovint/gairebé mai/ mai	*not very often/rarely/ never*

Grammar

A Regular verbs (3)

Third conjugation
Some of the verbs in Dialogues 1 and 2 belong to the third conjugation (infinitive ending in -ir): **fregir, llegir, sortir, venir** and **dormir**. Our model for this conjugation is **dormir**.

dorm-o (*I sleep*)   dorm-im (*we sleep*)
dorm-s (*you sleep*)   dorm-iu (*you sleep*)
dorm (*he/she sleeps*)   dorm-en (*they sleep*)

In fact, the set of regular verbs belonging to the third conjugation is relatively small. **Sentir** *to hear, to be sorry*, that we have already met, is one such verb.

Sortir (see Unit 3) and **venir** are irregular. Verbs like **fregir** and **llegir** are explained in the next section.

Inceptive verbs
Most third-conjugation verbs differ from the pattern seen in **dormir**, in that they introduce an additional syllable -**eix**- between the stem and ending in all parts of the verb except first- and second-person plural. We call these inceptive verbs and we can take **llegir** as our model:

lleg-**eix**-o (*I read*)   lleg-**im** (*we read*)
lleg-**eix**-es (*you read*)   lleg-**iu** (*you read*)
lleg-**eix** (*he/she reads*)   lleg-**eix**-en (*they read*)

Exercise 5
Complete each pair with the corresponding singular or plural form as in the example:

Example: (jo) fregeixo (nosaltres) fregim
            (ella) condueix (elles) condueixen

  1 llegeixo _____
  2 _____ deduïu
  3 construeix _____
  4 dirigeixes _____
  5 _____ descobrim

Grammar

B The gerund

Dialogue 1 introduces the use of the gerund, which, placed with the verb **estar**, expresses something equivalent to *to be -ing*, as explained in the introductory remarks to this unit. The gerund is formed by adding to the stem of the verb the ending for its conjugation **-ant**, **-ent** or **-int** (first, second and third conjugations).

stem		+	*ending*	>	*gerund*
preparar	prepar	+	ant	>	preparant
perdre	perd	+	ent	>	perdent
discutir	discut	+	int	>	discutint

C Reflexive verbs

A 'reflexive' verb is basically one whose subject and object are one and the same, that is the action is done 'to oneself'. This is true of **dir-se** which we have already met, and of a large number of verbs denoting daily activities. We can take **pentinar-se** *to do one's hair* as our model for how this type of verb is conjugated:

em pentino	ens pentinem
et pentines	us pentineu
es pentina	es pentinen

Note changes to some pronouns when the verb (for example **afaitar-se** *to shave*) begins with a vowel:

m'afaito	ens afaitem
t'afaites	us afaiteu
s'afaita	s'afaiten

Exercise 6

Put a verb in every blank space. Decide whether you need a simple present tense or a present continuous tense.

El senyor Carbonés normalment _____ (plegar, 1) a les sis en punt de la tarda, però ara mateix ja són les set i encara _____ (treballar, 2). _____ (preparar, 3) uns dossiers molt importants. De tant en tant _____ (mirar, 4) el rellotge.

En aquest mateix moment, la Rosa, la seva cunyada, _____ (esperar, 5) davant de la porta perquè aquest vespre tots dos _____ (anar, 6) al teatre.

Després d'esperar una bona estona la Rosa el truca per telèfon:

– Josep, que no _____ (venir, 7)? – Sí, d'aquí a cinc minuts _____ (baixar, 8).

Mentre _____ (esperar, 9), la Rosa aprofita el temps: _____ (maquillar-se, 10), _____ (pentinar-se, 11) els cabells i també _____ (patir, 12) perquè _____ (adonar-se, 13) que l'obra _____ (estar, 14) a punt de començar.

Insight

When a Catalan verb is used reflexively, the equivalent in English will often involve varying adjustments in the word pattern. **Aixecar** means *to lift, to raise* whereas **aixecar-se** is translated as *to get up*. The logic of the Catalan system is very simple, and, when this is properly understood, using the reflexive form becomes relatively straightforward for

(Contd)

the English-speaker. It is helpful to remind yourself that the correct pronoun forms are an integral part of the conjugation of reflexive verbs.

Daily activities

◀) **CD1, TR 17, 00:02**

despertar-se	to wake up
aixecar-se/llevar-se	to get up
dutxar-se/banyar-se	to take a shower/a bath
maquillar-se	to put on make up
afaitar-se	to shave
vestir-se	to get dressed
agafar el cotxe/l'autobús	to take/to catch the car/bus
començar/entrar a la feina	to start work
plegar/sortir de la feina	to finish/leave work
tornar a casa	to go/come home
rentar-se les dents	to brush one's teeth
rentar-se les mans/la cara	to wash one's hands/face
anar a dormir	to go to bed
pentinar-se	to do one's hair

Other activities

◀) **CD1, TR 17, 00:09**

sortir amb amics	to go out with friends
anar al cine/teatre/ concert/museu	to go to the cinema/theatre/ concert/museum
escoltar música/la ràdio	to listen to music/the radio
mirar la televisió	to watch television

anar a comprar	to go shopping
fer esport	to do sport
llegir un llibre/el diari	to read a book/the newspaper
netejar la casa	to clean the house
rentar/planxar la roba	to wash/iron clothes

Insight

Notice that what Pau says in line 3 of Dialogue 2 implies **i dijous què fas?** (equivalent to **i dijous, és possible?**) The verb **fer** has two meanings, *to do* and *to make*. We shall subsequently observe also that this verb figures in a large number of Catalan idioms like **fer mal** *to hurt*, **fer cas** *to pay attention*, **fer falta** *to be necessary,* etc. Sometimes **fer** is needed where in English we use other verbs, as in **fer esport** *to play/practise sport*, **fer bon temps** *to be good (the weather)*.

Exercise 7

Using the information above, together with what we have learnt about telling the time in Catalan, write a detailed account of what you normally (**normalment**) do on a weekday (**dia d'entre setmana**) and at the weekend (**cap de setmana**). This will be a reinforcement of Exercise 8 below and a very good way of practising the use of the various types of verbs represented here.

Exercise 8

Look at Quim's daily routine and write down a correct sentence for every picture (**a** to **j**) using the appropriate verbs and times. For further practice, express the same sequence of events in the first person.

Grammar

D The pronoun *hi*

One of the main functions of this word is to express the idea of *there* (as seen in Units 2 and 3), either as destination or location. Basically **hi** represents **a** (*to*, *at*, *in*) plus the idea of a place or activity already identified in the speaker's mind, as is seen clearly in Montse's **hi anem** in Dialogue 2, where **hi** means **a comprar**.

E Negation

In Catalan simple negation is expressed by **no** immediately preceding the verb, in both statements and questions.

No vol patates.	*S/he doesn't want any potatoes.*
No vol patates?	*Does s/he not want potatoes?*

Sometimes with **no** in the same sentence we can find other negative particles. **No** always goes before the verb, and all other adverbs are placed after. Some Catalan speakers use emphatic **pas**, situated after the verb too.

Vas sovint al teatre?	*Do you go to the theatre often?*
No, (no hi vaig **sovint).**	*No, (I don't go often).*
No, no hi vaig **mai.**	*No, I never go.*
No, no hi vaig **pas mai.**	*No, I never go.*
No, ja no hi vaig **més.**	*No, I don't go any more.*

More details on negatives will be given in Unit 6.

Exercise 9
Read these sentences and write down a question for every one.

1 No, no hi vaig avui.

2 Hi vaig tres cops per setmana.

3 Esmorzo a les vuit.

4 Els dimecres a la tarda.

5 Surt a les set.

6 Vaig d'excursió a la muntanya.

Reading

Try, first of all, to see how much of the following passage you can understand without referring to the **Catalan–English vocabulary** at the back of the book. Then use the vocabulary list to fill any gaps in your comprehension.

Publica un diari local que en la societat actual hi ha molt jovent que treballa més hores del normal per a poder marxar de casa dels pares. En Pere Molas n'és un exemple: serveix en un bar entre setmana i les nits del cap de setmana condueix un taxi. Treballa molt perquè està estalviant per poder pagar l'entrada d'un pis. Ell vol quedar-se a viure a Barcelona, però els preus de l'habitatge són molt alts. Com que treballa tant no té temps per a divertir-se, perquè sempre està cansat i prefereix quedar-se a casa i relaxar-se: mira alguna pel·lícula o llegeix llibres de ciència-ficció. Algun diumenge va a veure un partit de futbol i els dissabtes a la tarda els dedica a la forma física: passa unes dues hores al gimnàs fent exercicis i de tant en tant juga a tennis amb un amic del barri.

Exercise 10
Now answer these questions in English, or in Catalan if you feel confident enough.

1 Why does Pere Molas work in two different places?
2 What are property prices like in Barcelona?
3 What does he enjoy doing?
4 Does he take any physical exercise?
5 If so, when?

Insight

This is a good point at which to take stock of how far you have progressed since beginning the course. First of all read again the last Insight box in Unit 1. The advice given there still applies. The final sections of Units 1–5 supply the basis for reviewing your progress and then consolidating what you have learnt. Systematic revision is essential to extending linguistic competence, and it is especially constructive if you build in an overview of the situations in which you can communicate in Catalan plus your own audit of the vocabulary range and grammatical structures you have at your disposal.

Points to remember

1 **què fas/què estàs fent? estic llegint el diari** *what are you doing? I'm reading the newspaper*
2 **què fas aquest vespre? vaig al cinema** *what are you doing this evening? I'm going to the cinema*
3 **cada dia començo a treballar** a les 8 *every day I start work at 8*
4 **els caps de setmana sovint faig esport** *at weekends I often play sport*
5 Negative statements and questions: **vosaltres no aneu mai al teatre** *you never go to the theatre*; **que no vols venir-hi?** *don't you want to come (there)?*
6 Reflexive verbs for daily activities: **em dutxo, em vesteixo, em rento les dents...**
7 **estar** + gerund *to be ...-ing*: **estàs dormint** *you are sleeping.*
8 The pattern for the present tense of regular verbs of third-conjugation in **-ir.**
9 Inceptive verbs with the incremental **-eix-** syllable, like **llegir, fregir, conduir ...**
10 The pronoun **hi,** expressing the idea of *there*, referring to a place or activity already present in the speaker's mind.

6

Al restaurant
At the restaurant

In this unit you will learn
- *How to talk about preferences*
- *How to order meals and drinks*
- *How to ask for and give suggestions*

1 Menú o carta *Table d'hôte* or *à la carte*

Tim and his friends are in a typical restaurant, Can Sebastià. They have been looking at the menu for a while.

CD1, TR 18, 00:08

Cambrer	Què volen menjar?
Ester	Per a mi de primer peus de porc i de segon xai amb guarnició.
Cambrer	Em sap greu, però de xai no ens en queda gens. Tenim mongetes amb botifarra.
Ester	D'acord, agafo les mongetes.
Cambrer	I vostès?
Tim	Jo m'estimo més escollir de la carta. Què m'aconsella?
Cambrer	De primer li recomano el pastís de peix, especialitat de la casa, o el plat d'embotits de la comarca acompanyat de pa amb tomàquet.
Mireia	Per a mi el pastís i de segon llenguado a la planxa.

Tim	Doncs per a mi i en Jordi els embotits i després ànec amb naps.
Cambrer	I per beure?
Mireia	Vi de la casa, aigua i dues ampolles de cava.
Cambrer	El vi, el prefereixen rosat o negre?
Ester	Millor rosat. I l'aigua sense gas, sisplau.

menjar *to eat* (also, *to have lunch*)
els peus de porc *pig's trotters*
el xai amb guarnició *lamb with garnish*
*quedar *to be left, to remain*
*gens *(not) any*
les mongetes *beans*
la botifarra *Catalan pork sausage*
agafar *to take, to have*
estimar-se més *to prefer*
escollir *to choose*
aconsellar *to recommend, to advise*
el pastís de peix *fish pie*
el plat *dish, plate, course (of meal)*
els embotits de la comarca *local cured meats, ham* (or *salami*)
el llenguado a la planxa *grilled sole*
l'ànec amb naps (m.) *duck with turnips*
beure (irregular) *to drink*
el vi de la casa *house wine*
l'aigua (f.) **sense gas** *still mineral water*
el cava *cava (Catalan champagne-style sparkling wine)*
(el vi) rosat *rosé (wine)*
(el vi) negre *red (wine)*

QUICK VOCAB

Insight

de xai no ens en queda gens, *we don't have any lamb left*
illustrates well the function of the pronoun **en** as explained
in Unit 4 Grammar section B. The word order here shows
how **en** refers to a noun (**xai,** explicit in this case) already
identified in the speaker's mind. The same meaning could

(Contd)

have been expressed more simply as **no ens queda gens de xai**. What we hear in the dialogue, though, is characteristic of colloquial Catalan: an idea expressed at the beginning of an utterance 'picked up' and referred to again in pronoun form with the verb. Be prepared to meet further examples of this in Dialogue 3, and then subsequently as you progress through the units.

2 M'agrada el cava *I like cava*

During the dinner they talk about the food and drinks.

CD1, TR 18, 01:30

Ester	Què et sembla el llenguado, t'agrada?
Mireia	Sí que m'agrada, però està massa fet pel meu gust. I la botifarra, és bona?
Ester	És boníssima, de debò.
Jordi	A mi l'ànec em sembla que és una mica salat. El vols provar?
Ester	No, gràcies ... El que m'agrada més de tot és el vi.
Jordi	Està bé, tot i que jo m'estimo més el cava.
Tim	Doncs a mi ja m'agrada el vi i el cava també, però com la cervesa no hi ha res.

QUICK VOCAB

què et sembla ...? *what do you think about ...?*
***semblar** to seem*
sí que ... *sure ...*
***agradar** to please, to be pleasing/likeable*
massa *too much*
fet/-a *done, cooked*
pel meu gust *to/for my taste*
boníssim/-a *very good, really good*
de debò *really*
una mica *a little bit*
salat/-da *salty*

provar *to taste*
el que *what (that which)*
de tot *of all*
està bé *it's OK*
tot i que *although*
*ja see Grammar Unit 7
com ... no hi ha res *there's nothing like ...*

Insight

Boníssima, heard in Dialogue 2, is the superlative form of **bona** indicated by the suffix **-íssim/-a**. The meaning conveyed is even more emphatic than **molt bona** *very good*. Other examples: **petitíssim/-a**, *really small*, **ocupadíssim/-a** *extremely busy*...

Insight

Ja means basically *already*, but it often serves (as in the last sentence of the dialogue) simply to reinforce a verb and may not be translated into English.

---

3 El compte, sisplau! *The bill, please!*

Finally, it's time for the dessert and coffees.

Cambrer	Què els ve de gust de postres?
Jordi	Què teniu?
Cambrer	Crema catalana, flam, gelats, pastís de xocolata, de llimona i de formatge.
Mireia	Teniu gelat de vainilla?
Cambrer	Ho sento, de vainilla no ens en queda cap. N'hi ha de maduixa o de xocolata.
Jordi	I la crema, és de la casa?
Cambrer	Oh i tant!
Jordi	Decidit doncs: dos flams amb nata, un pastís de llimona i un gelat de xocolata.

(Contd)

CD1, TR 18, 02:32

QUICK VOCAB

*els *to you*
venir de gust *to appeal*
les postres *dessert*
la crema catalana *crème brulée*
el flam *crème caramel*
el gelat *ice cream*
el pastís *cake*
la llimona *lemon*
*cap *any*
de la casa *home made*
oh i tant! *of course!*
la nata *cream*
*la infusió *infusion, herbal tea*
ja n'hi ha prou *that's enough*

Insight

Did you understand what **en** means on the two occasions in the above dialogue, where this pronoun is combined with **hi ha: n'hi ha de maduixa …, ja n'hi ha prou**? In the first case what is referred to is **gelat**; in the second case, **aigua o cava**. If you understand how this construction works here, your listening and reading skills are coming on very well.

Exercise 1
True or false?

1 Ester is going to have lamb because there are no more beans.
2 Jordi and Tim eat the same dish.
3 Tim prefers beer to wine or cava.
4 At dessert time they order more cava.

Exercise 2

Read each dialogue again and make sure you can understand them in detail. Keep up the practice of repeating what you hear in the recording out loud, and of working with a partner (if you can) to act out each dialogue.

Insight

As explained in the section on word liaison (Pronunciation and spelling), some consonants placed at the end of the word are silent. Even if it is not a generalized picture for the whole Catalan-speaking area, this is common in the central dialect. Listen again to the dialogues and then do Exercise 3.

Exercise 3

Now listen again to the dialogues and say whether the last consonant of the words below is sounded or not.

1 menjar 2 primer 3 segon 4 sap 5 d'acord 6 escollir
7 gust 8 tant

Cultural information
Restaurants

The food of the Catalan-speaking areas is a notable example of the Mediterranean diet (la dieta mediterrània), in all its rich variety. The local cuisine is understood as a significant feature of the distinctive national culture. **Pa amb tomàquet**, for instance, is as genuine and distinctive an item of Catalan cuisine as is pizza for Italians. It is as simple as a slice of bread (or *toast*, **una torrada**) rubbed with tomato and garlic, with a good drizzle of olive oil and salt to taste. It can accompany cured meats, cheese or omelette, at any meal.

Not all restaurants offer Catalan or traditional food, and there are more and more places with foreign or cosmopolitan dishes. Traditional restaurants usually provide a **menú del dia** *table d'hôte*, with some starters (**primer plat**) to choose from, followed by a selection of main courses (**segon plat** or **plat principal**)

(Contd)

and desserts (**les postres**). Sometimes the **menú del dia** includes bread, drink and coffee. Always look carefully to see whether prices include VAT (**IVA, impost sobre el valor afegit**) or not. It is never obligatory but it is usual to leave a tip (**la propina**).

Insight
Can Sebastià

Can Sebastià (literally translated, **Sebastià's house/home**) is the name of the restaurant in the dialogues of this unit. Here **can** is a contraction of **ca** + personal article **en**, and the same feature occurs with **ca + el > cal** and **ca + els > cals** (but there is no contraction in **ca la, ca l'** or **ca les**). **Ca** itself is a contraction of **casa de** and, rather like its French counterpart **chez**, it appears regularly in the names of restaurants, country houses or estates. Note also that **ca** itself can be preceded by either **a** or **de**: **Vaig a cals pares** (*I'm going to my parents' (house)*); **Vénen de Ca l'Antònia** (*They have come from Ca l'Antònia*).

Cultural information
Catalan dishes

Here are some of the most common Catalan dishes (complementing those which already feature in the dialogues):

Primer plat *First course*

l'amanida (f.)	*salad*
la sopa (de peix, de verdures)	*(fish, vegetable) soup*
l'escalivada (f.)	*char-grilled vegetables*
l'esqueixada (f.)	*cold salad of flaked bacallà (see below)*
els cargols	*snails*
els calamars a la romana	*squid fried in batter*
les anxoves amb torrades	*anchovies with toast*
l'escudella i carn d'olla (f.)	*traditional stew*
la paella	*paella*
l'arròs (m.)	*risotto*

Some of these dishes are served with traditional **pa amb tomàquet** (bread rubbed with fresh tomato and seasoned with olive oil and salt). This is also the usual way a sandwich (**un entrepà**) is prepared.

Segon plat *Second course*

la carn	*meat*
el pollastre, el conill	*chicken, rabbit*
el (porc) senglar	*wild boar*
el bistec/l'entrecot de vedella (m.)	*steak*
la truita (de patates,	*(Spanish, asparagus, etc.)*
d'espàrrecs, etc.)	*omelette*
el peix (fresc o congelat)	*fish (fresh or frozen)*
el lluç	*hake*
el rap	*monkfish*
el bacallà (fresc, salat)	*(fresh, salt-dried) cod*

Meat can be served with **allioli** and garnished with fresh vegetables, potatoes or *French fries* (**patates fregides**). The most current cooking techniques are: *charcoal-grilled* (**a la brasa**), *grilled* (**a la planxa**), *roasted* (**rostit**), *fried* (**fregit**), *baked* (**al forn**) or *boiled* (**bullit**).

Postres *Desserts*

els fruits secs	*dried fruits*
el recuit, el flam	*cottage cheese, crème caramel*
(la) mel i (el) mató	*honey and cottage cheese*

Begudes *Drinks*

el vi (rosat,	*wine (rosé,*
negre o blanc)	*red or white)*
la cervesa	*beer*
el licor	*spirit*
el refresc	*soft drink*
l'aigua (amb gas/sense gas)	*water (fizzy, still)*
el suc de taronja, pinya ...	*orange, pineapple ... juice*
la infusió	*(herbal) infusion*
el te	*tea*
el cafè	*coffee*

el porró

Exercise 4

Look at these four restaurant advertisements and then answer the questions:

a Restaurant *La Guineu*
Cuina tradicional Catalana
Obert cada dia (excepte dimarts)
Acceptem grups

b Ca l'Andreu
• Restaurant amb productes •
de la comarca
• Menús i Carta •
• Ampli menjador •
• Obert cada dia •

c El Rebost d'en Quim
Cuina vegetariana
Menú del dia 9 €
Descans setmanal el dilluns

d *Mas Molinet*
ESPECIALITATS MARINERES
Productes frescos
Obert als vespres
Pàrquing privat

1 Quin o quins restaurants ofereixen plats vegetarians?
2 Quin o quins restaurants tanquen un cop per setmana?
3 Quin o quins restaurants tenen menús?
4 Quin restaurant és millor per a menjar peix?
5 Quin o quins restaurants s'especialitzen en cuina catalana?
6 A quin restaurant no hi pots anar a dinar?

Exercise 5
◀ CD1, TR 19, 00:02

Listen to the recording. A young couple are ordering a meal in a restaurant. Write **A** (woman) or **B** (man) next to each dish or drink according to the person who is speaking:

Primers		Segons	
Escalivada	____	Bistec amb patates	____
Esqueixada	____	Pollastre rostit	____
Amanida	____	Botifarra amb mongetes	____
Sopa de verdures	____	Lluç a la planxa	____

Postres		Begudes	
Crema catalana	____	Aigua	
Mel i mató	____	Vi negre	____
Gelat de vainilla	____	Cervesa	____

Key words and sentences

Asking about and ordering meals and drinks

Què teniu/tenen de primer?	*What do you have as starters?*
Què hi ha de postres?	*What is there for dessert?*
Què podem beure?	*What can we drink?*
Per a mi una cervesa. /	*For me, a beer. /*
Jo vull una copa de vi.	*I want a glass of wine.*

Asking for and giving suggestions

Què m'aconsella de segon?	*What do you suggest for my main course?*
Li aconsello agafar ...	*I suggest you try ...*

Expressing what you prefer

A mi m'agrada més el peix.	*I like fish best./I prefer fish.*
Jo m'estimo més la carn.	*I like meat best.*
M'estimo més beure aigua.	*I prefer to drink water.*
Com el peix no hi ha res.	*You can't beat fish.*
T'agrada el xai?	*Do you like lamb?*
No, no m'agrada (gaire/gens).	*No, I don't like it (much/at all).*
Sí, però és ...	*Yes, but it's ...*
salat/-da	*salty*
fat/-da	*tasteless*
cru/-a	*raw*
cuit/-a	*well cooked*

Saying how much you like things

massa	*too much*
molt	*very*
força	*quite a lot*
una mica	*a little*
poc	*not much*
no ... gaire	*not very much*
no ... gens	*not at all*
no .... gens ni mica	*not one tiny little bit*

Insight

Using **agradar** to express the idea of *to like* does take some getting used to. The main point to absorb is that **agradar** means *to please, to be pleasing*, so that the subject/object roles between English and Catalan are reversed, and the Catalan verb agrees in number with the object (what is liked). Note though that the order of the parts of the sentence generally remains the same (i.e. English verb + object, Catalan verb + subject): so, **m'agrada la música** *I like music*, **m'agraden les flors** *I like flowers*.

Exercise 6
◀) CD1, TR 19, 01:13

Match each sentence in the left-hand column with the correct one from the right.

1 T'agrada el menjar?

2 Què vols de postres?
3 Ens agrada molt el pollastre.
4 Hi ha molt poques patates amb el xai.
5 Què ens aconsella de segon?

a Doncs a mi no m'agrada gens.
b Sí, és força bo.
c M'estimo més no menjar res.
d Què prefereixen, carn o peix?
e En pots demanar més al cambrer.

Grammar

A Negatives: *gens* and *cap*

No ... gens (de) *none/not any (at all)* and no ... cap *none/not (a single) one* are used respectively in negative sentences to refer to an item in general, (no ... gens), and to an identifiable single item (cap). So, in Dialogue 1 we find de xai no ens en queda gens (= no ens queda gens de xai), where gens refers to the general and non-countable item xai. In Dialogue 3 there is de (gelats de) vainilla no ens en queda cap, where cap refers to gelat de vainilla. Here the speaker is thinking of individual ice cream servings. Otherwise he would have said (de gelat de vainilla) no ens en queda gens, understanding vanilla ice cream as a mass noun. The use of both terms tends to be emphatic and often one hears just no en queda or ja no me'n queda. Look at some other examples:

Tens pomes? No, no en tinc cap.

No tinc gens de por.

Do you have apples? No, I haven't got any at all / a single one.

I am not at all afraid.

Exercise 7
Complete the sentences using cap or gens (de) and a verb if required:

1 Portes el diari? No, a la botiga ja no en queda _____.
2 Em dones més vi? Ho sento però _____.
3 Vols dinar? Ui, no tinc _____ gana.
4 Vénen els teus germans al concert? No, no en ve _____.
5 Avui a la universitat no hi ha _____ professor. No hi ha classe.
6 En Pere és molt impacient: de paciència no en _____.
7 No _____ ampolla d'aigua a la nevera!

Grammar

B Indirect object pronouns

em	*to me*
et	*to you*
li	*to him/her; to you* (**vostè**)
ens	*to us*
us	*to you*
els	*to them; to you* (**vostès**)

Indirect object pronouns are used to represent a person who is the recipient or beneficiary of the action of the verb. In Dialogue 1 there is **Què m'aconsella? De primer li aconsello el pastís de peix ...** where **m'** means **a mi** *to me*, and **li** represents **a vostè** *to you* (formal). See the **Reference tables** for forms according to position and to spelling of the verb.

Insight

Note the word order and pronoun repetition in *a mi em sembla que l'ànec és ...* and *a mi ja m'agrada el vi ...*, in the light of what is said on this topic in Insight box above, after Dialogue 1.

C The verbs *agradar*, *semblar* and *quedar*

Expressing the idea of *to like* usually involves use of the verb **agradar** (*to please*). The form of **agradar** will vary according to whether what is liked is singular or plural. We often find the repetition of the person for emphasis, for example: **Doncs *a mi* ja *m*'agrada el vi** (Dialogue 2).

Li agrada aquest plat.	*S/he likes this dish.*
Ens agraden els vins del Penedès.	*We like wines from the Penedès district.*

A similar change in construction is seen in the use of the verb **quedar** (*to remain, be left*) to express the idea of *to have left*, and **semblar** (*to seem*) used to mean *to think (of)*. Note again agreement of the verb with what remains or what seems and also use of the indirect object pronoun (corresponding to the subject in English).

Només em queden vint euros.   *I have only 20 euros left* (lit. *only 20 euros are left to me*).

Aquest vi em sembla massa fort.   *I think this wine is too strong* (lit. *this wine seems too strong to me*).

De botifarra no ens en queda.   *We have no more sausage* (lit. (**botifarra**) *there is none of it remaining to us*).

Part of the complexity of this last sentence (a very common Catalan construction) is explained by the fact that **en** (combined with the other pronoun, **ens**) refers back to **botifarra**.

Venir de gust (literally *to appeal*) also behaves in a comparable manner: **Ara no em ve de gust ...** (*I don't feel like ... now*).

Exercise 8

Fill in the blanks with an indirect object pronoun and / or with a verb in the present tense, using the final vocabulary list to check the meaning of any word you are unsure of:

A la meva filla _____ (agradar, 1) molt sortir de nits. Cada cap de setmana _____ (gastar-se, 2) més de 50€ en begudes, discoteques i transport. A ella no _____ (3) sembla extravagant gastar-se tants diners. Jo _____ (4) dic que és millor fer altres coses però ella no _____ (escoltar, 5). Alguns amics seus _____ (venir, 6) a casa els divendres al vespre. Posen música o _____ (tocar, 7) la guitarra. Fan molt soroll i a mi i al meu marit _____ (molestar, 8) moltíssim. _____ (9) diem d'anar al bar però sovint no _____ (10) fan cas. A mi no _____ (semblar, 11) correcte el seu comportament.

Grammar

D Feminine article *l'* or *la*

In Unit 1 we introduced the use of articles with singular nouns.
We noted that **la** becomes **l'** before feminine singular nouns
beginning with a vowel or **h** + vowel. But, as seen in **la infusió**
(see the vocabulary box for Dialogue 3), there are some exceptions.
So, **la** is maintained when it is followed by a noun beginning with
unstressed **i, u, hi, hu**:

la universitat   la Isabel
la humanitat   la història

But the apostrophe appears before a stressed initial vowel: **l'illa** *the
island* or **l'ungla** *the (finger) nail*.

Reading

For this and subsequent reading exercises, see the guidance given in
Unit 5.

Estimada Marta,

*Sóc al Pirineu i estic esquiant amb uns amics. Em diverteixo molt. El
que més m'agrada és baixar per les pistes, però no m'agrada gens fer cua a
pujar-les. Als matins ens llevem aviat, tot i que a mi em costa molt, com
sempre. A la tarda passegem pel poble o ens estem en un bar. Al vespre
anem a menjar sempre al restaurant. Ahir a la pizzeria Don Antonio,
molt malament. Avui anem a Ca la Catarina: sembla que és el millor de
la comarca. Ja saps que a mi m'agrada molt la cuina elaborada.*

I per Tarragona, va tot bé?

Una abraçada,

Albert

Exercise 9

First, observe here the conventions followed in an *informal letter* (**carta**) or *postcard* (**postal**) in Catalan. Then read the text again carefully and make a list of Albert's likes and dislikes.

A Què li agrada fer a l'Albert?
B Què no li agrada fer a l'Albert?

For further practice you can compose a similar letter to a friend explaining your own tastes and preferences.

Things to remember

1 què tenen de primer / de segon? *what do you have as starters / main course?*

2 què hi ha de postres? *what is there for dessert?*

3 jo vull una copa de vi / per a mi una cervesa *I want a glass of wine / for me a beer.*

4 li aconsello agafar... *I suggest you try...* recomano... *I can recommend...*

5 m'agrada el peix *I like fish*; m'agraden els melons *I like melons.*

6 prefereixo / m'estimo més la carn *I prefer meat.*

7 a mi el que m'agrada més és el vi negre *what I prefer is red wine.*

8 no ens queda cap gelat *we don't have any ice cream left* (identifiable single item); de gelat no ens en queda gens, *we don't have any ice cream left* (generic product); no tenim gens d'aigua *we don't have any water* (item in general).

9 (a la carta) hi ha vins de tots els països /...de vins n'hi ha de tots els països (on the menu) *there are wines from every country.*

10 Indirect-object pronouns.

7

Els transports
Transport

In this unit you will learn
- *How to book a train or plane ticket*
- *How to express opinions about people and things*
- *How to make simple comparisons*

1 Vull un bitllet d'avió *I want a plane ticket*

Tim is making a booking at the travel agency (**l'agència de viatges**).

◈ CD2, TR 1, 00:10

Tim	Voldria comprar un bitllet d'avió d'anada i tornada a Palma de Mallorca.
Noia	Quin dia vols viatjar?
Tim	El quinze de setembre.
Noia	I la tornada?
Tim	El deu d'octubre.
Noia	Quantes persones?
Tim	Dues. El més econòmic possible, sisplau.
Noia	Hi ha una oferta per a estudiants. És un bitllet tancat, no reemborsable ni modificable.
Tim	Que puc reservar-lo ara i demà el vinc a pagar amb la targeta de crèdit?
Noia	Oh i tant!

el bitllet ticket
l'avió (m.) plane
l'anada (f.) outward journey
la tornada return journey
viatjar to travel
econòmic/-a cheap, economical
no ... ni neither ... nor
reemborsable refundable
reservar to book
pagar to pay for
la targeta card

Els mesos de l'any Months of the year
gener January, **febrer** February, **març** March, **abril** April, **maig** May,
juny June, **juliol** July, **agost** August, **setembre** September, **octubre**
October, **novembre** November, **desembre** December

Insight

You will have noticed that the sentence **demà el vinc a pagar**
tomorrow I'll come to pay for it has the verb in the present
tense although the meaning clearly refers to the future. This
idiomatic feature is quite common in everyday contexts: **on
anem el cap de setmana?** where shall we go at the weekend?
et truco demà a la nit I'll call you tomorrow night.

2 Segona classe i no fumador Second class and non-smoking

Esteve, meanwhile, has gone to make an enquiry at the railway station.

Esteve	Voldria informació sobre trens per a Castelló de la Plana.
Empleada	Per a quan?
Esteve	Demà o demà passat, m'és igual. Però al matí, eh!
	(Contd)

CD2, TR 1, 01:19

Empleada	Hi ha un tren directe, amb sortida de Barcelona-Sants a les 9.20 i arribada a Castelló a les 11.10. Aquest tren només accepta reserves.
Esteve	Quant val, anada i tornada?
Empleada	Primera o segona classe?
Esteve	Segona i no fumador.
Empleada	Són 32€60.
Esteve	I més barat, no teniu res?
Empleada	El més barat és agafar el tren que va a Tarragona i allà es fa el canvi cap a Castelló. Aquest tren para a totes les estacions.
Esteve	Quant dura el viatge?
Empleada	Depèn de l'estona d'espera a Tarragona. Al voltant de tres hores.
Esteve	Molt bé. Gràcies … mmm … l'estació d'autocars és a prop d'aquí?

QUICK VOCAB

l'empleat/-da employee
demà passat the day after tomorrow
m'és igual I don't mind
la sortida departure
l'arribada (f.) arrival
no fumador non-smoking
barat/-a cheap
*es fa el canvi one changes
parar to stop
dependre to depend
l'estona (f.) (short) time
l'espera (f.) wait, waiting
al voltant (de) around
l'autocar (m.) coach

Insight

Both **per** and **per a** translate English *for*. Their use overlaps to some extent, but they are best considered as two separate prepositions with distinct functions. We look at this topic in detail in Unit 9 (Grammar D). For the time being you are advised to observe examples as they arise and their meaning in context.

---

3 És tan antipàtica com sempre
She is as unfriendly as ever

Later, Tim meets Esteve outside the station.

Tim	Què, ja tens el bitllet?
Esteve	No, encara no. És que no sé què fer. Trobo que viatjar amb tren és còmode i també agradable perquè pots contemplar el paisatge i tot això, però és car. En canvi l'autocar és avorrit i cansat, però molt més barat.
Tim	Però tu pots escollir. Jo, per anar a Mallorca només tinc una opció, agafar l'avió. Ja sé que també s'hi pot anar amb altres mitjans, però gairebé tothom agafa l'avió: no hi ha res tan ràpid i segur com l'avió.
Esteve	A mi no em diverteix gens l'avió, més aviat em fa por.
Tim	Per cert, saps amb qui acabo de parlar?
Esteve	No, amb qui?
Tim	Amb la Marta Roura.
Esteve	Què dius ara! Aquella tan antipàtica i creguda? Què en penses tu?
Tim	Trobo que ara és més senzilla i agradable.
Esteve	La veritat és que a mi em cau molt malament. A més, no és gens divertida.

◀⬤ CD2, TR 1, 02:52

*ja *already*
encara no *not yet*
és que *the fact is that*
amb *by (means of transport)*
còmode/-a *comfortable*
agradable *nice*
el paisatge *landscape, scenery*

QUICK VOCAB

car/-a *expensive*
en canvi *on the other hand*
avorrit/-da *boring*
cansat/-da *tiring*
l'opció (f.) *option*
*s'hi *see Grammar C*
*altre/-a *other*
el mitjà *means, way*
gairebé *nearly*
*tothom *everybody*
*tan ... com *as ... as*
ràpid/-a *fast*
segur/-a *safe*
fer por *to frighten*
*acabar de (+ infinitive) *to have just*
què dius ara! *go on!, you are kidding!*
antipàtic/-a *unlikeable, unfriendly*
cregut/-da *conceited*
pensar *to think*
senzill/-a *simple, natural, straightforward*
la veritat *truth*
caure malament *to be disagreeable*
divertit/-da *amusing*

Insight

In the dialogue above we have seen some uses of the comparison: **És *tan* antipàtica *com* sempre; ara és *més* senzilla i agradable** (*que* abans implied). The basic structure of a comparison is: **més ... que** *more ... than*, **menys ... que** *less ... than* and **tan ... com** *as ... as*.

Exercise 1
Veritat o fals?

1 En Tim paga el bitllet d'avió amb targeta bancària.
2 Tots els trens de Barcelona-Sants a Castelló són directes.
3 A l'Esteve no li agrada gaire viatjar amb avió.
4 L'Esteve no coneix la Marta Roura.

Exercise 2

Read the dialogues in this unit again on your own, checking the words or sentences you don't understand. If possible, act them out with a partner.

Exercise 3

Listen again to the dialogues and say whether the s in these words sounds like s in English *see* or s in English *nose:*

1 setembre **2** quantes **3** persones **4** sisplau **5** reservar-lo
6 pots **7** paisatge

Then listen carefully and try to imitate the way this sound can be modified according to position and contact with other sounds:

el més econòmic   és un bitllet   el més barat és agafar
allà es fa el canvi   tres hores   només tinc

Exercise 4

Label the following illustrations with the words listed below. Try to do this exercise without looking at the vocabulary lists at the back of the book.

| moto (f.)   bicicleta (f.)   cotxe (m.)   tren (m.) |
| barca (f.)   vaixell (m.)   avió (m.)   autocar (m.) |

> ## Insight
>
> Explaining means of transport (*in, on, by*) is done in Catalan
> with the preposition **amb: van a treballar amb autobús** *they
> go to work on the bus,* **viatjo amb tren** *I travel by train* (but
> **hi anem a peu** *we go there on foot*). For additional practice
> you could make up some more sentences like these last ones,
> based on Exercise 4.

The seasons

🔊 **CD2, TR 2, 00:01**

Les estacions de l'any

la primavera *spring*   l'estiu (m.) *summer*
la tardor *autumn*   l'hivern (m.) *winter*

Key words and sentences

Booking or buying a plane/train ticket

Voldria un bitllet per a (lloc)   *I would like a ticket to (place)*
  pel (dia).   *for (day).*
Primera o segona classe?   *First or second class?*
Fumador o no fumador?   *Smoking or non-smoking?*
Anada i tornada?   *Return?*
Paga en efectiu o amb targeta?   *Will payment be by cash or*
                                           credit card?

Asking for and giving opinions (1)

Què et sembla ...?   *What do you think about ...?*
  Què en penses (de) ...?
Penso que ...   *I think that ...*
Trobo que ...   *I find that ...*

| Em sembla que ... | It seems to me that ... |
| Crec que ... | I believe that ... |

Making simple comparisons (1)

La Maria és tan simpàtica com la Neus.	Maria is as nice as Neus.
L'autobús és més barat que el metro.	The bus is cheaper than the underground.
La meva roba és menys cara que la seva.	My clothes are less expensive than theirs.

Insight

One of the main points in this unit is to establish the principles affecting the agreement of adjectives. While a basic feature is the ending **-a** as the feminine singular marker, with **-s** and **-es** as the masculine and feminine plural endings respectively, you will also encounter some variations on this pattern. Before going to the Grammar section F for more information, pay close attention to adjectives in the dialogues.

Some common descriptive adjectives

◀) **CD2, TR 2, 00:17**

avorrit/-da	boring, bored	tímid/-a	shy, timid
interessant	interesting	amable	kind
divertit/-da	funny, amusing	simpàtic/-a	nice
agradable	pleasant/nice	cregut/-da	big-headed
cansat/-da	tiring, tired	elegant	well-dressed
còmode/-a	comfortable	intel·ligent	intelligent, clever
maco/-a	nice	atractiu/-iva	attractive
alegre/-a	cheerful	llest/-a	clever, bright

Insight

Em cau malament as well as **no el/la puc veure** and **no el/la suporto** are very common ways of saying *I can't stand/bear someone*. Only the first of these constructions can be used with a positive meaning: **em cau (molt) bé** *I like him/her*.

Exercise 5

Which is **not** an appropriate answer for each question? Eliminate one sentence in each case.

1 Què et sembla en Miquel?
a Trobo que és massa tímid.
b Es prou divertit: a mi em cau molt bé.
c Jo crec que és molt amic.

2 Què prefereixes, el tren o l'autocar?
a Vull el tren.
b M'estimo més el tren.
c M'agrada més viatjar amb tren.

3 Què en penses del pis de l'Eloi?
a M'agrada més el meu.
b M'agrada, però és massa petit.
c M'agrada més que la meva.

4 No queden places a l'avió?
a No, no ens en queda cap.
b No, no n'hi ha gens.
c No, no hi ha cap plaça.

5 Quin dia vol viatjar?
a Entre el 10 i el 14 de desembre.
b Al voltant del mes de desembre.
c El 12 de desembre al matí.

6 Amb què viatges a Madrid?
a Amb ningú, viatjo sol.
b Sempre amb avió.
c Amb el cotxe o amb el tren.

Grammar

A Indefinite pronouns

	Things	*People*
Affirmative / interrogative	**alguna cosa**	**algú**
	something	*somebody / someone*
Negative / interrogative	**res**	**ningú**
	anything / nothing	*nobody / no one*
Affirmative / interrogative	**tot**	**tothom**
	everything	*everybody / everyone*

Tens **alguna cosa** a la maleta? Sí, hi tinc **alguna cosa**./No, no hi tinc **res**.

Que tens **res** a la maleta? Sí, hi tinc **alguna cosa**./No, no hi tinc **res**.

Que hi ha **algú** a casa?   Sí, hi ha **algú**./No, no hi ha **ningú**.
Que no hi ha **ningú** a casa?   Sí, hi ha **algú**./No, no hi ha **ningú**.
Qui ve a la festa?   Hi ve **tothom**.
Què hi ha a la festa?   Hi ha de **tot**.

Exercise 6

Complete the sentences with a negative or indefinite (**gens, cap, res, ningú ...**).

1 Qui hi ha al restaurant?   No hi ha _____.
2 Que tens segells?   No, no en tinc _____.
3 Queda aigua a la nevera?   No, no en queda _____.
4 Queda alguna cosa a la nevera? No, no hi queda _____.
5 No hi ha ningú al pis?   Sí, hi ha _____.

Grammar

B *Acabar de* with the infinitive

Acabar de + infinitive (as heard in Dialogue 3) is a frequently used way of expressing the idea of *to have just*, for example, **acabem d'arribar** *we have just arrived*. Note that **acabar** (without any preposition) means *to finish, to end*.

C Impersonal *es*

The particle **es** (**s'** before a vowel sound) is used to form an 'impersonal' expression in these sentences: **allà es fa el canvi cap a Castelló** (Dialogue 2) and **també s'hi pot anar amb altres mitjans** (Dialogue 3). In both cases **es** is a sort of equivalent of the English pronoun *one* as the subject of impersonal expressions. But the English translation of **es** is not always *one*:

Com s'escriu en català ...?   *(How does one write ... in Catalan?)*
                                   How do you write in Catalan ...?
                                   How is ... written in Catalan?

Here es/s' clearly behaves like the reflexive pronoun, but the impersonal construction has quite a different function. We will do more work with impersonal es/s' in Units 9 and 14.

D *Ja* and *encara*

Although the basic meaning of ja is *already*, we have seen other uses of this word, principally in Unit 2, where ja was accompanied by negative no: **Ja no hi viu** means *He no longer lives there*. In interrogative sentences ja can be translated by *yet*: **Ja tens el carnet?** *Have you got your licence yet?* The same happens with encara, literally translated by *still* (seen already in Unit 2), which has a different meaning in this sentence, from Dialogue 3: **Ja tens els bitllets? No, encara no** *Have you got the tickets yet? No, not yet*. In other cases ja corresponds to *(by) now*: **Tot això ja és molt diferent** *All this is very different now*.

As already seen, ja often serves to reinforce a verb, without any direct translation in English.

Cambrer! – Ja vinc.	*Waiter! – (I'm) coming.*
Ja veig que és molt difícil.	*I can see that it's very difficult.*
Ja n'hi ha prou.	*That's enough.*

Exercise 7
🔊 **CD2, TR 3, 00:03**

Listen carefully to the recording. You will hear a girl asking for a return ticket to Minorca by plane. Then answer the following questions:

1 Quin dia agafa l'avió?
2 Quin moment del dia viatja a l'anada?
3 Quant dura el viatge?
4 Quant val el bitllet?
5 Què opina del preu?

Grammar

E Comparisons (1)

Millor *better*, **pitjor** *worse*, **major** *bigger* and **menor** *smaller* are the only single-word comparative forms in Catalan. Like their English equivalents, these four instances are not made with **més** *more* + adjective/adverb. But we do also find even in these cases the comparatives formed with **més**: **més bó/més bé** *better*, **més dolent/més malament** *worse*, **més gran** *bigger*, **més petit** *smaller*.

Aquest llibre és **més bo** que aquell. *This book is better than that one.*
Aquest llibre és **millor** que aquell. *This book is better than that one.*
Aquest llibre és **el millor**. *This book is the best.*

Note that the superlative (*biggest, fattest*, etc. ...) is the same as the comparative in Catalan, and that reference is indicated by **de**: **la noia més llesta de la classe** (*the cleverest girl in the class*).

F Adjectives: forms of agreement

We have got used to the idea of agreement (number and gender) of adjectives in Catalan, and to the feature of the ending **-a** as the usual feminine singular marker, with **-es** for feminine plural. The most common pattern is:

m.s.	f.s.	m.pl.	f.pl.
	-a	-s	-es
fort	forta	forts	fortes

There may be modifications to the stem which the foreign learner soon becomes familiar with:

cregut	creguda	creguts	cregudes
menorquí	menorquina	menorquins	menorquines

Observe that adjectives ending with a vowel + ç are invariable in the singular but have distinctive masculine and feminine endings for the plural:

feliç	**feliç**	**feliços**	**felices**
dolç	**dolça***	**dolços**	**dolces**

*This is the main exception.

Other adjectives have an invariable singular form matched by an invariable plural:

fàcil	**fàcil**	**fàcils**	**fàcils**
igual	**igual**	**iguals**	**iguals**

As we are working here from the spoken language we need not worry too much about those spelling changes which reflect consistency of pronunciation, for example **feliços/felices, danès/danesa, simpàtics/simpàtiques.**

Reference table 1 presents the main patterns of forms/spellings for both nouns and adjectives.

Exercise 8

Look at the pictures (1–6) and write a comparison using the adjectives below, to make an expression like **A és més petit que B** or **A és tan bo com B.** Always begin with A.

feliç
modern
ràpid
alt
jove
gros

Exercise 9

Complete the following sentences with one of the adjectives from
the box. Remember to observe agreement as necessary.

1 La Montse i la Carme són bessones; són _____.
2 El carrer és massa estret, en canvi la carretera és massa _____.
3 La seva despesa és molt _____ a la meva.

4 Trobo que la seva cosina és _____ però _____.

5 Aquesta lliçó és _____ per a aprendre bé la llengua.

6 La carn d'aquesta carnisseria m'agrada; és molt _____.

| útil   igual   superior   bo   amable   ample   avorrit |

Exercise 10
Mots encreuats *Crossword*

Horitzontals:
1 Hi compro el pa.
2 Si no és solter pot ser _____.
3 El número més petit.
4 La meitat del dia.
5 Em _____ les dents.
6 Quant _____ tot plegat?

Verticals:
1 Via de comunicació o trànsit a la ciutat.
2 M'acomiado d'algú.
3 Primer àpat del dia.
4 Femení de morè.
5 Germà de la meva mare.
6 _____ reservar un bitllet d'avió.

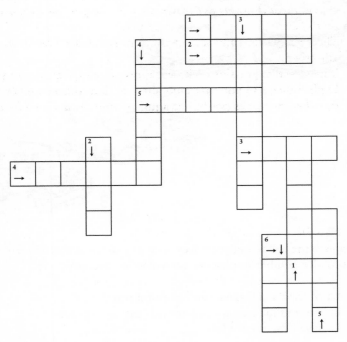

Points to remember

1 **voldria reservar un bitllet per a (lloc) pel (dia)** *I'd like to book a ticket to (place) for (day)*

2 **un bitllet de primera / segona classe, anada i tornada** *a first/ second class, return ticket*

3 **paga en efectiu o amb targeta?** *will payment be by cash or credit card?*

4 **què et sembla ...? què en penses (de) ...?** *what do you think about ...?*

5 **penso que ..., trobo que ..., em sembla que ..., crec que ...** *I think that ..., I find that..., it seems to me that ..., I believe that ...*

6 **la Maria és tan simpàtica com la Neus** *Mary is as nice as Neus*

7 **l'autobús és més barat que el metro** *the bus is cheaper than the underground*

8 **la carn no és tan cara com (= és més barata/menys cara que) el peix** *meat is not as expensive as (= is cheaper/less expensive than) fish*

9 The basic pattern and some variations in the agreement of adjectives.

10 Impersonal expressions with **es**, approximately equivalent to English *one*: **s'hi pot anar amb altres mitjans** *one can go there by other means;* **es pot fumar aquí?** *is smoking allowed here?*

8

De vacances
On holiday

In this unit you will learn
- *How to ask for or book a room in a hotel*
- *How to identify different kinds of accommodation*
- *How to ask someone to do something*
- *How to hire a car*

1 Voldria una habitació doble *I would like a double room*

Montse and Tim have gone on holiday and are looking for a room in a small hotel.

CD2, TR 4, 00:07

Tim	Bona tarda, teniu alguna habitació lliure?
Hostalera	Individual o doble?
Tim	Dues d'individuals.
Hostalera	Amb dutxa o bany complet?
Tim	Dutxa ja va bé.
Hostalera	Per a quantes nits?
Tim	Set, fins el divendres dia 24.
Hostalera	En tinc dues a la part de darrere; hi ha menys soroll i tenen vistes al mar.
Montserrat	Perfecte! L'esmorzar va inclòs en el preu?

Hostalera	No, va a part. Val 5€70.
Tim	Teniu pàrquing?
Hostalera	Sí, tenim un garatge privat. També es paga a part. Val 4€50 per dia. Si voleu, immediatament després de veure l'habitació us l'ensenyo. Podeu deixar l'equipatge aquí.

l'hostalera (f.) *hotel owner*
la dutxa *shower*
anar bé *to be fine, all right*
la part *side, part*
el soroll *noise*
la vista al mar *sea view*
inclòs/-osa *included*
a part *separately*
el garatge *garage*
*immediatament *immediately*
ensenyar *to show*
*us l'ensenyo *I'll show you (it):* see Grammar E Unit 9
deixar *to leave*
l'equipatge (m.) *lugagge*

QUICK VOCAB

Insight

A slightly more polite way of asking for something than **vull** *I want*, when shopping, is the use of the conditional tense of **voler, voldria** *I should/would like* + an infinitive or a noun. Well done if you have already spotted this in Dialogue 1 of Unit 7!

Insight

Correct pronunciation of both **ny** and **ll** at the end of words (including the corresponding plural forms in **-nys** and **-lls**) demands a bit of extra practice: notice **bany** and **soroll** in Dialogue 1 and work at getting your tongue round the sounds.

2 Assegurança inclosa *Insurance included*

Next, Montse and Tim decide to hire a car.

CD2, TR 4, 01:48

Empleat	Bona tarda.
Montserrat	Bona tarda. Volem llogar un cotxe petit per a una setmana. Que en teniu cap?
Empleat	Sí, de la categoria A podeu escollir entre un Ford Ka i un Peugeot 106. Tots dos van amb gasolina sense plom.
Montserrat	I quant val el lloguer?
Empleat	La tarifa per a set dies és de 221€ amb quilometratge il·limitat. L'assegurança està inclosa.
Montserrat	Preferim agafar el Ford.
Empleat	Entesos! Us fa res deixar-me el carnet de conduir i una targeta de crèdit? ... Aquí teniu les claus. A dins del cotxe hi ha un mapa de carreteres. No oblideu tornar-lo amb el dipòsit ple abans de les 12 del migdia de dijous.

QUICK VOCAB

llogar *to rent, to hire*
tots dos *both*
la gasolina/benzina sense plom *unleaded petrol*
el lloguer *rent(al), hire charge*
la tarifa *tariff*
el quilometratge *mileage*
il·limitat/-da *unlimited*
entesos! *OK, fine*
*us fa res ...? *do you mind ...?*
el carnet de conduir *driving licence*
la clau *key*
no oblideu *don't forget*
el dipòsit *tank*
ple/-na *full*
abans (de) *before*

Exercise 1
Veritat o fals?

1 En Tim i la Montse volen quedar-se una setmana a l'hotel.
2 L'esmorzar val 4€50.
3 El Ford KA i el Peugeot 106 no tenen el mateix preu.
4 El mapa de carreteres és gratuït.

Exercise 2
Listen again to the dialogues and repeat them out loud, preferably
with a partner.

Exercise 3
Focus on the words below, taken from Dialogue 2, and say
whether the underlined letters sound like *g* in English *give* or *s*
in English *measure*.

1 llogar 2 categoria 3 Peugeot 4 gasolina 5 lloguer
6 assegurança 7 targeta 8 dijous

Exercise 4
This dialogue in a car-hire agency has to be put in order for it to
make sense.

1 M'és igual.
2 Per a quants dies?

3 Hi ha una oferta de cap de setmana a 123€.
4 Categoria B o C? Tots dos són grans.
5 Amb quilometratge il·limitat?
6 D'acord, ja em va bé.
7 Li fa res deixar-me el seu carnet de conduir?
8 Pel cap de setmana.
9 No, hi ha un límit de 250 quilòmetres.
10 Hola, vull llogar un cotxe gran.

Insight

Related to **carnet de conduir**, note also **el carnet de la biblioteca/d'identitat/de soci** *library card, identity card, membership card.*

Key words and sentences

Types of accommodation

el càmping	*camp site*
l'alberg de joventut (m.)	*youth hostel*
el refugi de muntanya	*mountain lodge*
l'agroturisme (m.)	*farmhouse accommodation*
la pensió	*guest house*
l'hostal (m.)	*budget hotel*
l'hotel (m.)	*hotel*
la fonda	*inn*

Asking for or booking a room in a hotel

Hi ha habitacions lliures?	*Are there any free rooms?*
Voldria reservar una habitació, sisplau.	*I'd like to book a room, please.*
Vull una habitació doble/individual.	*I want a double/single room.*
Amb llit doble/individual/dos llits.	*With a double/a single/two beds.*

Amb bany/dutxa/vistes al mar.	With a bath/shower/sea views.
Per a quantes nits?	For how long?
Per a tres nits/una setmana/ quinze dies.	For three nights/a week/ a fortnight.
Pensió completa o mitja pensió?	Full board or half board?
El preu per habitació i nit és de 75€.	The (room's) price per night is 75€.
L'esmorzar i el pàrquing van a part.	Breakfast and parking are charged separately.

Items in your hotel

dins l'habitació	inside the room	fora de l'habitació	outside the room
el sabó	soap	el bar	bar/cafeteria
la tovallola	towel	l'ascensor (m.)	lift
la finestra	window	la recepció	reception
el llum	light (lamp)	l'aire condicionat (m.)	air conditioning
l'armari (m.)	wardrobe	la pista de tennis	tennis court
la tauleta	bedside table	la piscina	swimming pool
el mirall	mirror		

Hiring a car

Voldria llogar un cotxe.	I would like to rent a car.
De quina categoria, A, B o C?	Which category/price band, A, B or C?
Quant val el lloguer?	What is the hire charge?
Tenim una tarifa de cap de setmana/setmanal.	We have a weekend/weekly tariff.
quilometratge il·limitat	unlimited mileage (measured in kilometres)
assegurança inclosa	insurance included

Exercise 5

Complete the following with words from the box below (singular or plural, with or without article, as appropriate).

Entrem a l'habitació 28 i com que és de nit encenem _____1, però no funciona. A les fosques fem córrer les cortines i veiem que _____2 estan obertes. Jo les tanco. Decideixo trucar a _____3 però _____4 no funciona tampoc. Entro al bany i trobo a terra dues _____5 completament molles i a més, no hi ha _____6 per rentar-se les mans al lavabo. Finalment agafem _____7 i anem a parlar amb el director de l'hotel. Diu que hi ha un error i que la nostra _____8 és una altra. Ens dóna una altra _____9.

sabó	clau	llum	habitació	tovallola	finestra
	recepció		ascensor	telèfon	

Insight

Even before looking at the Grammar section B below, you will most probably have worked out how Catalan forms its own adverbs corresponding to English ones ending in -ly. Think of **immediatament** that occurred in Dialogue 1. All you need to remember is that the suffix **-ment** is added to the feminine form of the Catalan adjective. Examples in Exercise 5 are **completament** and **finalment**.

Exercise 6
◀) CD2, TR 5, 00:02

You will hear four people (A to D) booking a room in a hotel. With all the information try to complete the grid below. Some details have already been written in for you.

	🛁	🌙	🛏	🍽
A	*bany complet*			
B				
C				*esmorzar i sopar*
D			*dos llits*	

Grammar

A Li fa res …?

A very common way of making a polite request is with the expression **fer res** + infinitive, with the pronoun indicating the person addressed: thus **et fa res …?** means something like *do you mind …?* The Catalan infinitive expresses the action requested (*…ing*, in English) as in **Us fa res deixar-me …** (*Do you mind letting me have …*) in Dialogue 2. Note also how the (indirect object) pronoun functions here and in these other examples.

Et fa res (a tu) obrir la finestra?	No, ara l'obro.
Li fa res (a vostè) pagar ara mateix?	No, no em fa res.
Us fa res (a vosaltres) baixar del cotxe?	No, ara mateix baixem.
Els fa res (a vostès) parlar en anglès?	No, no ens fa res.

Note also **no oblideu** *don't forget to*, in Dialogue 2, as another way of making a request. For the singular **tu** this would be **no oblidis** and for **vostè(-s)** **no oblidi(-in)**. The Grammar Section D in Unit 15 extends this point.

B Adverbs ending in '-ly'

There is quite a close correspondence between the way in which English forms adverbs ending in *-ly* and the Catalan system which is to add **-ment** (such as **immediatament** in Dialogue 1) to the feminine form of the adjective. Other examples are **exacte > exacta > exactament** *exactly*; **ràpid > ràpida > ràpidament** *quickly*.

C Prepositions

In Unit 2 we saw how some prepositions (**a, de** and **per**) contract when they are placed before the articles **el** and **els**. Now we are going to study when we use these and other prepositions and how the translations may vary at times.

a

▶ with the meaning of *at* (time)	**Arribo a les deu.**	*I arrive at ten o'clock.*
▶ with the meaning of *to/towards* (direction)	**Vaig a/cap a l'estació.**	*I go to the station.*
▶ with the meaning of *at* (place, location)	**Ara és a casa.**	*S/he's at home now.*
▶ with the meaning of *in* (place, location)	**Sóc a la piscina.**	*I am in the swimming pool.*
	És a l'armari.	*It is in the cupboard.*

en

with the meaning of *in/at* (place, location), replacing **a** in this function before the indefinite article (**un**, etc.) and the demonstrative adjectives, which begin with vowels. Compare:

▶ **Les nenes són a l'escola.**	*The girls are at school.*
▶ **Les nenes són en una escola.**	*The girls are in a school.*
▶ **Les nenes són en aquesta escola.**	*The girls are at this school.*

de

▶ with the meaning of *of* (including possession)	**el guanyador de la copa**	*the winner of the cup*
	el pis de la Sara	*Sara's flat*
▶ with the meaning of *from* (origin)	**Vinc de Reus.**	*I come from Reus.*
▶ with the meaning of *in* (comparison)	**la (noia) més llesta de la classe**	*the cleverest girl in the class*
▶ with the meaning of *in* (time)	**Són les deu del matí.**	*It's ten in the morning.*

amb

▶ with the meaning of *with* (company)	**Treballo amb la Sònia.**	*I work with Sònia.*
▶ with the meaning of *in/by* (vehicle)	**Hi vaig amb bicicleta.**	*I go there by bike.*

entre

- ▶ with the meaning of *between* (place)

  La casa és entre la farmàcia i l'estanc.

  The house is between the chemist's and the newsagent.

- ▶ with the meaning of *among* (place)

  Passeja entre els arbres.

  He walks among the trees.

fins (a)

- ▶ with the meaning of *until*

  Sóc a Madrid fins demà.

  I'm in Madrid until tomorrow.

- ▶ with the meaning of *as far as*

  T'acompanyo fins a la cantonada.

  I'll come with you as far as the (street) corner.

Further treatment of prepositions, mainly the uses of **per/per a**, comes in Unit 9.

Note that the pronouns used after prepositions (strong pronouns) are the same as the subject pronouns, except in the first-person singular where **mi** is used, not **jo: Vols venir amb mi?; Puc anar-hi amb tu.**

Exercise 7
🔊 CD2, TR 5, 02:24

Look at this text. Some of the prepositions shown in bold are wrongly used. You should be able to identify and correct them. Note that not all of them are wrong.

Arribo **en** 1 Sóller amb 2 el meu cotxe i entro **d'** 3 un bar. Demano un tallat i miro **a** 4 fora mentre espero la Mercè. Diu que torna de Palma **en** 5 les sis. La música **del** 6 bar m'agrada. Hi ha gent: uns homes parlen **entre** 7 ells **en** 8 la barra. Dues noies **amb** 9 vint anys beuen cervesa. **En** 10 dos quarts de 11 set arriba la Mercè. Ve **amb** 12 un amic. Es diu Pau i és **a** 13 Eivissa. Esperem **entre** 14 que tanquen el bar i després sortim.

Exercise 8

Look carefully at this advertisement and then answer the questions in Catalan:

1 Quin tipus d'allotjament és aquest?
2 Tenen obert tot l'any?
3 Hi pots menjar?
4 Les habitacions, són totes iguals?
5 Quines possibilitats ofereix el lloc

Points to remember

1 hi ha / teniu habitacions lliures? *are there/have you got any free rooms?*

2 voldria reservar una habitació doble / individual, amb bany / dutxa / vistes al mar *I'd like to book a double / single room, with a bath / shower / sea views*

3 per a tres nits / una setmana / quinze dies *for three nights / a week / a fortnight*

4 pensió completa o mitja pensió? *full board or half board?*

5 el preu per persona / habitació i nit és de 62€ *the room rate is 62€ per person / per night*

6 l'esmorzar i el pàrquing estan inclosos *breakfast and parking are included*

7 voldria llogar un cotxe de categoria alta *I'd like to hire a top-of-the-range car*

8 tenim/oferim una tarifa de cap de setmana amb quilometratge il limitat *we have/offer a weekend tariff with unlimited mileage*

9 l'assegurança es paga a part *insurance is charged separately*

10 *Polite requests made with the construction* fer res (de) + *infinitive:* et/li/us fa res (de) tancar la porta? *would you mind closing the door?*

9

Gira a la dreta
Turn right

In this unit you will learn
- *How to identify public places*
- *How to ask for and give directions*
- *How to give instructions and distances*

Insight

In this unit we shall practise understanding and giving commands in Catalan, with verbs in the imperative form. The formation of imperatives is laid out in Grammar section B. The only form not introduced in the dialogues is the one corresponding to **vostès**, which has the ending **-in**. You might wish at this point to look ahead to Grammar section A in Unit 14 where you will find an explanation of the constructions involving **haver de +** infinitive (*to have to*), a way of expressing obligation in a tone which is less abrupt than the simple imperative.

1 Com s'hi va? *How do I get there?*

Tim and Montserrat are talking to an employee in a local tourist office (**oficina de turisme**).

Montserrat	Bona tarda. Acabem d'arribar al poble i volem saber què es pot visitar.
Empleat	Mireu, en aquest mapa està tot indicat. Podeu començar visitant la plaça de l'Ajuntament, que no és gaire lluny d'aquí. Després us recomano entrar al Museu Municipal i també visitar les esglésies de Sant Antoni i Sant Miquel. Un dels llocs més interessants és el pont romà, sense oblidar el castell. Ambdós són monuments històrics.
Tim	I la platja?
Empleat	Home, sens dubte la nostra badia és preciosa. A peu s'hi pot anar.
Tim	Com? Quin és el camí més ràpid?
Empleat	Agafeu aquest carrer fins al final de tot. Un cop al parc, gireu a la dreta, allà on hi ha una bústia, i continueu caminant tot dret. Just al costat de la comissaria de policia hi ha una indicació. No és gaire lluny, a uns deu minuts.
Montse	Moltes gràcies … Per cert, hi ha algun caixer automàtic a prop d'aquí? Necessito treure diners.
Empleat	Sí, n'hi ha un al carrer de dalt, a davant de la biblioteca municipal.

QUICK VOCAB

*que *which, that*
l'església (f.) *church*
el pont *bridge*
ambdós/-dues *both*
la platja *beach*
home! *well!* (exclamation)
sens dubte *definitely*
la badia *bay*
preciós/-osa *lovely, beautiful*
el final de tot *the very top/end*
girar *to turn*
la bústia *mailbox*
continuar *to continue, to keep (doing something)*
caminar *to walk*

tot dret *straight ahead*
la comissaria de policia *police station*
la indicació *sign*
el caixer automàtic *cash machine*
treure (irregular) *to take out, to withdraw*
dalt *above, (higher) up*
la biblioteca *library*

Insight

The statement **a peu s'hi pot anar** deserves attention for the pronoun combination **s'hi**, already encountered in Unit 7. What is involved here is impersonal **es** (**s'** before a vowel or **h** + vowel), English *one*, combined with **hi** meaning *there* (in this case = **a la badia**). For reinforcement of this point see Grammar E.

Insight

The mild exclamation **home!** (and **dona!** if a woman is being addressed) is very frequently used to give gentle emphasis to what is being said.

---

2 És a uns 300 metres *It's about 300 metres away*

Some hours later Tim and Montse are in their car.

CD2, TR 6, 01:59

Tim	Perdoni, per anar a Vilajoana?
Vianant	Mmm ... És força complicat des d'aquí! A veure ... surt del poble per aquest carrer.
Tim	Aquest de la dreta?
Vianant	Sí, el Carrer de l'Església. El del costat és direcció prohibida. Baixa el carrer fins al capdavall i a la rotonda gira a l'esquerra, en direcció a l'hospital. Al segon semàfor agafa el carrer de la dreta i a uns tres-cents metres entra a la carretera comarcal.

Tim	El semàfor és abans o després de l'hospital?
Vianant	Després. L'hospital queda a mà esquerra del carrer.
	Un cop a la carretera està tot indicat.
Tim	És lluny el poble?
Vianant	No, deu ser a uns catorze quilòmetres d'aquí.
Tim	Moltes gràcies.
Vianant	A disposar, i bon viatge!

el/la vianant *pedestrian*
a veure ... *let's see ...*
la direcció prohibida *one way (traffic)*
al capdavall (de) *to/at the (very) bottom (of)*
la rotonda *roundabout*
el semàfor *traffic lights*
comarcal *local district*
quedar *to be situated* (here)
un cop *once*
***deure** (irregular) *to owe, must:* see Grammar A
a disposar! *you are welcome!*

Insight

As in the title of Dialogue 2, the plural indefinite article (**uns, unes**) can express an approximate number or quantity. *Some* can be the English translation, but other equivalents like *about* or *around* may sound more natural, according to context. How would you translate **un document d'unes tres-centes pàgines**?

Exercise 1

Go through Dialogues 1 and 2 and make sure you understand everything. Act them out with a partner, if possible.

Exercise 2

Match the signs with their meanings:

a Prohibit passar
b Prohibit estacionar

c Prohibit fumar
d Prohibit girar a l'esquerra
e Prohibit tirar fotos
f Prohibit banyar-se

Reading

Read the following instructions you find on a parking meter:

Decideixi el temps d'estacionament que necessita.
Selecioni el temps prement el botó de dalt.
Col·loqui la quantitat de diners exacta.
Recordi que el parquímetre només accepta monedes de 2€, 1€,
0,50€, 0,20€ i 0,10€.
Premi el botó de sota.
Reculli el tiquet i col·loqui'l en un lloc visible dins el cotxe.

a Listen to a conversation on the CD about the parking-meter instructions above and say whether the following words below are stressed on the final syllable, on the next to last or two before the last.

1 estacionament 2 botó 3 col·loqui 4 quantitat
5 parquímetre 6 monedes 7 tiquet

b Listen again to Dialogue 1 paying careful attention to how the following groups of words run together.

acabem d'arribar al poble – què es pot visitar? – us recomano entrar – les esglésies de Sant Antoni i Sant Miquel – hi ha algun caixer automàtic?

Key words and sentences

Asking for and giving directions

Per anar a la platja, sisplau?	*The way to the beach, please?*
Com es va a l'Ajuntament?	*How do I get to the town hall?*
Sap com puc anar a l'hospital?	*Do you know the way to the hospital?*
Com s'hi va?	*How do I get there?*
És lluny/És a prop d'aquí?	*Is it far from/near here?*
És a uns deu quilòmetres.	*It is about ten kilometres away.*
És a deu minuts caminant.	*It is ten minutes' walk away.*
Deu ser a uns 300 metres.	*It is probably about 300 metres from here.*

Useful verbs

agafar	*to take*
pujar (per)	*to go up, come up*

baixar (per)	*to go down*
continuar (per)	*to keep…/to continue*
seguir (per)	*to continue/to go on…/to follow*
girar/tombar	*to turn*
travessar	*to cross*

Useful adverbs (direction)

amunt/avall	*up(wards)/down(wards)*
tot dret	*straight ahead/on*
endavant/endarrere	*ahead/back(wards)*

Useful adverbs (situation)

a baix/a dalt	*down/up, below/above*
al capdamunt/al capdavall (de)	*at the (very) top/bottom (of)*
(a) sobre/(a) sota	*above/below*
(a) dins/(a)fora	*inside, in/outside, out*

Exercise 4

Look at the shapes below. Then, complete the sentences using (without repetition) one of the adverbs seen in this unit and in Units 2 and 3, such as **a la dreta, (a) sota, davant, lluny,** etc.

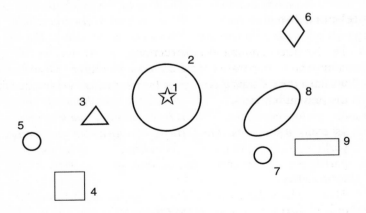

Example: El número 3 és entre el 5 i el 2.

1 El número 7 és a _____ del 9 i aquest és _____ del 6.
2 Els números 5 i 4 són _____ del 8.
3 El 6, 7, 8 i 9 són a _____ del 2, 3, 4 i 5.
4 L'1 és a _____ del 2 i el 8 és _____ del 7.
5 El 6 és _____ de tot.

_____

Grammar

A Expressions of probability

The most frequent way of expressing supposition or probability in Catalan involves the irregular verb **deure** introducing an infinitive, as in **deu ser a uns vuit quilòmetres**, heard in Dialogue 2.

La Maria *deu viure* a prop de casa perquè la veig cada dia.
Maria must live near my home because I see her every day.

Els seus amics *deuen anar* molt sovint a la platja perquè sempre que hi vaig ells hi són.
Their friends must go to the beach very often because every time I go (there) they are there too.

B Imperative

1 To give direct commands, instructions, etc. we use the command or imperative form of verbs. For **tu** and **vosaltres** we have the following scheme (where some parts coincide with the present tense):

1st conj.	2nd conj.	3rd conj.	
parla	pren	dorm	llegeix
parleu	preneu	dormiu	llegiu

Then see how the **vostè** form is used in the more formal/official instructions for the parking meter in the Reading section (i.e. **decideixi, seleccioni** ...). Look at the examples from the dialogues: **agafeu aquest carrer** ... from Dialogue 1, and **baixa el carrer** ... from Dialogue 2. In the first one the speaker is talking to Tim and Montserrat (**vosaltres**) and in the second one just to the driver, Tim (**tu**).

2 Any pronoun accompanying an imperative verb has to be placed after it. Remember the form of direct-object pronouns after the verb that we have seen in Unit 4. A full review is provided in the **Reference tables**.

Agafeu **aquest carrer** (*Take this street*) > Agafeu-lo.
Baixa **el carrer** (*Go down the street*) > Baixa'l.
Fica **el peu** a l'aigua (*Put your foot in the water*) > Fica'l a l'aigua.
Recorda **aquesta adreça** (*Remember this address*) > Recorda-la.

You have now seen that pronouns are attached after the verb (by an apostrophe or a hyphen) in the following three cases:

a with an infinitive: Et fa res dir-me ...? *Do you mind telling me ...?*
b with a gerund: Estic maquillant-me. *I am putting on*
  (*also* m'estic *make-up.*
  maquillant)
c with a direct command, as in the examples above.

C Relative pronoun *que*

The unstressed relative pronoun **que** is invariable and can refer to persons, things or concepts. It can stand as subject or as direct object. Look at some examples from this unit:

La plaça de l'Ajuntament, *The town-hall square, which is*
  que no és lluny ... *not far ...*
El temps d'estacionament *The parking time you need ...*
  que necessita ...

Note that Catalan, unlike English, never omits the relative pronoun in a relative clause. For example:

la noia que estimo   *the girl I love*

(The same is also true for **que** as conjunction *that*: **Diu que vindrà** *S/he says (that) s/he will come.*)

Exercise 5

Make a single sentence from each of the following pairs, using the relative pronoun **que**:

Example: La casa és petita. La casa és a la vora del riu.
         La casa que és a la vora del riu és petita.

1 La finestra està tancada. La finestra és a la dreta.
2 El cotxe té set anys. El cotxe és de la família d'aquí davant.
3 El museu és molt interessant. Volem visitar el museu.
4 El noi treballa a l'estació. El noi viu al pis de dalt.
5 El tren porta retard. El tren surt a dos quarts de sis.

Cultural information
Montserrat

The name of one of our characters, abbreviated to Montse, comes from an important Benedictine monastery in the hills close to Barcelona. Montserrat, which dates back to the Middle Ages, has had a significant role in the religious life and in the history of Catalonia from the earliest times until the present. The monastery and its associated buildings occupy a commanding site high up among the jagged pinnacles of the Montserrat massif. It is still a special place of worship and pilgrimage, centred on the figure of the Black Virgin (**La Moreneta**), the Mother of God of Montserrat, while being also nowadays a big attraction for secular tourism from far and near.

Grammar

D per/per a

Both prepositions **per** and **per a** can translate *for*, but they must not be confused. The difference between the two can best be appreciated by seeing **per a** as a distinct preposition with its own range of meaning. Basically **per a** indicates a destination or an object:

No hi ha prou fruita per a tots.	*There isn't enough fruit for everybody.*
La casa és massa gran per a nosaltres.	*The house is too big for us.*

A difference between **per** and **per a** is distinguishable

a in expressions of time:

Per a is used only for specific arrangements or fixed appointments in the future.

Ho podem deixar per a dijous.	*We can postpone that for/until Thursday.*

Per indicates for how long something is intended or the time during which something happens.

Hi anem per Pasqua.	*We are going there for Easter.*
L'he llogat per un any.	*I have rented it for a year.*

b introducing an infinitive:

Per translates (*in order*) *to* before an infinitive:

Ho fem per entretenir-nos.	*We are doing it to amuse ourselves.*
Vull anar-hi per visitar el castell.	*I want to go there in order to visit the castle.*

Certain verbs and expressions do admit **per a** to introduce an infinitive. You will most probably observe instances of this, but remember that in practice **per** + infinitive will always sound authentic.

E Pronoun combinations

We have already met some instances of two pronouns combined (**n'hi**, Unit 3; **us l'ensenyo**, Unit 8). The heading for Dialogue 1 in this unit **Com s'hi va?** is another case: here you see impersonal **es** (Unit 7) going together with **hi** (Unit 5), expressing destination/ location. Here are some other examples:

No s'hi pot entrar.   *You can't go in there.*

En aquest restaurant la gent menja molt bé *(In this restaurant people eat very well)*, where **en aquest restaurant** could be represented as **hi** and **la gent** *as* **es > s'**, giving (**Aquí**) **s'hi menja molt bé**, equivalent to *The food is good here.*

This important area of grammar is returned to in Unit 13 and Unit 14.

Exercise 6
🔊 **CD2, TR 7, 01:06**

Look carefully at the map. In the recording you will hear four people explaining the way to get to each of the museums. For each statement (1 to 4), identify the correct museum and give its name. Your starting point is the railway station.

Insight

Note how **agafar** *to take* is often used in giving directions. This coincides approximately with English usage, as well as **agafar** occurring in the same context for taking or catching a means of transport (see Dialogue 3 in Unit 3).

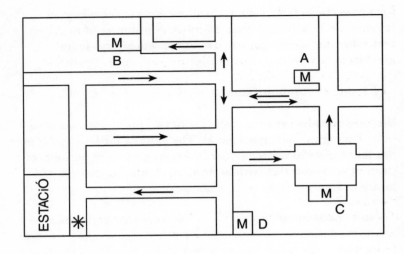

Reading

Read the following recipe (**recepta de cuina**) and observe the use of the imperative. (Remember that you can always use the vocabulary list at the back of the book to check any unfamiliar words.)

COCA DE TARONJA

Per fer una coca de taronja seguiu aquestes instruccions:

▶ Unteu un recipient amb mantega i farina.
▶ Barregeu els ous amb el sucre en un bol fins a obtenir una massa espessa.
▶ Afegiu el suc de taronja, la farina amb el llevat, una mica de sal i la llet.
▶ Treballeu la massa i poseu la mescla dins el recipient.
▶ Col·loqueu el recipient dins el forn i espereu vint-i-cinc minuts.

Mentre es cou la coca:

- ▶ Poseu a coure durant tres o quatre minuts el suc de les taronges, el sucre i la pell de la taronja.
- ▶ Retireu el líquid del foc.
- ▶ Afegiu el licor.

Un cop la coca és cuita:

- ▶ Tireu el suc pel damunt de la coca.
- ▶ Poseu la coca a gratinar al forn durant uns minuts.

Exercise 7
Tell a friend about the recipe above, filling in the gaps with words from the text, changing the forms of verbs as well as using pronouns:

En primer lloc agafa un recipient i unta _____ 1 amb mantega i farina. Per fer la massa, _____ 2 els ous amb el sucre en un bol i afegeix _____ 3 el suc de taronja, la farina, el llevat, la sal i la llet. _____ 4 la mescla i posa _____ 5 dins el recipient. _____ 6 el recipient dins el forn i _____ 7 vint-i-cinc minuts. Mentre es cou la coca _____ 8 a coure durant tres o quatre minuts el suc de les taronges, el sucre i la pell de la taronja. Un cop acabat, _____ 9 el líquid del foc i _____ 10 -hi el licor. Per acabar _____ 11 el suc sobre la coca i posa _____ 12 a gratinar durant uns minuts.

Points to remember

1 **per anar a la platja, sisplau?** *the way to the beach, please?*
2 **com es va a l'Ajuntament?** *how does one/do I get to the town hall?*
3 **com s'hi va?** *how do I get there?*
4 **és lluny? / és a prop d'aquí?** *is it far away? / near here?*
5 **és a uns deu quilòmetres** *it is about ten kilometres away*

6 us recomano visitar el museu / el castell / l'església / el monument

I recommend you to visit the museum / the castle / the church / the monument

7 The verb **deure** in expressions of probability: **deu ser a uns vint minuts caminant** *it is probably about twenty minutes' walk away*

8 The formation of the imperative for regular verbs.

9 Object pronouns attached after commands.

10 Use of the relative pronoun **que** *who, which*.

10

Vaig néixer a Eivissa
I was born in Ibiza

In this unit you will learn
- *How to talk about key events in your past*
- *How to say how long ago something happened*
- *How to talk about someone's job/profession*
- *How to greet someone on a special occasion*

Before you start

So far you have been working with situations and materials that involve almost exclusive use of the present tense. From this unit onwards you will be meeting the other main parts of the tense system in Catalan, beginning here with the (past) preterite. This is the tense used to talk about actions, events or states occurring in a time which is past and finished, a time not regarded as being connected to the present. The past time represented by the preterite tense is thus *a period that does not include 'today'*. You will be reminded of this important distinction in Unit 12, when you are introduced to the tense for past actions completed 'today' and when the contrast with English usage is looked at in detail.

The form of the preterite tense you are studying here is properly called the 'periphrastic preterite tense' ('periphrastic' referring merely to a 'roundabout' formation). This is a very easy tense to construct and use since it involves dealing with only a very limited set of variables – the parts of a single auxiliary verb – as follows:

(jo)	vaig	+infinitive
(tu)	vas (sometimes vares)	+infinitive
(ell/ella/vostè)	va	+infinitive
(nosaltres)	vam (sometimes vàrem)	+infinitive
(vosaltres)	vau (sometimes vàreu)	+infinitive
(ells/elles/vostès)	van (sometimes varen)	+infinitive

Once you have learnt these easily recognizable forms, and once you are familiar with the basic principles explained above, the past preterite tense of any verb (provided that the infinitive is known, of course) can be expressed with ease.

Va tancar la porta.	*S/he closed the door.*
Vaig arribar ahir.	*I arrived yesterday.*
Vam portar males notícies.	*We brought bad news.*

By the end of this unit (taking on board the supplementary information given in Grammar A), you will have a good command of this tense.

1 Vaig estudiar a la universitat *I studied at university*

Tim is talking for the first time with Lluïsa, an old friend of Montserrat.

◆ CD2, TR 8, 00:09

Lluïsa	Escolta Tim, parles molt bé el català, no?
Tim	És que vaig néixer a Barcelona, la meva mare és catalana. Vaig viure a Catalunya fins als sis anys. Després, els meus pares van decidir tornar a Anglaterra i allà vaig continuar parlant català. Recordo que durant la meva infància vam voltar molt, d'un poble a un altre. Fa cinc anys em vaig independitzar, quan vaig entrar a la universitat, i vaig anar a viure a Bristol.

Lluïsa	Què vas estudiar?
Tim	Vaig fer tres anys de Turisme i quan vaig acabar la carrera vaig estar dos anys treballant de guia turístic a Oxford.
Lluïsa	Deus parlar moltes llengües, oi?
Tim	A part del català i l'anglès parlo francès i també portuguès, però com que no el practico ... I tu Lluïsa, d'on ets?
Lluïsa	Sóc d'Eivissa, vaig néixer a Sant Antoni, però de petita els meus pares van canviar de feina i vam venir tots a viure a Palma.
Tim	Vas estudiar a la universitat?
Lluïsa	Sí, vaig estudiar a la facultat de medicina. Però jo de llengües només en parlo dues: el mallorquí i el castellà.
Tim	A què et dediques?
Lluïsa	Sóc metgessa. Des de fa un any treballo a l'hospital públic, però també vaig treballar un temps en una consulta privada. Com l'Antoni. Per cert, vas anar ahir a la seva festa d'aniversari?
Tim	Sí, ens hi vam divertir molt ... vam ballar i beure tota la nit.
Lluïsa	Jo no vaig poder venir perquè vaig tornar ahir mateix de Madrid. I tu, quan fas els anys?
Tim	Els vaig celebrar una setmana abans de venir cap aquí, el divuit d'agost ...
Lluïsa	Doncs jo els faig demà, trenta-dos!
Tim	Felicitats!

*... no? *isn't that so?*
néixer (irregular) *to be born*
*durant *during, for*
la infància *childhood*
voltar *to go (travel) around*
*fa ... ... *ago*
independitzar-se *to become self-sufficient*
la carrera *university studies*
el/la guia *guide*
*... oi? *isn't that so?*
a part *except for, apart from*

com que *as*
de petit/-a *when I was (a) young (boy/girl)*
canviar *to change*
la facultat *faculty*
*de ... *see Grammar C*
*dedicar-se *to be occupied/employed (as)*
la metgessa *(female) doctor*
des de *since*
la consulta *surgery*
la festa d'aniversari *birthday party*
ballar *to dance*
ahir mateix *(just) yesterday*
fer anys *to have one's birthday*
felicitats! *congratulations!, happy birthday! (here)*

Insight

Note that, unlike in English, the indefinite article is not
needed after **ser** when saying what one's job/profession is:
sóc metgessa, ets arquitecte? The same applies to **fer de** *to
be employed/have a job as*: **faig de recepcionista,** *I'm working
as a receptionist.* A particular line of work is often indicated
with **dedicar-se a** (e.g. ... **a l'ensenyament, al disseny gràfic,**
teaching, graphic design).

Exercise 1
Veritat o fals?

1. En Tim parla molt bé el català perquè viu a Barcelona des de
   fa molt de temps.
2. El francès és la llengua que en Tim menys practica.
3. La Lluïsa no té experiència professional.
4. En Tim es va divertir molt a la festa d'ahir.

Exercise 2
Familiarize yourself with the dialogue and then, if you can, act it
out with a partner.

Exercise 3

Listen again to the dialogue, focusing on the words listed below, and say whether the *r* sounds with a single or a double trill or whether it is silent.

1 parles **2** néixer **3** Anglaterra **4** recordo **5** voltar **6** altre **7** viure **8** mallorquí

Insight

You will have observed that in standard Catalan the final **-r** of infinitives is silent. Apart from this there is no comprehensive rule which covers every case: **per** (pronounced), **ahir** (silent).

Cultural information
Mallorquí

Lluïsa, in the Dialogue, says she speaks **mallorquí** rather than **català**. You will find some people using the name of Catalan dialects to refer to the language itself, especially in the case of **valencià**. Some complex 'political' issues are involved here, concerning the position of the Catalan-speaking areas within other established states (in this case Spain). In objective terms there is no question that Catalan is a coherent single language with its own particular system of dialects.

Cultural information
Greetings for special events

Most Catalan-speakers celebrate both their birthday and their 'Saint's day' (that is the **festa** *feast-day* of the saint after whom they are called). For both occasions the usual greeting offered is **Per molts anys!** (literally *For many years!*) corresponding to *Many happy returns!*. You can also use,

(Contd)

as in the dialogue, **felicitats!**. Specific events like Christmas have other expressions: **Bon Nadal!** or **Bones festes!** *Merry Christmas* and **Feliç any nou!** *Happy New Year!*.

Insight

Refer to the Introduction (where we explain why the 'prop' of the Key words and sentences is no longer supplied in Units 10–16. Its function should now be covered by the final summaries and by your own competence in self-expression.

Grammar

Insight

You are advised to study the Grammar section A in conjunction with the preliminary remarks presented at the beginning of this unit. A point that cannot be stressed too much is that the Catalan *preterite* tense is used for actions completed in *a period that does not include today*, a past time that is seen as cut off from the present. Actions and events that have taken place *today* or *in a past time that is understood to be still connected with the present* are expressed in the *perfect* tense, introduced in Unit 12.

A The preterite tense

1 You must be careful to distinguish between the auxiliary for the preterite (**vaig, vas,** etc.) and those parts of **anar** *to go* (Unit 5) which coincide with it. Also watch out for possible confusion between the periphrastic preterite and the construction **anar a +** infinitive, meaning *to go (to/and)*. There is, of course, a vast difference between **Vaig trobar un amic** *I met a friend* and **Vaig a trobar un amic** *I am going to meet a friend*.

2 Position of pronouns
With the preterite tense, object pronouns (including reflexive)
can either be placed before the auxiliary **vaig, vas,** etc. or
attached after the infinitive, with no change of meaning.
Remember that, after the infinitive, pronouns are linked
to it either with an apostrophe or a hyphen (see Unit 9,
Grammar B).

Es van casar el 1990 or   *They got married in 1990.*
   Van casar-se el 1990.

El formatge? El vaig posar or   *The cheese? I put it in the*
   Vaig posar-lo ahir a   *fridge yesterday.*
   la nevera.

Els papers? Els van perdre   *The papers? They lost them*
   or **Van perdre'ls** fa molts   *many years ago.*
   anys.

3 The form of the simple preterite
As well as the periphrastic preterite, Catalan has a single-
word version of this tense. Except in Valencia and to a lesser
extent in the Balearics you will not encounter this simple
(or synthetic) preterite in the spoken language, where the
periphrastic form prevails. However, since it does appear
frequently in written texts (where it may alternate freely with
the **vaig, vas** form), you can study here the conjugation
pattern for regular verbs:

	portar	**perdre**	**dormir**
(jo)	port-í	perd-í	dorm-í
(tu)	port-ares	perd-eres	dorm-ires
(ell/ella/vostè)	port-à	perd-é	dorm-í
(nosaltres)	port-àrem	perd-érem	dorm-írem
(vosaltres)	port-àreu	perd-éreu	dorm-íreu
(ells/elles/vostès)	port-aren	perd-eren	dorm-iren

The Reading exercise for this unit contains a few examples.

B Temporal expressions

Remember that **fa** corresponds to *ago* for actions situated in the
remote past, as heard in **fa cinc anys em vaig independitzar.**

Va venir a veure'm fa només un mes.	*He came to see me only a month ago.*
Es van divorciar ara fa tres anys.	*They got divorced three years ago.*

You should not confuse this with other temporal expressions
involving **fa**, for actions begun in the past and continuing into the
present. Here, English emphasizes the 'pastness' of the action's
beginning, whereas Catalan uses the present tense, focusing on the
action's continuation until 'now'.

Fa dues hores que t'espero. = T'espero des de fa dues hores.
I have been waiting for you for two hours.

Exercise 4
And now, for reinforcement, write a brief account of your own life,
using the constructions illustrated in the sections above and in the
dialogue.

Grammar

C The pronoun *en* and 'partitive' *de* in conjunction

In the dialogue we heard **Però jo *de llengües només en* parlo dues.**
In constructions like this the pronoun **en** refers back to **llengües**

which appears just before it in the same sentence. The consistent pattern is for a noun represented by **en** + verb to be preceded by **de**. This is not affected by the order of the sentence, but any natural pause will be indicated by a comma:

En vaig veure moltes, de persones = De persones en vaig veure moltes.	*I saw a lot of people.*
En té quatre, de gossos i de gosses.	*He has four, dogs and bitches.*

Similarly, when a noun is already represented by **en**, any adjectives referring to that noun will be preceded by **de**.

Si voleu peres *en* tenim *de* verdes i *de* madures.	*If you want pears we've got green ones and ripe ones.*

Exercise 5

For each of the following questions mark just one appropriate answer.

1 Quants convidats vénen a sopar?
    a En vénen cinc, de convidats.
    b De convidats vénen cinc persones.
    c Vénen cinc de convidats.

2 Quin tipus de vi voleu?
    a En volem negre.
    b Volem vi de negre.
    c En volem de negre.

3 Saps anglès?
    a D'anglès, no sé gens.
    b No en sé gens, d'anglès.
    c No en sé, anglès.

4 Només compra productes locals?
    a No, també en compra estrangers.
    b No, també compra estrangers.
    c No, també en compra d'estrangers.

5 Vas trobar alguna parada de bus?
  a No, no en vaig trobar cap parada.
  b No, no en vaig trobar cap, de parada.
  c No, de parada no vaig trobar cap.

Grammar

D Tag questions (*oi?, no?*)

At several points you have heard what are called 'tag questions', used to reinforce direct yes/no questions. In Catalan just two words, **oi?** and **no?** (plus, colloquially, **eh?**) cover the whole set of tag questions in English.

En Pere fuma, no?	*Pere smokes, doesn't he?*
Véns amb tren, oi?	*You come by train, don't you?*

Notice, though, that **no?** cannot follow a negative question, just **oi?**

No és pas tan dolent, oi?   *It's not so bad, is it?*

Exercise 6
◆) CD2, TR 9, 00:01

Listen to the recording. You will hear some people talking about their lives. As you listen, fill in the blanks below with what you hear (2–3 words).

Marta: Jo vaig néixer a Perpinyà però només **a**_____ del meu naixement el meu pare **b**_____ un accident i **c**_____ tots a viure a Barcelona. **d**_____ a casa de la meva àvia i la meva mare **e**_____ a treballar en una pastisseria. No **f**_____ mai anar a l'escola, així que amb setze anys **g**_____ els llibres i vaig crear la meva pròpia pastisseria. **h**_____ que la tinc i cada dia tinc més clients.

Miquel: Jo **a**_____ a estudiar enginyeria a França. És clar que
b_____ vaig estudiar molt de francès. Allà **c**_____ molts
estudiants estrangers. L'any després de la graduació **d**_____ una
feina a París i allà m'hi **e**_____ un pis. **f**_____ tres mesos
estic casat amb la Marie.

Pilar: Jo **a**_____ vaig decidir que volia ser pilot d'avió.
b_____ un dia que el meu pare **c**_____ a l'aeroport. Durant
uns mesos **d**_____ l'aeroport cada diumenge fins que un dia
la meva tia **e**_____ a visitar-la a Suïssa. **f**_____ un avió i
em va fer tanta por que mai més **g**_____ parlar d'avions ni
d'aeroports. Ara treballo de periodista.

Reading

Study this article taken from a Catalan newspaper. Remember that
you can check any unfamiliar vocabulary in the vocabulary list at
the back of the book.

Roben a la Biblioteca Amat

Una part important i valuosa del fons de llibres de la Biblioteca
Salvador Amat de Girona va desaparèixer ahir a la nit arran d'un
robatori. Els fets van tenir lloc al voltant de les 11 de la nit quan
uns desconeguts entraren a la biblioteca saltant-se les mesures de
seguretat. El robatori no va durar més de quinze minuts, just el
temps que tardà la policia a arribar al lloc dels fets. De les obres
desaparegudes destaquen llibres dels segles XVIII i XIX, així com
una peça de gran valor, *El somni dels estels,* de 1687. Sembla ser
que els lladres van poder desconnectar l'alarma i entrar directament
a la sala d'obres especials. Quan la policia va arribar a la part de
darrere de la biblioteca va poder veure desaparèixer els lladres. De
moment no se sap on són. Just després del robatori el director de la
biblioteca mostrà la seva sorpresa i ràbia davant d'aquest incident.

Exercise 7

Mark all verbs in the reading passage which are in the preterite tense.

Exercise 8

Answer the following questions in Catalan, making as much use of the language of the text as you can.

1 When did the robbery occur?
2 How long did the police take to arrive?
3 What kind of objects were missing from the library?
4 Which way did the thieves go out of the library?
5 What was the reaction of the library director?

Insight

We have reached another point where a review of progress is in order. Refer back, first, to the advice given in the Insight boxes at the end of Unit 1 and of Unit 5. You will surely be gratified now to consider how your competence in Catalan has evolved since you first began to 'teach yourself'. Progress will be accelerated in the next six units. Before proceeding, you may feel that you do not need to do any revision and consolidation work on the material covered so far. If you want to reassure yourself, however, and in order to strengthen your position, we recommend that you study the Points to remember sections for Units 1–10, referring to material in the relevant unit to clarify any points that you feel less than fully confident about.

Points to remember

1 **vas estudiar a València, oi?** *you studied in Valencia, didn't you?*
2 **vam anar a Tàrrega fa tres setmanes / abans d'ahir / l'any 2004** *we went to Tàrrega three weeks ago / the day before yesterday / in 2004*

3 a què et dediques? / de què fas? *what is your occupation?*
what do you work as?

4 treballo de recepcionista / sóc paleta / faig de cambrer *I work*
as a receptionist / I am a bricklayer / I am working as a waiter

5 es dediquen a la venda de material esportiu *their job is selling*
sporting goods

6 en Xavier és lampista però fa de camioner *Xavier is a plumber*
but he works as a lorry driver.

7 va estar deu anys contractat per aquella empresa *he/she spent*
ten years under contract with that firm.

8 des de fa un mes treballo en un banc / fa un mes que treballo
en un banc *I have been working in a bank for one month.*

9 es van divorciar fa dos anys / fa dos anys que es van divorciar
they got divorced five years ago.

10 The preterite tense, constructed with auxiliary verb **vaig**, etc.
and the infinitive.

11

Quin vestit més bonic!
What a nice dress!

In this unit you will learn
- *How to talk about clothes in a shop and try them on*
- *How to talk about sizes and colours*
- *How to describe a person's physical appearance*

---

1 Com em queda? *How does it suit me?*

Montse has decided to go shopping.

Dependenta	Et puc ajudar?
Montserrat	Sí, estic buscant un vestit.
Dependenta	Alguna cosa elegant?
Montserrat	Sí, un vestit elegant i llarg.
Dependenta	De quin color?
Montserrat	Blanc o d'algun color clar.
Dependenta	Aquesta temporada es porten molt els colors pastel: rosa,

CD2, TR 10, 00:09

8 4230212 9578101

ARTICLE	TALLA
BRUSA SENYORA	**42**

MODEL **XZ78**
PVP **53**

TEXTILS FUSTER
Avda. dels eibarresos n° 17–19
08450 Mont Palau

blau, groc ... Totes les noies duen els mateixos colors ... Mira't aquests.

Montserrat Que bonic, aquest groc! Me'l puc emprovar?

Dependenta Els emprovadors són al costat del taulell.

Montserrat Com em queda?

Dependenta Et queda preciós, però vols emprovar-te una talla menys?

Montserrat Sí, em sembla que no em va pas a la mida, em va massa ample de la cintura.

Dependenta Si necessites una jaqueta a joc amb el vestit, també en tenim. Aquesta hi va de conjunt. Posa-te-la i mira com et va.

Montserrat Gràcies. Ara que sóc aquí faig un cop d'ull als jerseis també.

ajudar *to help*
llarg/-a *long*
clar/-a *light* (coloured)
la temporada *season*
portar *to wear* (here)
***dur** (irregular) *to wear* (here)
mateix/-a *same*
***que + adj.** *how ...!*
emprovar-se *to try on*
l'emprovador (m.) *fitting room*
el taulell *counter*
quedar (here) *to suit*
preciós/-a *beautiful, lovely*
la talla *size*
anar a la mida *to fit*
ample/-a *full* (here), *wide*
la cintura *waist*
a joc = de conjunt *together, matching*
posar-se *to put on* (clothes)
fer un cop d'ull *to have a look*

QUICK VOCAB

*Els colors *The colours*
verd/-a *green*
blanc/-a *white*
gris/-a *grey*
vermell/-a *red*
roig/-ja *red*
blau/-va *blue*
groc/-ga *yellow*
negre/-a *black*
rosa *pink*
taronja *orange*
marró *brown*

Insight

Pay attention in Dialogue 1 to the two sentences, **me'l puc emprovar?** *can I try it on?* and **posa-te-la** *put it on*, noting that the pronouns precede the verb in one case and are attached after it in the other. The basic rule is that object pronouns follow the infinitive, the gerund and affirmative commands: otherwise they go before the verb. (The alternative **puc emprovar-me'l** is thus available for the first example above. Further explanation will come in Unit 15.) Keep looking out for this feature as we proceed, observing modifications in form and spelling of the pronouns according to particular positions and combinations.

Exercise 1

Read the dialogue again making sure you understand it all. Then, if you can, act it out with a partner, trying to imitate the speakers as much as you can.

Exercise 2
🔊 **CD2, TR 11, 00:05**

You are going to hear a list of words (written below). Put them in the correct column depending on the pronunciation of the **x**.

1 as in ta**xi** **2** as in **x**avi **3** as in e**x**amen **4** as in co**tx**e

mateix, excursió, baixar, dutxa, xai, exercici, peix, màxim, exacte, marxar, exemple

Insight

Observe that the sound represented by **-tx-** in **cotxe** is written **-ig** when this same sound comes at the end of a word: **faig, roig, maig,** etc.

Exercise 3

Look at these pictures and match them with the correct word. Look up those you don't know.

1 la brusa
2 les sabates
3 els texans
4 els guants

5 la camisa
6 els pantalons
7 la jaqueta
8 la corbata

9 la faldilla
10 la samarreta
11 les sandàlies
12 el vestit

Grammar

A The verbs *dur* and *portar*

Dur is an irregular verb (whose conjugated forms can be checked in the **Reference tables**) that we use as a synonym of **portar**. In fact both **dur** and **portar** have a lot of different meanings such as *to take*, *to bring*, *to carry*, *to drive*, *to transport*, as well as *to wear*, which is what we mainly practise in this unit.

B *Que ... !* *quin ... !* in exclamations

In the dialogue and in the unit title we have seen the use of **que ...!** and **quin...!** as a structure to express opinion or just exclamation. But, look again at these sentences: **quin vestit més bonic** and **que bonic, aquest groc!** (referring to a yellow dress) and you realize that we use **que** before an adjective (or an adverb, too) and **quin/-a/-s/-es** before a noun. Here are a few more examples with the corresponding translations:

que gran!	*how big!*
quines cases més grans!	*what big houses!*
quina sort!	*what (good) luck!*
que ràpid!	*how quick!*

Més (or **tan**) always precedes the adjective in the construction **quin + noun + més/tan + adjective.**

C Uses and forms of colours

The main Catalan words for 'simple' colours are straightforward adjectives that agree in number and gender with the noun they qualify (**uns pantalons blaus/unes camises blaves**). Exceptions are colours like **rosa** *pink*, **taronja** *orange*, **marró** *(chestnut) brown* which have only the one form. This is because these words are originally nouns that have taken on an adjectival function, so that **rosa**, for example, signifies (**de color**) **rosa: les sabates rosa**. Note also that when **clar** *light* or **fosc** *dark* qualify a colour these words too are invariable: **uns pantalons blau clar** *light blue trousers*.

Exercise 4

Here is a list of nouns with some adjectives (in the masculine singular form) in brackets. As in the example, you have to make a correct expression with all of them. You will be practising agreement of adjectives and two other features: the use of **i** to complete sequences of adjectives and use of the intensifier **ben** (see Grammar F).

Example: Uns arbres (alt, vell, ben verd). Uns arbres alts, vells i ben verds.

1 Unes jaquetes (car, curt, blanc).
2 Una beguda (fresc, vermell, ben bo).
3 Uns cafès (descafeïnat, negre, congelat).
4 Uns dies (gris, llarg, ben avorrit).
5 Unes galetes (marró, salat, barat).
6 Una bicicleta (nou, groc, modern).
7 Uns animals (salvatge, gros, lliure).
8 Unes camises (blau fosc, econòmic, ben elegant).

Insight

Failure to make a Catalan adjective agree in number and gender with the noun it qualifies is something which grates on the ear or offends the eye of the native speaker. Remember what has been said already, beginning in Unit 1, about the

(Contd)

basic pattern of adjective endings. The Reference table shows the main variations, of the kind exemplified in Exercise 4 by **blanc** (feminine plural **blanques**), **groc** (feminine singular/plural **groga/grogues**) and **blau** (feminine singular **blava**).

Exercise 5

Look carefully at this advertisement. Note that **calçat** means *footwear* while **espardenyes** are *trainers*. Then answer the questions below.

1 Aquesta empresa ven només calçat?
2 A quin moment de l'any es publica aquest anunci?
3 Quantes botigues tenen?
4 Com es diu en català a *leather belt*?

2 És alta, morena i té els ulls blaus *She is tall, dark-haired and has blue eyes*

Some friends of Montse are in a cybercafé (**cibercafè**), looking at an Internet page and talking about other people's looks.

Joan	Mireu qui surt al web d'aquesta agència de viatges!
Antoni	A veure! Ostres, però si és la Mercè!
Mònica	Que no! No ho és pas!

CD2, TR 11, 01:05

Joan	Sí que ho és. Porta un pentinat diferent i està més prima.
Mònica	Com s'ho fa la gent per aprimar-se? Jo estic tan grassa ...
Antoni	Fer règim, és clar!
Joan	Coneixeu el seu xicot? És un noi ros, d'ulls verds i fa un metre noranta.
Mònica	Nòrdic, no? A mi m'agraden més els nois morens, arrissats i de pell fosca. I el teu amic anglès, Montse, com és?
Montse	No el coneixes? És força alt, porta el cabell curt i és pèl-roig. Té la pell ben clara i els ulls clars també. Duu ulleres. És molt simpàtic ...
Joan	Bé, prou xerrar ... Deixeu-me entrar al meu portal de correu electrònic, que vull enviar un missatge a un amic.

sortir (here) *appear*
que no *no* (emphatic)
*ho see Grammar D
el pentinat *hairstyle*
prim/-a *slim, thin*
fer-s'ho (here) *to manage*
aprimar-se *to get thin, to lose weight*
gras/-sa *fat*
el règim *diet*
el/la xicot/-a *boyfriend/girlfriend*
ros/-sa *fair-haired/skinned*
arrissat/-da *curly-haired*
la pell *skin, leather*
fosc/-a *dark*
el cabell *hair*
curt/-a *short*
pèl-roig/roja *red-haired*
*ben *very*
les ulleres *glasses*
xerrar *to chat*
el portal *access, doorway*

QUICK VOCAB

Insight

The verb **conèixer** means *to know* in the sense of *to be acquainted with*. The idea of *to meet/have met* is sometimes the English equivalent: **encantat de coneixe't**, *pleased to meet you*; **coneixes en Santi? – sí, ja ens coneixem** *do you know/have you met Santi? – yes, we do know each other/we have met*. Be careful not to confuse this verb with **saber** which expresses the other meanings of *to know*: **no sé com es diu** *I don't know what s/he is called*.

Exercise 6
Veritat o fals?

1 La Mònica no reconeix la Mercè perquè sembla una altra.
2 El xicot de la Mercè és estranger.
3 La Mònica encara no coneix en Tim.
4 En Joan vol obrir el seu correu electrònic per saber si hi té cap missatge.

Insight
Height and weight

Like other languages Catalan uses metres and centimetres to talk about physical dimensions such as *height* (**alçada**), *width* (**amplada**), *length* (**llargada**), etc. Note the use of **fer** in such expressions:

Aquest edifici fa cent metres d'alçada.
La meva germana fa un metre i setanta-dos centímetres.

For *weight* (**el pes**) (verb **pesar**), whether talking about things or people, we use **quilo** *kilo*, **gram** *gram* and even **tona** *tonne*. Some examples:

Quant pesa en Miquel?
Ara pesa setanta-tres quilos. Quan va néixer va pesar tres quilos i set-cents grams.

Grammar

D The object pronoun *ho*

Ho is a weak object pronoun, invariable like **hi**. It means *it*, when
standing for a neuter demonstrative (**això, allò**) or for a whole
sentence: **Em preguntes si sé *quant val el quadre* i jo et dic que no
ho sé** *You're asking me if I know how much the picture is worth,
and I'm telling you that I don't know*. Note, though, that it does
not always appear in English equivalents: **no ho sé** *I don't know*;
ho sento *I'm sorry*. Remember **ho pots lletrejar** or **ho pots repetir**
from Unit 1.

Dialogue 2 in this unit illustrates another function of **ho**: **Aquesta
noia ... és la Mercè. –No, no ho és pas. –Sí que ho és.** Then look
at: **No és boig però ho sembla** *He's not mad but he looks it*. Here
ho represents an adjective or noun complement of **ser, estar** and
semblar.

Note too that *so* is sometimes the translation of **ho**: **Això és veritat:
ho diu el capità** *This is true: the captain says so*; **No ho crec** *I
don't think so*. When *everything* is the object of a verb, then the
combination **ho ... tot**, cf. *it all*, must be used: **Ho saben tot** *They
know everything*; **Pots repetir-ho tot?** *Can you repeat it all?*.

Exercise 7

Fill in the blanks with an item from the list that is represented by the pronouns **ho** (neuter) or **lo** (direct object pronoun, Unit 4).

> calent, que aquest és el seu cotxe, el disc compacte, que fumar és dolent, aquest llibre, és teu això d'aquí?, alt i ros, el jersei de llana

1 Llegeix-**lo**, és molt divertit. _____
2 El cafè **ho** està molt. _____
3 Vaig escoltar-**lo** una sola vegada. _____
4 Diu que vol donar-**lo** a una amiga. _____
5 La Marta no **ho** vol entendre. _____
6 **Ho** és més el meu germà. _____
7 Com **ho** saps? _____
8 Sí que **ho** és. _____

_____

Grammar

E *Portar* and *tenir* in descriptions

The standard way of describing physical attributes is with **ser** and **tenir**, as in **La senyoreta Marí és morena i té els ulls verds**. Both verbs serve to present permanent characteristics, while **portar/ dur** refer to something that can be changed or worn, like in **porta ulleres i du un vestit rosa**. But, be careful, because we can find sentences like **porta els cabells arrissats** and **té els cabells arrissats / és arrissada**, which are different: while the first one refers to a result of hairdressing, in the second one she has natural curly hair.

F Position of adjectives and adverbs

The normal position of qualifying or descriptive adjectives is after the noun, as illustrated in the dialogues. The adverb (unless standing at the beginning of a sentence) is usually positioned directly after the verb: **Això s'arregla ràpidament** *This can be quickly sorted out.*

Remember that when the verb is in a compound tense, the adverb will not divide the auxiliary from the main verb: **El problema es va resoldre fàcilment**.

An exception to this is **ben** *well, really, very, quite* which is the form taken by **bé** when it precedes an adjective, infinitive or participle: **Em van ben sorprendre** *They really surprised me.*

Exercise 8
An Internet friend has just e-mailed you, wanting to know what you look like, before she comes to meet you. Read the e-mail carefully and then answer the questions which follow.

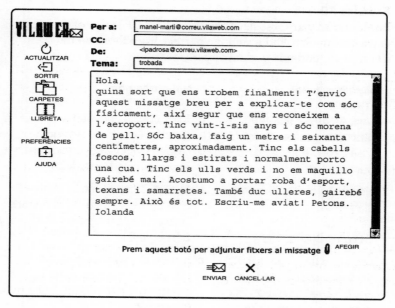

Per a:	manel-marti@correu.vilaweb.com
CC:	
De:	<ipadrosa@correu.vilaweb.com>
Tema:	trobada

Hola,
quina sort que ens trobem finalment! T'envio aquest missatge breu per a explicar-te com sóc físicament, així segur que ens reconeixem a l'aeroport. Tinc vint-i-sis anys i sóc morena de pell. Sóc baixa, faig un metre i seixanta centímetres, aproximadament. Tinc els cabells foscos, llargs i estirats i normalment porto una cua. Tinc els ulls verds i no em maquillo gairebé mai. Acostumo a portar roba d'esport, texans i samarretes. També duc ulleres, gairebé sempre. Això és tot. Escriu-me aviat! Petons.
Iolanda

Prem aquest botó per adjuntar fitxers al missatge 🔗 AFEGIR

✉ ❌
ENVIAR CANCEL·LAR

1 Quina alçada fa la Iolanda?
2 Com té els cabells?
3 Què és el que no acostuma a fer?
4 Com vesteix?
5 Què duu molt sovint?

Exercise 9

Now send Iolanda an e-mail describing, in Catalan, your own appearance. Take as much vocabulary and language structure as you want from Exercise 8.

Exercise 10

Look carefully at these newspaper small ads. For five of the six entries on the left find a suitable partner from those on the right. There is an 'odd one out' on either side.

Noia busca noi

1 Laia, 44 anys i separada. Busco noi per a compartir coses. Zona Barcelona. Bústia: 3124

2 Neus, 41 anys, 1,75, prima, ulls foscos, romàntica i molt dinàmica. Busco home. Truca'm. Bústia: 6597

3 Separada de 32 anys, 1 fill. Busco relació amb noi entre 32–40 anys, bon físic i agradable. Bústia: 1276

4 Eva, 42 anys, atractiva i simpàtica. Cerco home atractiu, sensible, nivell cultural mig-alt, fins a 46 anys. Bústia: 7435

Noi busca noia

a Jordi, casat i apassionat, divertit i atractiu. Busco noia casada o liberal per a relacions esporàdiques. Bústia: 4367

b Miquel, 32 anys, maco. Busco noia entre 27–33 anys, simpàtica i alegre, per a relació seriosa. Bústia: 4581

c Noi, 34 anys, busco noia maca i simpàti-ca per a conèixer-se, amistat o futura relació. Truca'm. Bústia: 6217

d Jove de 37 anys, separat i sense fills busca noia semblant per a possible relació. No importa edat. Barcelona. Bústia: 8539

5 Senyora de 55 anys busca persona educada i amant de la música clàssica per a possible relació. Bústia:1827

6 Mireia, jove, bonica i agradable. Desitjo conèixer noi compatible entre 18–35 anys per a relació seriosa o amistat. Bústia: 7591

e Cerco estabilitat amb noia entre 35–43 anys. M'agraden les activitats esportives i d'aventura. Si ets activa, truca'm. Bústia: 6429

f Jaume, 40 anys, simpàtic. Nivell cultural elevat. Cerco noia senzilla de bon físic, per a relació estable. Bústia: 4248

Exercise 11

For each of the following words choose a synonym from the box below.

1 atractiva   **4** simpàtica
2 buscar   **5** actiu
3 compatible   **6** estable

maca,	seriosa,	agradable,	semblant,	cercar,	dinàmic

Points to remember

1 necessito uns pantalons llargs i negres *I need some long, black trousers*

2 me'ls puc emprovar?/puc emprovar-me'ls? *can I try them on?*

3 com em queden? et queden bé *do they suit me? they suit you well*

4 la faldilla et va massa llarga/curta, ampla/estreta...*the skirt is too long/short, full/tight ... on you*

5 treu-te els texans i posa't aquests altres *take your jeans off and put these others on*

6 com és ella? és jove? sí que ho és *what does she look like? is she young? yes, she is*

7 fa un metre setanta-dos i pesa 68 quilos *s/he is 1.72 metres tall and weighs 68 kilos*

8 porta/té els cabells arrissats i duu ulleres *s/he has curly hair and wears glasses.*

9 Various functions of the neuter pronoun **ho**, translating *it* but present also in other constructions and in numerous idioms.

10 Combinations of object pronouns: position with the verb, forms and spelling of pronouns in combination.

12

Festa major
Local festivities

In this unit you will learn
- *How to talk about events in the recent past*
- *How to talk about incidents in the city*
- *How to talk about your pastimes*

Before you start

In Unit 10 you learnt how to express actions completed in a distant past, using the preterite tense with **vaig, vas,** etc. plus infinitive. In this unit we deal with actions completed in a past time which is understood to be still connected to the present. This is the perfect tense (sometimes called the 'present perfect') and it is formed with the auxiliary verb **haver** *to have* introducing the past participle. **Haver** is conjugated thus: **he, has, ha, hem, heu, han.**

The past participles of regular verbs are formed as follows:

1st conj. (-**ar**)	*2nd conj.* (-**er**/-**re**)	*3rd conj.* (-**ir**)
parlar > parl +**at**	perdre > perd +**ut**	dormir > dorm +**it**
parlat (*spoken*)	perdut (*lost*)	dormit (*slept*)

(Participles of irregular verbs are introduced in Grammar A of this unit.)

As in English, the perfect tense is associated with time references conveyed by demonstrative **aquest** meaning this: **Aquesta setmana ha fet bon temps** *The weather has been fine this week*.

Catalan, however, always uses the perfect tense for an action which has taken place *today* (the past seen invariably as still connected to the present). In this case (actions completed today) Catalan must have a perfect tense where English may have a preterite: **Avui/ Aquest matí he vist la Carme** *Today / This morning I saw Carme*; **M'he aixecat d'hora (avui) i així he pogut arribar abans del migdia** *I got up early (today) and so I was able to arrive before noon*.

---

1 Hi ha hagut un robatori a la joieria
There has been a robbery at the jeweller's shop

Montse and Tim are at a town festival. It's 5.00 p.m. and they are in the street when they meet a friend.

CD2, TR 12, 00:08

Eduard	Hola nois, ja sou aquí?
Montse	Sí, hem arribat aquesta matinada. I tu què, ja has anat a l'exposició de pintures?
Eduard	Ara en vinc i m'ha agradat molt ... Sabeu que han entrat a robar a la joieria de la Judit?
Tim	Què dius ara! I què ha passat? Com està ella? S'han endut moltes coses?
Eduard	Encara no se sap ben bé. Per sort no hi ha hagut cap ferit, però la Judit, pobra, està molt espantada. L'han portada a la comissaria i ara la policia l'està interrogant.
Tim	És una noia valenta, però ...
Eduard	Ja ho pots ben dir ...! Enguany no sé què passa. Fa un mes hi va haver aquell accident de trànsit just davant de casa. Uns dies després l'incendi al mercat i avui aquest robatori.
Montse	Tens raó, ha estat un any dolent ... I a la festa, ja hi has participat?
Eduard	Home, i tant! Aquest matí he tocat a la cercavila. I abans de dinar he muntat l'escenari per al concert.

l'exposició (f.) *exhibition*
la pintura *painting*
passar *to happen* (here)
endur-se (irregular) *to take away*
per sort *good luck*
ferit/-da *injured*
pobre/-a *poor*
espantat/-da *frightened*
valent/-a *brave*
ja ho pots ben dir! *you can say that again!*
enguany *this year*
el transit *traffic*
l'incendi (m.) *fire*
tenir raó *to be right*
tocar *to play an instrument* (here)
la cercavila *street serenading (in groups)*
muntar *to assemble, to set up*
l'escenari (m.) *stage, set*
***pensar** + infinitive *to intend to*
tenir ganes de ... *to be keen to ...*

QUICK VOCAB

Insight

The presence of demonstrative **aquest/-a** *this* in temporal expressions qualifying a past action is always associated with the perfect tense in Catalan. Where English can say *we went* or *we have been there this lunchtime* (depending on the speaker's perspective), the Catalan version can only be **hi hem anat aquest migdia** (not **hi vam anar...**). Remember the rule about actions taking place *today*.

Another rule of thumb is that adverbs like **sempre** *always* and **(no) mai** *(n)ever* have a strong tendency to go with the perfect tense where English may have the perfect or the simple past: **has vist mai tal cosa?** *did you ever see/have you ever seen such a thing?*

Exercise 1

Go through the dialogue again and act it out, preferably with a partner.

Exercise 2
◀) CD2, TR 13, 00:02

You are going to hear some words, partially written below. Listen carefully and decide whether the sound corresponding to the missing part has to be written with **g**, **gu** or **gü** + vowel. The first word has been done for you.

Example: guerra

1 ai_____   **7** llo_____r
2 _____a   **8** se_____nt
3 _____tarra   **9** _____st
4 pin_____í   **10** boti_____ra
5 ve_____da   **11** se_____n
6 car_____l

....
Insight
Here we focus on a distinctive feature of Catalan pronunciation and spelling. The **g/gu/gü** pattern tested here is replicated in the behaviour of **c/qu/qü**. Remember that **g/gu** and **c/qu** variations are important in the correct spelling of different parts of a good number of verbs: **toco, toques, toca**, etc; **jugo, jugues, juga**, etc.
....

....
Cultural information
Festa major

Each town or village celebrates annually a particular date or occasion, often the feast of the local patron saint. The occasion is not to be missed if you are in the area, and locals living away will take great pains to be back home for the festive period. The religious origins and contents of the

184

festa major are conspicuous: in the south **moros i cristians**, recalling historical religious conflict, figure prominently. Municipal authorities, neighbourhood and recreational groups organize diverse activities centred on processions, music, sporting competitions, fireworks, etc. Among these there may well be a session of human-tower building by well-supported groups of **castellers**. Many places, including very small villages, have colourful and spectacular (and usually noisy) rituals: **La Patum de Berga** is perhaps the most famous of these. The **ball de festa major** will usually be the highlight of the social programme, complemented by performances by the local **orquestra** or **cobla** (the latter playing traditional instruments and accompanying the 'national' dance, **la sardana**). The festive spirit which accompanies all the activities (**partits de futbol o bàsquet** *football* or *basketball matches*, **exposicions** *exhibitions*, **fires** *markets*, **danses tradicionals**, **espectacles teatrals o musicals**) is stimulated by the **cercavila**, when various groups wander the streets playing lively music. Night-time parades and processions, with **gegants** *giants* and grotesque animal figures, often end with dramatic **focs d'artifici** *fireworks* and the **correfoc** in which braver spirits run among the flashes and bangs.

2 Aquest cap de setmana he jugat a futbol
This weekend I played football

Montse	Què heu fet aquest cap de setmana?
Eduard	La Roser ha anat a nedar a la piscina, com sempre, i jo he jugat a futbol.
Tim	I a tennis, ja no hi jugues?
Eduard	Aquest mes només hi he jugat un parell de vegades. Ara m'he afeccionat a anar a pescar. M'estimo més fer això que anar a la platja a parar el sol.

(Contd)

QUICK VOCAB

nedar *to swim*
jugar *to play*
com sempre *as usual*
afeccionar-se *to grow fond*
pescar *to fish*
parar el sol *to sit in the sun*
el curset *short course*
aprendre (irregular) *to learn*
actualment *at the moment*
passar estona *to spend time*
els escacs *chess*
apuntar-se *to enrol, to sign up*
el campionat *championship*

Insight

Refer back to Grammar section D in Unit 7 and then observe the different functions of **ja** *already*, *yet* and of **ja no** *no longer*, *not any more* as they appear in Dialogue 2.

Insight

Make sure that you understand the function and meaning of the pronouns **ho** and **hi** as they are used in Dialogue 2.

Exercise 3
Veritat o fals?

1 La Roser va a nedar a la piscina cada cap de setmana.
2 L'Eduard ara va més a pescar que a jugar a tennis.

3 La Monste toca la guitarra des que va a un curset.
4 En Tim encara no s'ha apuntat al campionat d'escacs.

Insight

You will have noticed the distinction made in Catalan between **jugar** *to play* (games and sports) and **tocar** *to play* (musical instrument, piece of music). The main meaning of **tocar** is *to touch* but this verb is also found in various idioms. Think of **a qui toca? – em toca a mi**, used in the context of queuing (Unit 4, Dialogue 3). **Tocar** also expresses the idea of winning a prize in a lottery or competition: **l'any passat li va tocar la grossa** *last year he won the jackpot*, **m'han tocat tres mil euros** *my winnings were 3,000 euros*.

Grammar

A The past participle

1 The formation of past participles for regular verbs has been explained at the beginning of this unit. There are some consistent patterns for participles of irregular vebs, notably those showing the ending -**gut**.

venir > vingut	beure > begut	tenir > tingut
haver > hagut	conèixer > conegut	deure > degut
poder > pogut	voler > volgut	valer > valgut

And, for verbs whose infinitive ends in -**endre**, the ending is -**ès**:

entendre > entès	comprendre > comprès
encendre > encès	(*but* prendre > pres)

Participles of other common irregular verbs are:

escriure > escrit	veure > vist	treure > tret
obrir > obert	fer > fet	viure > viscut
ser > estat/sigut	oferir > ofert	prometre > promès
respondre > respost		

2 Auxiliary **haver** is never separated from the participle:

> **Vostè ha viscut sempre aquí?/**   *Have you always lived here?*
> **Sempre ha viscut aquí vostè?**

except in the simple case of **ben: M'has ben confòs** You have really confused me.

3 The past participle may optionally agree with third-person direct-object pronouns coming before **haver**: as in Dialogue 1 (**L'han portada...**, where **la = Judit**).

> **Les claus? Les he perdut/**   *The keys? I have lost them.*
> **perdudes.**

Exercise 4

Here is an official letter inviting you to a special event, a book launch. All the verbs in the past tense have been removed from the text. Choose the appropriate tense (preterite or perfect) to fill in the blanks. Also you can compare the formal composition of this letter with the more familiar tone used in the texts you saw in Units 6 and 11.

Cornellà del Terri, 3 de maig del 2010

Benvolgut senyor Piramon,

L'Ajuntament de Cornellà es complau a convidar-lo a la presentació del llibre *La meva vida i l'esport* de Jesús Miqueló, el proper diumenge dia 15 al Saló d'Actes de l'Ajuntament. L'Editorial Tresveles i l'autor _____**1** (decidir) presentar-lo públicament al nostre poble. Com vostè ja sap, el senyor Miqueló _____**2** (passar) una llarga etapa de la seva carrera esportiva en el nostre poble i per això mateix _____**3** (acceptar) la nostra invitació. Miqueló _____**4** (entrar) a formar part del club de patinatge de Cornellà l'any 1998 i un any després _____**5** (proclamar-se) campió de Catalunya en la seva categoria. Des de llavors i fins fa poc no _____**6** (parar) d'entrenar-se a les instal·lacions del nostre club. Just aquest mes _____**7** (participar) en els campionats d'Europa i el mes de gener passat _____**8** (quedar) en sisena posició als mundials que _____**9** (tenir lloc) al Brasil.

Esperem la seva assistència a l'acte.

Atentament,

L'alcalde
Àngel Bartra i Casacuberta

P.D. Preguem confirmació.

Exercise 5

Read the letter again and write the corresponding Catalan
expressions used in formal letters.

1 Dear Mr/Mrs
2 The town council is pleased to …
3 We hope you can attend the ceremony.
4 Yours sincerely/faithfully
5 RSVP
6 P.S.

Grammar

B *Pensar* + infinitive

You will study the Catalan future tense in the next unit. Both
dialogues here, however, introduce a way of expressing the idea
of a future action with **pensar**. Here **pensar** + infinitive means *to
intend to*: **Penso respondre demà** *I mean to/shall reply tomorrow*.

C Review of *en* and *hi*

You are in a good position to appreciate the importance of these
little words in the machinery of Catalan grammar.

En represents **de** (*of, from*) combined with a pronoun or reference
to a noun. In Unit 4 you used expressions in which **en** refers to

a quantity of something: **De farina no en tenim.** Similarly, when de means about: **N'has parlat amb en Terenci?** *Did you speak to Terenci about it?*

Notice, in Dialogue 1 of this unit, Eduard's **Ara en vinc**, where **en** now conveys the idea of *from* (the exhibition). Another example of this use: **He entrat a la feina a les 8 i no n'he sortit fins a les 9 del vespre** *I went into work at 8 o'clock and I didn't leave until 9 this evening.*

In Dialogue 2 we are reminded of how **hi** represents **a** + pronoun (or reference to a noun), in **ja no hi jugues?** and **hi he jugat un parell de vegades** (where **hi** = **a tennis** in both cases). Here are some more examples:

Ja has anat al lavabo? – No, encara no hi he anat.	*Have you been to the toilet yet? – No, I haven't been (there) yet.*
Si vas a l'estació puc acompanyar-t'hi, si vols.	*If you're going to the station I can give you a lift there, if you like.*

You will find it useful to look again at the section on **ho** (Grammar D, Unit 11), another small but essential 'cog' in Catalan grammar. When you feel confident in using **en**, **hi** and **ho** you can be sure that your fluency is very well advanced.

D *Ser* and *estar* with adjectives

You have seen that *to be* is expressed by two different verbs in Catalan, **ser** and **estar**. Here we focus on distinctions in the way these verbs combine with adjectives.

Ser expresses a quality that is understood to be inherent or permanent: **En Jaume és llest i treballador** *Jaume is clever and hard-working;* **Aquesta proposta és atractiva** *This proposal is attractive.*

Estar, on the other hand, expresses a state or condition that is seen as subject to or the result of change: **Ara està trista** *She is sad now;* **Estic més prim que abans** *I am slimmer than before.*

This basic contrast is seen clearly in Dialogue 1, where we hear **La Judit està espantada ... és (una noia) valenta**. In Unit 11 Dialogue 2 we heard **La Mercè està prima**, conveying the idea that she has lost weight, whereas **és prima** would mean that she is a slim person. Because **ser** and **estar** offer different ways of viewing quality or properties in a subject, a number of adjectives (like **prim/-a** just here) can be introduced by either verb, with clearly differentiated nuances. If **som alegres** means *we are happy/cheerful (people)* and **estem alegres** means *we are happy/cheerful* (now, because of something that has happened), you should be able to make up similar contrasting pairs with adjectives like **dèbil** *weak*, **nerviós/-a** *nervous*, **tranquil/-il·la** *calm*, etc.

A final review of **ser** and **estar** is made in Unit 16.

Exercise 6
For every sentence, choose the correct verb (**ser/estar**).

1 La Montse _____ força blanca de pell, però a l'estiu sempre _____ més morena.
2 La camisa _____ de color blau i a més _____ molt barata.
3 _____ una ciutat industrial, però m'agrada perquè _____ molt ben situada.
4 En Jordi _____ un jove molt tranquil. Avui, que té un examen, _____ poc tranquil.
5 _____ contentíssims perquè han guanyat un premi!
6 _____ rossa la Margarita? No, no ho és pas, _____ tenyida.

Exercise 7
◄♬ CD2, TR 14, 00:01

Look at this diary of events and listen to the recording. You will hear four people talking about one of the activities listed in which they have participated. You have to match each person (A–D) to one of these towns (Igualada, Maldà, Sabadell, Tarragona, Tàrrega and Terrassa). Note that two of them are not needed.

IGUALADA
22.00:
'No et vesteixis per sopar'. Representació teatral de l'obra de Marc Camoletti. A càrrec de la companyia Greta & Aurora. Teatre Municipal l'Ateneu. Sant Pau, 9.

MALDÀ
19.30:
Festa infantil. Amb balls, jocs i cercavila. A càrrec del grup d'animació De Pata.

SABADELL
12.00:
'El parxís màgic'. Espectacle de teatre musical per a tots els públics de Jaume Esquius, amb música de Quim Serra. A càrrec de la Companyia Teatre de Paper. Teatre del Sol. C/ del Sol, 99.

TARRAGONA
23.00:
Actuació del grup El Cortijo de los Callaos. Dins del programa Tarragona Cultura Contemporània. Sala Zero. Sant Magí, 12.

TÀRREGA
Mercat mensual de segells, monedes i pins. Vestíbul del Teatre Ateneu. Durant el matí.

TERRASSA
23.00:
Actuació de Jorge Pardo (saxòfons i flauta), Carles Benavent (baix) i Tino di Geraldo (bateria i percussió). Concert de jazz-flamenc. Nova Jazz Cava. Passatge Tete Montoliu, 24.

Adapted from Avui, 5 January 2003.

Exercise 8

Here are the outlines of a story. Write a proper narrative with the correct form of the perfect tense for each infinitive. You can use expressions of time like **després**, **tot seguit**, **immediatament** and also make connections with **i**.

L'ANDREU AVUI (llevar-se a les 9, llegir el diari, acompanyar la filla a la ciutat, veure un client, jugar un partit d'esquaix, guanyar el partit, dutxar-se, fer el dinar, recollir la nena, treballar a l'ordinador, connectar-se a Internet, anar a una festa, ballar, beure cervesa)

Exercise 9
For further practice rewrite the story, using the preterite, as if all these events took place yesterday.

Points to remember

1 **què heu fet avui? – aquesta tarda hem anat a fer un volt amb bici** *what did you do / have you done today? this afternoon we went / have been for a bike ride*
2 **heu estat mai a Dènia?** *have you ever been to Dènia?*
3 **què ha passat? – han entrat a robar al banc** *what has happened? – someone has broken into the bank*
4 **hi ha hagut un incendi / una explosió / un atracament / un accident** *there has been a fire / an explosion / a hold-up / an accident* (but **ahir / l'any passat va haver-hi un incendi**, etc.)
5 **t'ha agradat el concert d'avui?** *did you enjoy the concert today?* – **sí, però em va agradar molt més el d'ahir** *yes, but I much preferred yesterday's*
6 **que has rebut el missatge d'en Toni? – sí, i penso respondre-hi ben aviat** *have you received / did you receive Toni's message? – Yes, and I mean to reply (to it) very soon*
7 The perfect tense, formed with the auxiliary verb **haver** to have introducing the past participle.
8 Past participles of regular (stem + **-at, -ut, -it**) and irregular verbs.
9 Optional agreement of past participles with third-person direct-object pronouns coming before **haver**.
10 Different aspects of *to be* expressed by **ser** and **estar** used with adjectives.

13

Demà plourà
Tomorrow it is going to rain

In this unit you will learn
- *How to talk about projects and events in the future*
- *How to talk about the weather*
- *How to ask for services in a bank*
- *How to reply to an invitation*
- *How to send apologies*

---

1 Fa molta calor *It's really hot*

Montse, Roser and Eduard are on the beach.

Roser	Estic farta de parar el sol! Fa massa calor. Me'n vaig a l'aigua.
Eduard	Aprofita-ho, que l'home del temps diu que demà plourà.
Montse	Ah sí? i per quants dies?
Eduard	Sembla que farà mal temps durant un parell de dies i baixaran les temperatures, però divendres tornarà a fer sol.
Roser	El meu cosí demà se'n va al Pirineu a escalar, segur que allà també hi trobarà pluja.
Eduard	O neu!
Roser	Sí home, al mes d'agost!
Eduard	La veritat és que a l'estiu hi ha moltes tempestes fortes a la muntanya, amb calamarsa i tot.

fart/-a *fed up*
fer calor/sol/mal temps *to be hot, sunny, bad weather*
*anar-se'n *to go (away)*
*que *because* (here)
l'home del temps *weather man, forecaster*
ploure *to rain*
tornar a + infinitive *to ... again*
escalar *to climb*
la pluja *rain*
la neu *snow*
la tempesta *storm*
fort/-a *heavy, strong, powerful*
la calamarsa *hail*
... i tot *even*
el creuer *cruise*
calent/-a *hot*
la bossa *bag*
la crema *sun cream* (here), *cream*

QUICK VOCAB

Insight

The verb **fer** is essential when talking about the weather. In these expressions **fer** is used impersonally, always in the singular because the unstated subject is really the weather. Something similar applies to **ploure** *to rain*, **nevar** *to snow* and **tronar** *to thunder* and in expressions with **estar** and **hi ha** seen in Exercise 3. Note that **fer** remains in the singular even when reference is objectively plural: **està fent uns dies bons** *we've been having some nice days*.

Exercise 1
Veritat o fals?

1 L'home del temps ha pronosticat que hi haurà nevades al Pirineu.
2 L'Eduard i la Roser no marxen aquest mes de vacances.
3 L'aigua del mar està molt calenta.
4 La crema pel sol és a dintre de la bossa de la Montse.

Exercise 2
Read the dialogue again and act it out, preferably with a partner.

Exercise 3
Now that you know some weather-related vocabulary, you can match each of the symbols below with the appropriate phrase:

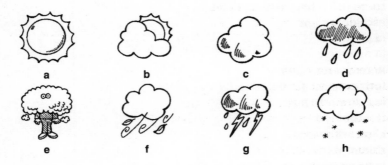

1 Plou.
2 Fa sol.
3 Està núvol.
4 Està nevant.
5 Fa vent.
6 Fa boira.
7 Està cobert.
8 Hi ha tempesta.

2 Quan m'ho ingressaran? *When will it be credited to my account?*

Tim is in a bank.

🔊 CD2, TR 15, 01:48

Tim	Bon dia, tinc uns vuit-cents dòlars i els vull ingressar al meu compte.
Empleat	Em deixa el carnet? ... Gràcies. A quin compte els posem, al corrent o al d'estalvi?
Tim	Al compte corrent, sisplau. Aquí té la meva llibreta ... A quant està el canvi?
Empleat	Avui un euro val 1,15 dòlars.
Tim	I quan els tindré ingressats, els diners?
Empleat	Acostuma a tardar un parell de dies feiners. Demà passat ja estaran disponibles al seu compte.
Tim	Moltíssimes gràcies.
Empleat	De res. Passi-ho bé.

QUICK VOCAB

ingressar *to pay in*
el compte *account*
l'estalvi (m.) *saving*
acostumar a *to happen (to do) usually*
el dia feiner *working day*
disponible *available*
passi-ho bé *goodbye (formal)*

Insight

Notice how many pronouns, single and in various combinations, occur in Dialogues 1 and 2: **ens hi estarem ...**, **passa-me-la ...**, etc. From their contexts you will most probably have understood the meaning they convey, without having to think too hard about their precise grammatical functions. However, the more you reflect on how pronouns behave (functions and forms) in examples as you meet them, the more your own proficiency in using them will develop.

Exercise 4

Answer these questions:

1 En Tim, vol treure diners del banc?
2 L'empleat li demana la llibreta?
3 Un euro val més d'un dòlar i mig?
4 Els diners estaran disponibles immediatament?

Insight

Before beginning the next activity refer again to the Pronunciation and spelling section, mainly to remind yourself of when Catalan words take written accents. Even if written accents may not be a priority in the early stages of learning the language, their relevance needs to be appreciated. They make the written language conform to the sound system of Catalan: compare, for example, the pronunciation and the spelling of **perdo** *I lose*, **perdó** *pardon, forgiveness*.

Exercise 5
◆ CD2, TR 16, 00:03

a Listen to the following words and say whether the underlined vowels sound as one syllable or two separate syllables.

Example: feina (*one syllable*) veïns (*two syllables*)

1 sisplau 2 raïm 3 ploure 4 país 5 neu 6 mai 7 dia 8 cuina
9 Pirineu 10 Suïssa

b Decide from what you hear whether these words require a written accent:

1 parlara, vindran, canço, cargol, bonic, anire, donem
2 parla, arriba, platan, donen, rapid, sabates, regim
3 esglesia, secretaria, musica, pagina

3 No podré venir *I'm not able to come*

Montse has been invited to an exhibition, but she will not be able to attend. She calls the painter, a friend of hers, to let him know, by leaving a message on his answering machine.

colors

Martí Llansó i Rosset

Us convida a la inauguració de l'exposició **colors** de pintures a l'oli i aquarel·les.

A la Sala Les Coves d'Olot, el dimecres 4 de setembre a partir de les 20 h.

Horaris de visita: de dimarts a dissabte de 17 a 21 h., fins el 15 de novembre.

Contestador	(Aquest és el contestador automàtic d'en Martí Llansó. Ara no sóc a casa però si voleu podeu deixar un missatge després de sentir el senyal.)
Montse	Martí, sóc la Montse. Gràcies per la invitació, però no podré venir a la inauguració. Em sap molt de greu, però seré tot el dia amb uns clients visitant fàbriques al Vallès i al vespre els portaré a sopar al port olímpic. Et prometo que passaré a veure els teus quadres un altre dia. Sort i molt d'èxit! Adéu.

CD2, TR 17, 00:04

l'aquarel·la (f.) *watercolour*
el contestador *answering machine*
el senyal *signal, tone*
la inauguració *opening*
prometre *to promise*
passar a + infinitive *to go/come and ...*
l'èxit (m.) *success*

> **Cultural information**
> **Banks**
>
> The word for bank is **el banc** and also **la banca**, which means
> an investment *bank* or *banking* in general. More prevalent
> than either of these, however, is **la caixa** (**d'estalvis**), literally
> *savings bank*, locally based institutions, part of whose
> profits goes into social and cultural activities. Most branches
> (**oficines, sucursals**) will transact currency exchange,
> sometimes at a special counter, while in busy and strategic
> places you will find separate **oficines de canvi**.

Grammar

A The future tense

The future tense in Catalan behaves basically like the
corresponding *shall/will* equivalent in English. The future tense
is formed by adding the appropriate ending for each person to
the infinitive. These endings are the same for the three regular
conjugations and for irregular verbs.

estar + é > estaré	estar + em > estarem
estar + às > estaràs	estar + eu > estareu
estar + à > estarà	estar + an > estaran

Although the endings do not vary, adjustments to the infinitive
are often involved, especially for irregular verbs, e.g. **fer > farà**,
anar > anirem (Dialogue 1), **tenir > tindré** (Dialogue 2) and **poder
> podré** (Dialogue 3). As a general rule, verbs ending in -e lose this
before the addition of the endings: **prometre > prometré, treure >
treuré**, etc.

Insight

Remember that, as well as the future tense itself, there is another way to talk about future events, using **pensar** + infinitive, as explained in the last unit: **penso tornar-hi aviat** *I intend to/will go back there soon*. Unit 14 Grammar section A introduces another alternative for the future tense.

Exercise 6

Take the conversation exchange below as a model, and complete the ones that follow:

Example:

> Que teniu el nou compacte d'en Lluís Llach?
> No, encara no *ha sortit* a la venda (**sortir**).
> I quan *sortirà*?
> A principis de setembre.

1 Que teniu la darrera novel·la de la Maria Barbal?
> No, encara no _____ (**arribar**).
> I quan _____?
> A finals d'aquest mes.

2 Que teniu la revista El Cornetí d'aquesta setmana?
> No, encara no _____ (**distribuir-se**).
> I quan _____?
> Demà al matí.

3 Que teniu la nova edició del Mapa comarcal dels Països Catalans?
> No, encara no _____ (**publicar-se**).
> I quan _____?
> L'any vinent.

4 Que teniu el nou model de telèfon mòbil?
> No, encara no _____ (**posar-se a la venda**).
> I quan _____?
> No ho sabem.

Grammar

B *Que* meaning 'because'

When Eduard says in Dialogue 1 **Aprofita-ho, que l'home del temps diu …** we hear a construction involving **que** which is very common in colloquial Catalan. As in this case, **que** is often inserted to connect one idea to another where English might use a more explicit link word or perhaps supply the connection with just a pause (sometimes represented in writing by a dash):

Corre, home! que farem tard!	*Get a move on, man! We're going to be late.*
Calla, que ens escolten aquells.	*Be quiet – that lot can hear us.*

Perquè *because* and not **que** will be used in more formal contexts.

C *Anar-se'n* 'to go (away)'

This verb means *to go (away)* and it appears in contexts where simple **anar** might be expected. It is rather similar to French *se'n aller* in that a combination of two pronouns (reflexive + en) is an integral part of the infinitive and all conjugated parts. The position and spelling of the pronouns in the different tenses require special attention, e.g. **te'n vas, te'n vas anar, te n'has anat, vés-te'n** or **ens n'anem, ens en vam anar, ens n'hem anat, anem-nos-en**, etc.

D Combination of two pronouns

Anar-se'n illustrates this feature very well. However, it is difficult to absorb all at one go the principles and the multiple combinations found in this complex aspect of Catalan grammar. For this reason you are being introduced gradually to it, through naturally occurring cases in the dialogues, etc. Remember **ens hi vam divertir molt** and **me'l puc emprovar** or **com s'ho fa la gent per aprimar-se**, from Unit 10, Dialogue 1 and Unit 11, Dialogues 1 and 2. Then look again at **ens hi estarem** and **passa-me-la** in Dialogue 1 of this unit.

If you analyse these sentences you should be able to identify the function of each pronoun involved. In the first case **hi** refers back to **pel Mediterrani** integrated with reflexive **estar-se** (*to be, to stay*). In the case of **-me-la** (after the command **passa** *give*) we see that **-me** is indirect object to me combined with **-la** which refers back to **la crema**.

Using this approach you will progressively grasp the principles involved and thus acquire a sound basis for being accurate and fluent yourself. You will be given more practice and guidance in this area in Unit 14.

Exercise 7

Substitute pronouns for the elements in italics in each of the following sentences, as in the examples. (Before beginning you might like to revise Unit 6, Grammar B and to look ahead to Unit 14, Grammar B).

Examples:

Demà acompanyaré *els teus pares a l'aeroport*.	Demà **els hi** acompanyaré.
Ahir no vaig explicar *a en Joan això*.	Ahir no **li ho** vaig explicar/vaig explicar-**li-ho**.

1 La Dolors col·loca *els papers al calaix*.
2 No va poder comprar *a mi la faldilla*.
3 Els meus amics convidaran *a nosaltres a la festa*.
4 Diré *als estudiants que demà no hi ha classe*.
5 Tornem *a tu les claus del cotxe*.
6 Porto *a elles flors*.
7 Ha repartit *a nosaltres invitacions*.

Exercise 8
◀) CD2, TR 18, 00:04

Listen to a radio presenter – with a Valencian accent – announcing a popular race. From what you hear, complete the written announcement below.

CURSA POPULAR CIUTAT DE VALÈNCIA

Dia 1 _____

Hora 2 _____

Recorregut 3 Eixida _____

4 Arribada _____

Lloc i termini d'inscripcions 5 _____

Premis 6 Primer _____

7 Segon _____

8 Tercer _____

Insight

As shown on the map at the beginning of the book and as explained at other points (see especially the section on **mallorquí** in Unit 10) the Valencian dialect is one of the western varieties of Catalan. While listening to the announcement in Exercise 8 you may have noticed the pronunciation of final **r** and **t**, as in **proper** and **consistent**, or the absence of the relaxed pronunciation of unstressed **a** and **e**. The use of **eixida** instead of **sortida** illustrates the interesting, minor particularities of vocabulary at the dialect level.

Exercise 9

Imagine you have been invited to a party but you cannot go. Complete the dialogue writing your part as indicated:

Amic	Què, vindràs a la festa dissabte?
1	*(Say you are sorry but you will not be able to attend.)*
Amic	On seràs?
2	*(Say you are going to Andorra, to visit your cousin who is in hospital.)*
Amic	I quants dies t'hi estaràs?
3	*(Say you will stay there for a couple of days.)*
Amic	Ens veurem la setmana que ve?
4	*(Say 'yes' and say you will call him.)*

Exercise 10

Have a look at the map and, according to the symbols, complete the text below using either weather vocabulary or the future tense of the verbs indicated.

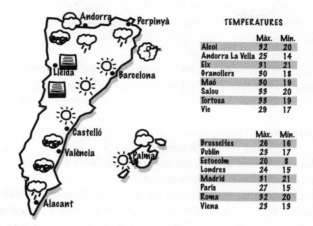

TEMPERATURES		
	Màx.	Mín.
Alcoi	32	20
Andorra La Vella	25	14
Elx	31	21
Granollers	30	18
Maó	30	19
Salou	33	20
Tortosa	33	19
Vic	29	17

	Màx.	Mín.
Brussel·les	26	16
Dublín	23	17
Estocolm	20	8
Londres	24	15
Madrid	31	21
París	27	15
Roma	32	20
Viena	23	13

Pronòstic per a demà:

Al nord dels Països Catalans hi _____(haver, 1) molta nuvolositat amb possibilitat de _____(2) al final del dia. Les temperatures _____(baixar, 3) dels 28 graus d'ahir als 20. A Andorra, tot i que el dia _____(iniciar-se, 4) amb sol, cap a la tarda pot haver-hi pluges dèbils. Al centre de la zona _____ (dominar, 5) el sol, sobretot a la costa, amb _____(6) que _____(arribar, 7) als 35 graus. A la costa nord _____ (bufar, 8) vent de tramuntana i a les terres de l'interior hi pot haver _____(9). A les Illes també hi _____(fer, 10) sol, alternant-se amb algun _____(11) a mitja tarda. A les terres del sud, el cel _____(estar, 12) cobert amb possibilitat de pluja. Les temperatures _____(mantenir-se, 13) com els darrers dies.

Exercise 11

Now you can practise on your own, writing a weather forecast for your area tomorrow.

Points to remember

1 **quin temps fa/farà?** *what is the weather like / going to be like?*
2 **fa fred/calor, fa vent/sol, plou/neva/trona** *it's cold/hot, it's windy/sunny, it's raining/snowing/thundering*
3 **està núvol/cobert, hi ha boira/tempesta** *it's cloudy/overcast, it's foggy/stormy*
4 **anireu de vacances? sí, ens n'anirem el mes que ve** *are you going on holiday? yes, we are going away next month*
5 **vindreu a sopar a casa?** *will you come to dinner at my house?*
6 **em sap molt de greu però no podrem venir / ho sento però no tindré temps** *I am really sorry but we shan't be able to come / I am sorry but I won't have time*
7 **ingressar/treure diners, fer una transferència** *to deposit/to withdraw money, make a transfer*
8 **penso tancar el meu compte corrent i obrir-ne un d'estalvi** *I intend to close my current account and to open a savings one*
9 The future tense of regular and irregular verbs: infinitive + future endings. Adjustments to some infinitives.
10 Further study of pronouns and pronoun groups, including use of **anar-se'n** *to go away.*

14

Oferta de treball
Work opportunity

In this unit you will learn
- *How to discuss requirements for and details of a job*
- *How to talk and write about obligations and responsibilities*

1 És una empresa privada *It's a private company*

Montse has been dismissed from her former job and now she wants to apply for a new one. She has found an interesting opening in a list of situations vacant.

Montse	Has llegit el diari d'avui?
Anna	No. Per què?
Montse	Hi ha una oferta de treball que sembla interessant.
Anna	Ah sí! I de què es tracta?
Montse	És una feina en una empresa privada. Busquen un llicenciat en químiques per treballar al seu laboratori.
Anna	I a què es dedica aquesta companyia?
Montse	Fan productes nutricionals per a animals. És una empresa gran, filial d'una marca internacional.
Anna	I quines condicions de treball ofereixen?

(Contd)

◀) CD2, TR 19, 00:09

Montse	No ho diu l'anunci. Però hi puc trucar i els ho demanaré.
Telefonista	Laboratoris Suprix, digui?
Montse	Bon dia. Voldria parlar amb la senyoreta Sílvia Serrat.
Telefonista	Què diu? No la sento bé. Pot parlar més alt, per favor?
Montse	Em pot posar amb la senyora Serrat?
Telefonista	Ara sí que la sento. De part de qui, sisplau?
Montse	Ella no em coneix. Truco perquè estic interessada en l'oferta de treball que anuncieu al diari.
Telefonista	Ah sí, ara l'hi passo (...) Ho sento, però en aquest moment està parlant per l'altra línia. Pot tornar a trucar d'aquí a cinc minuts?
Montse	D'acord!

QUICK VOCAB

*per què? *why?*
tractar-se *to be about, to involve*
llicenciat/-da *graduate*
la química *chemistry*
la filial *subsidiary*
la marca *(trade) mark, brand*
l'anunci (m.) *advertisement*
alt (here) *loud*
per favor *please*
*l'hi see Grammar B
passar (here) *to put on (telephone)*

Insight

The telephonist's statement **ara l'hi passo** *I'll put you through to her now* involves a rather special combination of pronouns: one of them refers to a direct object (Montse) and the other to an indirect object (Sílvia). Here the indirect object **li** has been replaced by **hi**, with **la** contracted to and heard as **l'**. This is the usual solution in standard central Catalan, and a fuller explanation of this and of similar pronoun combinations is provided in Grammar section B.

2 S'ha de tenir experiència *Experience is required*

CD2, TR 19, 02:19

Montse	La senyoreta Serrat, sisplau?
Telefonista	Un moment, ara s'hi posa.
Sílvia	Sí, digueu?
Montse	Bon dia. Truco perquè he vist el seu anunci de treball i abans d'enviar el meu currículum voldria saber-ne més coses.
Sílvia	El que et puc dir ara mateix és que és una plaça per a un any, amb possibilitat de renovació a contracte indefinit. Les persones interessades han de ser llicenciades en químiques i si és possible amb domini de l'alemany escrit i parlat.
Montse	S'ha de tenir experiència?
Sílvia	Sí, és imprescindible tenir experiència en laboratori, tot i que la persona escollida haurà de passar un curs de formació pagat per l'empresa.
Montse	I en què consisteix exactament la feina? Què haurà de fer la persona designada?
Sílvia	Necessitem una persona capaç de crear nous productes en el camp de l'alimentació per a animals: vaques, conills i cavalls, fonamentalment. Tindrà la responsabilitat de posar a prova i elaborar un producte adaptat a les demandes del mercat.
Montse	I pel que fa a les hores de treball i al sou?
Sílvia	L'empresa té un horari de treball força flexible, però s'han de fer 40 hores setmanals i el treballador té dret a 30 dies laborables per any de vacances. El sou està estipulat en uns 2.200€ bruts, però és negociable i s'haurà de discutir.
Montse	Bé, moltes gràcies per la seva informació.
Sílvia	A disposar.

posar-se (al telèfon) *to come (to the phone)*
la plaça (here) *position*
la renovació *renewal*

QV

*haver de + infinitive *must, to have to*
el domini *command*
alemany/-a *German*
imprescindible *essential*
el curs de formació *training course*
capaç *able, capable*
el camp *field*
l'alimentació (f.) *food*
la vaca *cow*
el cavall *horse*
posar a prova *to test*
elaborar *to prepare, to make*
la demanda *request, demand*
pel que fa a ... *about ..., concerning ...*
el sou *salary*
el treballador *worker*
el dret *right*
laborable *working*
brut/-a *dirty,* (here) *gross/before tax*

Insight

Compare **ara s'hi posa** *she's coming on the line now* with **ara l'hi passo** in Dialogue 1. The meanings are very similar, but the constructions are quite different. The **hi** (joined with the reflexive pronoun **s'**) in **ara s'hi posa** stands for an idea of location, **al telèfon**, and does not function as an indirect object in the way we encounter it in **ara l'hi passo**.

Exercise 1
Familiarize yourself with these dialogues and then act them out, preferably with a partner.

Exercise 2
Answer these questions:

1 Quin tipus d'empresa busca un científic?
2 A què es dedica aquesta empresa?

3 Quins són els requisits bàsics per a demanar aquesta plaça?

4 Quina aptitud es considera important però no imprescindible?

Exercise 3
🔊 **CD2, TR 20, 00:02**

In a spoken sentence you don't hear a sequence of isolated words; what you hear is a sequence of sounds running into each other. In this exercise, listen to these sentences and repeat them focusing on the intonation and on the way words 'run together'.

1 S'ha de tenir experiència?

2 Transports Dalmau, digui?

3 Oh i tant!

4 Tanca el calaix!

5 Què dius ara!

6 De què es tracta?

Insight
Making and receiving telephone calls

Here we revise and extend the simple conventions of telephone conversations that were introduced in Unit 3. **Puc parlar amb ...?** *Can I speak to ...?* or **Em pot posar amb ...?** *Can you put me on to ...?* are the usual ways of asking to be connected with someone on the phone. Don't forget to be polite: **sisplau** *please*. If the person answering is not the one you wish to speak to they may well ask **de part de qui?** *who (shall I say) is calling?* On answering the phone the most common response is **(sí,) digui** equivalent to *hello*. **Digueu** is also heard, corresponding to an old-fashioned polite form **vós** (the one which also appears in **sisplau = si us plau**). In formal contexts, a name (company, institution or individual) often precedes these formulae: **Institut Ramon Llull, digui?**. The usual way to keep someone on hold is to say **No pengi, sisplau** *Don't hang up, please* or **Un moment, sisplau** *One moment, please*. Pronoun combinations appear frequently in telephone exchanges and you will look again at this matter in Grammar B.

Exercise 4
◀) CD2, TR 20, 00:49

Complete the phone conversations below, orally or in writing:

1 Bon dia, _____ a amb la senyoreta Garcia, sisplau?
   _____ b però està _____ c (on another line). Pot
   _____ d més tard?

2 Assegurances Solà, digui?
   _____ a amb el senyor Riera, _____ b?
   De _____ c?
   Sóc en Santi Roura.
   Un moment, no _____ d.

3 _____ a
   És la pastisseria Bunyol?
   _____ b
   Que _____ c en Xavier?
   Un moment, ara _____ d.

Exercise 5
Write a correct question for every sentence. Some of them will start
with a question word and in some cases there will be more than
one possible option.

Example:

| S'ha de saber parlar | Quines llengües són necessàries?/ |
| anglès i portuguès. | Quines llengües s'han de saber parlar? |

1 Hauràs de començar immediatament, a principis del
   mes vinent.
2 L'empresa té un total de 136 treballadors.
3 Sí, el sou es podrà discutir.
4 No, no és necessari tenir experiència en el sector.
5 Tindràs 28 dies de vacances pagades a l'any.
6 Sí, ja tornaré a trucar més tard.

Grammar

Insight

Before studying the next grammar point, observe that the verb **haver (de)** used in expressions of obligation is the same one as the auxiliary for the perfect tense. Sometimes, though, you will hear **haig de** instead of **he de** for the first person singular (but always **he +** participle for the perfect tense).

A Haver *de* + infinitive (obligation and recommendation)

This is the most usual way to express obligation. It can have the force of a 'toned down' imperative: compare **Neteja els vidres** and **Has de netejar els vidres**. At other times the 'imperative' value of **haver de** is so dilute that it overlaps with the meaning of the future tense: **Demà me n'he d'anar a Sueca** *Tomorrow I have to (shall) go to Sueca*. Impersonal **es** (Unit 7) frequently combines with **haver de** in a construction whose equivalents are *you/one must, have to*, etc. or *it is necessary to*. Note the agreement of the verb: **S'ha de pagar amb anticipació?** *Does it have to be paid for in advance?* and **S'han hagut de rentar tots els llençols** *All the sheets have had to be washed.*

Exercise 6
Here are some suggestions on environmental matters. For each sentence choose the appropriate verb from the list and write an impersonal suggestion.

Example: S'ha d'evitar comprar esprais que destrueixen la capa d'ozó.

1 _____ menys el transport i caminar més o anar amb bicicleta.
2 _____ la natura: els rius, els boscos, la muntanya.
3 _____ les deixalles sempre a la paperera i no a terra.
4 _____ el paper, el vidre, el cartró i les llaunes.

5 _____ els productes ecològics als que fan mal al medi
ambient.

6 _____ només cotxes amb gasolina sense plom.

7 _____ encendre foc al bosc a l'estiu.

> conduir, preferir, tirar, utilitzar, reciclar, respectar, evitar

Insight

Remember the impersonal **es** as seen in previous units and
how it is used here for obligation and recommendation,
s'ha d'evitar comprar… This construction has a rather
more formal and polite tone than equivalents with **haver
de** addressed directly to someone, as in **has/heu d'evitar
comprar…**

Grammar

B Pronoun combinations: *li* (+ direct object) > *hi*

Look again at **els ho demanaré** in Dialogue 1 and **ara s'hi posa** in
Dialogue 2. Try to work out the function of the individual pronouns
in each of these combinations. You will see that in the first case
els refers, as indirect object, to 'the people' who placed the advert,
where **ho** is the direct object of **demanar** and stands for **quines
condicions … ofereixen**. In the case of **s'hi posa** we have reflexive **es**
combining with **hi** (= **al telèfon**): similarly, with different subjects,
we might say or hear **ara m'hi poso** or **per què no t'hi poses?**, etc.

A general rule for the order of pronouns in groups can be
summarized as follows: (where any of the elements appear)
they come in the order of:

1 reflexive   **4** en
2 indirect object   **5** hi
3 direct object

Now look at the spelling modifications (reflecting pronunciation) entailed when indirect object **em** (> **me**) precedes a third person direct object:

me +		>		me +		>	
	el		me'l		els		me'ls
	la		me la				
	ho		m'ho		les		me les

Now substitute for yourself **et** (> **te**) in these same combinations (making **te'l**, etc.).

Third person **li** (invariable for masculine and feminine singular) can combine in exactly this way with the same direct-object pronouns (in Valencian Catalan it is the norm). However, in Dialogue 1 we hear what is the usual solution in standard central Catalan for the **li** + direct object group. The telephonist says 'Ah, sí, ara **l'hi** passo …' Here **l'hi = la + hi**: **la** stands for direct-object Sílvia Serrat, the indirect object is expressed as **hi**; **a vostè** is understood (= **l'hi passo a vostè**). This can be shown graphically as:

li +		>		This can be understood as:	
	el		l'hi		li + el/la/ho
	la		la hi / l'hi		
	ho		li ho / l'hi		l'+ hi

You can observe, first of all, that we have here an exception to the 'rule' that the normal order is indirect object + direct object. Also to be remembered is that this indirect-object function supplements the other uses of **hi** with which you are familiar (e.g. **s'hi posa** where **hi = al telèfon**, etc.).

This information will help you to get your ear attuned to this feature of pronoun behaviour which occurs spontaneously in all levels of speech. Equally important, grasping the principles just explained and imitation of native practice will enable you to express yourself with increasing accuracy and confidence.

Exercise 7
Match the words on the left with an item from the right to form a complete question:

1	El vestit,	**a**	me'n compraràs?
2	La faldilla,	**b**	me'ls rentaran?
3	De mitjons,	**c**	me'l penges, sisplau?
4	Les camises,	**d**	me la planxes?
5	Els pantalons,	**e**	m'ho deixes?
6	Això que duus,	**f**	me les poses a l'armari?

Exercise 8
Here you have some sentences where you should be able to replace the direct object and the indirect object with the corresponding pronouns in combination.

Example:
El meu fill ha de donar el resultat del problema al seu professor.
> El meu fill l'hi ha de donar.

1 Cada dia paga *el cafè al seu director*.
2 L'Antoni posa *les sabates a la seva neboda*.
3 Recomana *a nosaltres aquesta pel·lícula*.
4 Ensenya *la corbata nova a la seva xicota*.
5 Hem de deixar *els diners a vosaltres*.

Grammar

C Main verb with dependent infinitive
You will have noticed that some Catalan verbs are followed directly by a dependent infinitive: **voler** *to want to*, **poder** *to be able to, can*, etc. Remember too expressions of probability with **deure** + infinitive (**Deuen arribar aquest vespre** *They'll probably arrive this evening*), as discussed in Unit 9. **Saber** with the infinitive translates *can* but with the sense of intellectual or inherent capability rather than physical ability (**poder**): **No saps sumar** *You can't (don't know how to) add up*.

Then there are a number of constructions in which the main verb takes a preposition before the infinitive, as in:

tornar a + inf.	*to ... again*	anar a + inf.	*to go and/to ...*
passar a + inf.	*to go and/to ...*	venir de	*to (have)*
acabar de	*to have just ...*	+ inf.	*come from ...*
+ inf.		acostumar	*to be in the*
		a/de + inf.	*habit of ...*

D *Per què* vs. *perquè*

These two items sound alike and are obviously related. In writing, though, the distinction between **per què?** *why?* and **perquè** *because* is carefully maintained.

On another level **perquè** also means *in order that*, related to **per** + infinitive *in order to*. The point is best illustrated by comparing **Ho faig per divertir-me** *I do it to amuse myself* with this other construction:

Ho faig perquè et diverteixis.   *I do it in order for you to be amused.*

In the latter case the subject of the second part of the sentences (**tu**) is not the same as that of the main verb (**jo**), whereas in **ho faig per divertir-me** there is only one subject (**jo**). This kind of construction involves use of what is called the subjunctive mood of the verb: a topic to which you will be introduced briefly in Grammar E and Unit 15.

Exercise 9
Imagine you have seen a job advert in a paper and you are interested in it. You write them a letter asking for more information. Having in mind the composition of a formal letter (as seen in Unit 12, Exercise 4) order the sentences below.

a Atentament.
b Em pot enviar, sisplau, informació sobre les condicions de treball.
c He llegit el seu anunci al diari, que ofereix una plaça de ...

d També voldria saber l'horari i el sou.
e Benvolgut senyor.
f Espero la seva resposta ben aviat.
g M'ha semblat que és una feina que em pot interessar.

Reading

A bookshop manager has left a note for her sales assistant, giving some instructions. You will observe how the order of tasks is clearly expressed through the use of 'temporal connectors': **abans de, primer de tot,** etc.

Marcel,

Abans de començar a ordenar els llibres, recorda que primer de tot has d'engegar els ordinadors de la botiga. Llavors has d'etiquetar els nous exemplars, els preus són al calaix del despatx. Tot seguit s'ha de trucar a la distribuïdora i encarregar les obres que els clients ens han demanat. Finalment, pensa també que has de connectar la caixa! Arribaré a mig matí. Truca'm si hi ha algun problema.

Clàudia

Exercise 10
1 Identify all the different ways of saying what has to be done in the Reading passage, and then convert them into direct commands (imperatives) using the **tu** form. Note that there is already one verb in the imperative, **truca'm**.
2 List the 'temporal connectors' (**abans de,** etc.).

Exercise 11
Taking as a model the Reading text, write a note from a teacher giving instructions to his/her students. Cover all the indications in the list below, alternating between imperatives and **haver de**. You will find that the use of some connectors will make your instructions clearer.

- corregir els exercicis de la setmana passada.
- agafar el llibre de Ciències i obrir-lo a la pàgina 125.
- copiar els dos primers paràgrafs i respondre a les preguntes.
- anar al laboratori i acabar l'experiment.
- escriure els resultats a la llibreta.
- deixar les llibretes al meu despatx.

Exercise 12
◀) CD2, TR 20, 01:57

Listen to the radio news bulletin and then answer the questions. The main subject is the recent rise in unemployment, **la pujada de l'atur**.

1 Quines són les causes principals de la pujada de l'atur?
2 Quins sectors són els més perjudicats?
3 Quines mesures vol adoptar el govern?
4 En què consisteix aquest pla?
5 Què opina un dels aturats sobre el pla?
6 Segons les previsions oficials, en quin percentatge baixarà l'atur?

Grammar

E The present subjunctive of regular verbs

For the three regular conjugations the present subjunctive is formed as follows:

parl-ar	**perd-re**	**dorm-ir**
parl-i	perd-i	dorm-i
parl-is	perd-is	dorm-is
parl-i	perd-i	dorm-i
parl-em	perd-em	dorm-im
parl-eu	perd-eu	dorm-iu
parl-in	perd-in	dorm-in

Note that the forms of the first and second person plural coincide in the present indicative and subjunctive. 'Inceptive' verbs of the third conjugation (see Unit 5, Grammar A), retain -eix- for the subjunctive in the parts where this appears in the present indicative. Thus for **llegir** we have **lleg-eix-i, lleg-eix-is, lleg-eix-i, llegim, llegiu, lleg-eix-in**.

Insight

The subjunctive mood of verbs has an important function at all levels of Catalan, occurring with a frequency of perhaps 25% more than the indicative mood. Because it is used less in English, you will have to make a special effort to get used to how the subjunctive is used. Here you are introduced to its forms after being presented (Grammar section D above) with an initial example of how it performs. Units 15 (especially Grammar section D) and 16 will build on these foundations, and the subjunctive mood will be established in your own range of comprehension and expression.

Points to remember

1 **a què es dedica aquesta empresa? fabrica electrodomèstics** *what does this company do? they manufacture electrical appliances*

2 **puc parlar amb el director, sisplau? un moment, ara l'hi passo** *can I speak to the director, please? one moment, I'll put you through*

3 **la plaça és oberta a llicenciats/graduats** *the position is open to graduates*

4 **es tracta d'una plaça de metge/infermera** *the post/vacancy is for a doctor/nurse*

5 **el sou/salari brut/net és de...** *the salary before/after taxes is...*

6 **no és necessari tenir experiència i el contracte és temporal/indefinit** *no experience is necessary, and the contract is temporary/open ended*

7 s'ha de netejar tota la classe/has de netejar tota la classe
*the whole classroom must be cleaned/you have to clean the
whole classroom*

8 Haver de + infinitive for obligation and recommendation.

9 The general rule for the order of pronouns in groups (reflexive +
indirect object + direct object + **en** + **hi**, when any of the
elements appear), and the particular combination **l'hi**, where
hi has the function of **li**.

10 An introduction to the subjunctive mood of verbs and the
pattern for the present subjunctive.

15

No em trobo bé
I don't feel well

In this unit you will learn
- *How to express moods and physical feelings*
- *How to say what is wrong with you*
- *How to give and listen to advice*

---

1 Hauries de tranquil·litzar-te *You ought to calm down*

Montse has gone to visit the doctor (**el metge / la metgessa de capçalera**), because she doesn't feel very well.

Metgessa	Hola, Montse, bon dia. Seu aquí. Bé, què tens? Què et passa?
Montse	Darrerament no em trobo massa bé. Tinc mal de cap, sobretot aquí, a sobre dels ulls, i vaig estar uns dies amb mal de ventre i vòmits i encara em sento com marejada. Però no he tingut pas febre.
Metgessa	Que has estat molt enfeinada o desmotivada, potser?
Montse	Sí, estic buscant feina i això em fa estar nerviosa. Fins i tot algunes nits no he pogut dormir gens.
Metgessa	Déu n'hi do! I t'has pres algun medicament?
Montse	No, només unes infusions.

Metgessa	I el menjar?
Montse	La veritat és que no tinc gaire gana i molts dies no tinc ni temps per a menjar com cal.
Metgessa	Seguir una bona dieta és importantíssim. Hauries de trobar temps per als àpats i, el més important de tot, no hauries d'agafar-te les coses tan a pit. Relaxa't. Fas esport?
Montse	No, en aquests moments no.
Metgessa	Jo de tu dedicaria com a mínim una hora diària a fer exercici. Cal mantenir-se en forma!
Montse	I pel mal de cap?
Metgessa	Et receptaré un medicament per treure el dolor, però sobretot no prenguis més de tres pastilles al dia. Segur que d'aquí a uns dies ja et trobaràs més bé.

seure (irregular) *to sit down*
darrerament *lately*
el mal de cap/ventre *headache/stomach ache*
l'ull (m.) *eye*
estar marejat/-da *to feel sick*
tenir febre *to have a temperature*
enfeinat/-da *busy*
desmotivat/-da *dispirited*
em fa estar *makes me feel*
fins i tot *even*
Déu n'hi do! emphatic affirmation or agreement
el medicament *medicine*
*caldre (irregular) *to be necessary, to be right*
*hauries de ... *you ought to ...*
agafar les coses a pit *to take things to heart*
jo de tu *if I were you*
com a mínim *at least*
receptar *to prescribe*
el dolor *pain*
*no prenguis see Grammar D
la pastilla *tablet, pill*

QUICK VOCAB

Exercise 1

Veritat o fals?

1 La Montse té un problema als ulls.
2 Ella ha passat algunes nits sense dormir bé.
3 La metgessa li aconsella menjar de manera regular.
4 També li recomana que faci esport cada dia.

Exercise 2

Go through the dialogue again and then act it out, preferably with a partner.

Cultural information
The Catalan stereotype

Because of the way Catalan society has evolved in the modern era the people have earned a reputation for thrift and economic prudence. This image, especially when viewed from other parts of Spain, has turned into the stereotype or caricature of the money-conscious, niggardly Catalan, with as much basis in truth as the corresponding stereotype of the 'penny-pinching' Scot within the British tradition. The subject occurs in many popular expressions and jokes like the following one:

**Què fa un català quan té fred? – S'apropa a una estufa.
I quan té molt, molt i molt fred? – L'encén!**

2 Li fa mal l'esquena *His back hurts*

Tim notices that Anna is concerned.

CD2, TR 22, 00:03

Tim	Què et passa Anna, et veig preocupada?
Anna	És que han ingressat a l'hospital el meu germà.
Tim	Què li ha passat?
Anna	Ha tingut un accident a la feina. S'ha trencat una cama i s'ha donat un cop fort a l'esquena.
Tim	I què han dit els metges?
Anna	Diuen que no és greu, però li caldrà fer repòs i bondat durant uns mesos. Està tan desanimat que no vol parlar amb ningú. A més l'esquena li fa mal i pateix molt. I per postres, la meva cunyada té la grip i el meu nebot està refredat. Estan tots ben fotuts!

ingressar (here) *to admit to hospital*
trencar *to break*
la cama *leg*
el cop *blow, knock*
l'esquena (f.) *back*
greu *serious*
el repòs *rest*
fer bondat *to behave oneself*
desanimat/-da *discouraged, downhearted*
fer mal *to hurt*
patir *to suffer*

QUICK VOCAB

per postres *on top (of all that)*
la grip *influenza*
el nebot/la neboda *nephew/niece*
estar refredat/-da *to have a cold*
fotut/-da *in a (bloody) bad way* (colloquial)

Insight

Remember what was explained in Unit 12 Grammar section
D about the use of **ser** and **estar** with adjectives. Moods
and physical feelings are inherently subject to or the result
of change, and thus **estar** is used in such expressions: **estar
cansat/enfadat/de mal humor/deprimit**, etc. *to be tired/angry/
in a bad mood/depressed*, etc. Note, however, that certain
conditions of this kind involve using **tenir** + noun: **tenir set/
son/fred/por**, etc. *to be thirsty/sleepy/cold/frightened*, etc.

Insight

A footnote to the preceding box: we should distinguish
between references to temperature in different contexts: **el vi
és fred / el nen té fred / avui fa molt fred** *the wine is cold / the
boy is cold / it is very cold today.*

Exercise 3
🔊 **CD2, TR 23, 00:03**

Remember how words run together, often affecting pronunciation
at the points of contact. Listen again to these examples from
Dialogue 1 observing that the main effects are assimilation
(alteration) in Column 1 and elision (suppression) in Column 2.

tinc mal de cap	què et passa?
a sobre dels ulls	no em trobo massa bé
i vaig estar	això em fa estar
uns dies amb mal	una hora
només unes infusions	treure el dolor
seguir una bona dieta	

Exercise 4

Select the corresponding word from the box below for each of the pointers in the drawings.

El cos humà

La cara humana

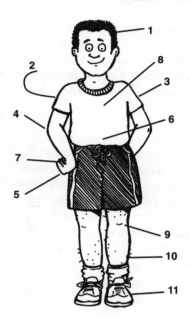

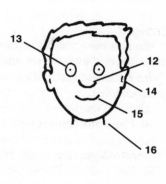

la boca, el braç, l'orella, el colze, el nas, el peu, el coll, el pit,
la cama, l'esquena, el cap, l'ull, la mà, el dit, el genoll, el ventre

---

Grammar

A Possession

Dialogue 2 reminds us of how things done to oneself or to another person involve, in Catalan, use of a reflexive or indirect object pronoun rather than a possessive adjective: **S'ha trencat una cama i s'ha donat un cop fort a l'esquena** *He has broken his leg and received a bad knock to his back*. Here are some more examples:

Li van agafar la pistola.   *They took **his** gun (away from him).*
Els va lligar les mans.   *He tied **their** hands.*
Treu-te els mitjons.   *Take off **your** socks.*

Note also that English often uses a possessive where in Catalan possession is understood and not made explicit: **On tinc la cartera?** *Where is my wallet?*; **Ha perdut el passaport** *S/he has lost her/his passport*.

B The conditional tense

You were already introduced to **voldria** *I would like* in earlier units and now you are shown the full conjugation of the conditional tense in Catalan. The stem used for the conditional is, in every case, that used for the future tense (based on the infinitive). The set of endings for the conditional are likewise the same for every class of verb.

parl-ar	**permet-re**	**sent-ir**
parlar-ia	permetr-ia	sentir-ia
parlar-ies	permetr-ies	sentir-ies
parlar-ia	permetr-ia	sentir-ia
parlar-íem	permetr-íem	sentir-íem
parlar-íeu	permetr-íeu	sentir-íeu
parlar-ien	permetr-ien	sentir-ien

In the conditional, irregular verbs also behave as they do for the future tense: **anar > anir-ia**, etc., **venir > vindr-ia**, etc.

Exercise 5
Complete the following sentences by placing the verbs in brackets in the conditional tense.

1 Jo _____ (deixar) de treballar, però no puc.
2 Hem pensat que l'August _____ (poder) guanyar el partit.

3 Elles van decidir que no _____ (canviar) de feina.

4 El metge li va dir que bevent tant _____ (tenir) una greu malaltia.

5 Nosaltres _____ (fer) tantes coses amb més temps!

6 Ens va dir que la reunió _____ (durar) més de dues hores.

Exercise 6
🔊 **CD2, TR 23, 01:06**

Fill in the following dialogues with verb + adjective or verb + noun expressing a recommendation in the conditional tense. The first one has been done for you.

1 Què et passa, Teresa?
  a Estic preocupada.   (*to be worried*)
  b Jo de tu no em preocuparia.   (*not to worry*)

2 Què tens, Imma?
  a _____.   (*to be cold*)
  b Jo de tu _____.   (*to put on a pullover*)

3 Què tens, Joan Carles?
  a _____.   (*to be hungry*)
  b Jo de tu _____.   (*to eat something*)

4 Què et passa, Lídia?
  a _____.   (*to be sleepy*)
  b Jo de tu _____.   (*to go to bed*)

5 Què et passa, Jordi?
  a _____.   (*to be nervous*)
  b Jo de tu _____.   (*to relax*)

6 Què et passa, Marc?
  a _____.   (*to be thirsty*)
  b Jo de tu _____.   (*to drink water*)

Grammar

Insight

Related to what is discussed in the second Insight box of this unit, Grammar section C completes our coverage of the various resources Catalan possesses to express obligation. Those who are familiar with how French does this with impersonal *il faut*, will have no problems with its Catalan equivalent which uses the verb **caldre**.

C *Cal* + infinitive

As well as **haver de** expressing obligation, see Unit 14, Grammar A, there is also **caldre**, an impersonal verb meaning *to be necessary,* often translating *must*. As its subject is *it* we use only the third-person form **cal** (occasionally plural **calen**). This can introduce either an infinitive or a noun: **No cal cridar** *There is no need to shout,* **Ha calgut una fortuna per a comprar allò** *A fortune was necessary to buy that.* The person on whom the obligation falls can be expressed with the indirect-object pronoun:

M'ha calgut corregir els errors.	*I have had to correct the mistakes.*
Si et calen consells, hauries de parlar amb ...	*If you need advice, you should speak to ...*

You may also encounter another construction with **caldre**, where it is followed not by the infinitive but by **que** introducing a verb in the subjunctive mood the scheme for which is set out in Unit 14 Grammar E: **No cal que t'ho repeteixi** *There is no need for me to repeat it (to you).* Compare also **recomana que faci ...** in Exercise 1. Further mention is made of the subjunctive in the next section.

D Negative commands and more on the subjunctive mood

Revise how commands are given in Catalan using the imperative (see Unit 9). Negative commands for **tu** (*Don't ...*) are expressed in forms with different endings.

1st conj.-**ar**	2nd conj.-**re/-er**	3rd conj.-**ir**
crida/no cridis	promet/no prometis	dorm/no dormis

These negative commands for **tu, vosaltres** and **vostè(s)** coincide
with the form of the subjunctive mentioned in Grammar C; and seen
in Unit 14. In fact for **vostè(s)** both direct and negative commands
coincide in taking this form **truqui(n)/no truqui(n), vingui(n)/no
vingui(n), vagi(n)/no vagi(n)**. The verb lists in our **Reference tables**
show you the present subjunctive forms for all verbs included there.
From these you can take the negative imperative as required. This
will also help you to get used to meeting subjunctives in other areas
of use. Here are a few examples to open up this subject:

Volem que ens escriguis sovint.	*We want you to write to us often.*
No crec que siguin tan inútils.	*I don't think they are so useless.*
T'estimo, encara que sembli mentida.	*I love you, even if it does not seem so.*

In the majority of cases you find the subjunctive appearing
after **que** and certain other linking words (conjunctions). The
components **que ens escriguis, que siguin, encara que sembli**
above are called subordinate clauses, and it is in certain types
of subordinate clause that the subjunctive appears:

1 when the subject of the subordinate clause is different from that
of the main clause (like **Volem, No crec** and **T'estimo**, above).
2 when the meaning of the subordinate verb is affected by an
idea of influence, subjective response or uncertainty conveyed
by the main verb.

It can be helpful to consider that the subjunctive comunicates
the idea that the action of a subordinate clause is not viewed by
the speaker as a fact or reality, but rather as an uncertainty, a
hypothesis or as a future possibility. This latter case is clearly seen
in expressions of future time:

Quan vinguis ja en parlarem.	*When you come we'll discuss it.*
Així que ho sàpigues, m'ho diràs, oi?	*As soon as you find out you'll tell me, won't you?*

Exercise 7

Transform these commands into negative ones. Note that **més** has to be changed into **tan**.

Example:

Parla més fort.   No parlis tan fort.

1 Aprèn anglès.
2 Tanca la finestra.
3 Condueix més ràpid.
4 Escriu més a poc a poc.
5 Truca al metge.
6 Pren aquest medicament.

Grammar

E *Tant* vs. *tan*

As the final -t of **tant** *so much* is silent, this word is pronounced exactly like **tan** *so*. However, in writing you must be careful to make the spelling distinction: **No vagis tan de pressa** *Don't go so quickly*; **No corris tant** *Don't run so (much / fast)*. Notice that **tan** precedes what is qualified, while **tant** can stand alone or agrees in number and gender with the noun it qualifies.

Exercise 8
🔊 **CD2, TR 23, 02:18**

You are going to hear a conversation in a surgery between Paula, who is ill, and a doctor. As you listen to the recording choose the correct answer.

1 La Paula fa uns dies que té ...
   a mal de coll i mal de cap.
   b mal de coll i mal d'orelles.

2 El metge creu que la Paula …
   a s'ha refredat.
   b té la grip.

3 Quina és la causa de la malaltia?
   a La Paula va passar fred.
   b Va dormir a fora tota la nit.

4 El metge li aconsella:
   a Que es quedi a casa i s'abrigui.
   b Que s'abrigui i prengui el medicament.

5 Quantes pastilles pot prendre al dia?
   a Tres aspirines i algunes pastilles pel coll.
   b Tres pastilles pel coll i una aspirina.

Reading

Look at these responses from a health survey. These are the reasons
(**els motius, la motivació**) why eight people have given up smoking.

a Voler estalviar diners em va ajudar a prendre la decisió.
b El meu pare va morir d'un càncer de pulmó.
c Una pneumonia em va apartar del tabac.
d Les campanyes antitabac em van influir molt.
e Vaig decidir que ja era hora de cuidar la meva salut.
f Vaig tenir problemes durant l'embaràs.
g El tabac és el pitjor si t'agrada fer esport.
h Vaig deixar-ho quan vaig quedar embarassada.

 Generalitat de Catalunya
Departament de Sanitat
i Seguretat Social

Exercise 9

Answer the following questions, based on the Reading passage above.

1 Quins motius del text anterior estan relacionats amb una malaltia?
2 Quins altres estan relacionats amb l'embaràs?
3 Quins creus que són el resultat de voler millorar la qualitat de vida?
4 Com es tradueix al català *to look after one's health*?

Insight

Some final advice, leading on from what you have already learnt about the subjunctive. Your understanding of how the subjunctive works will be reinforced by considering how virtually all subordinate clauses after an impersonal main clause formed by **és** (or other tenses of **ser**) + adjective/noun + **que** take the subjunctive, as in **és trist que no hagin pogut venir** *it is sad that they haven't been able to come*, **és increïble que sigui tan complicat** *it is incredible that it is so complicated*, **és important que s'hi inscriguin** *it is important that they sign up for it*, **és (una) llàstima que l'hagin acomiadada** *it is a pity they have dismissed her.* The only exceptions to this are subordinate clauses after main clauses like **és veritat/cert que...** *it is true that...*, which have the subordinate verb in the indicative. Now you can relate this explanation to the two basic principles for subjunctive use laid out in Grammar section D.

Points to remember

1 **què et passa? què tens?** *what is wrong with you?*
2 **com estàs? com et trobes?** *how are you? how do you feel?*
3 **estic fatal: cansada i deprimida** *I feel rubbish: tired and depressed* **no em trobo gaire bé** *I don't feel very well*

4 tinc mal de cap / d'estómac / de coll *I have a headache / stomach-ache / sore throat*

5 tinc febre / la grip / estic refredat/-da *I am feverish / I have flu / I have a cold*

6 hauries de descansar / menjar més *You should rest / eat more*

7 cal dormir més / jo de tu aniria a dormir *sleep is what's needed / if I were you I would go to bed*

8 Formation of the conditional tense, using the same stem (based on the infinitive) as for the future tense.

9 Verb forms for and various functions of the subjunctive mood, including negative commands.

10 Indirect object pronouns (including reflexives) used to indicate possession, for actions done to oneself or to another person.

16

Això no era així
It wasn't like this before

In this unit you will learn
- *How to discuss how things used to be*
- *How to ask for and give opinions*

Before you start

In this unit you are introduced to the imperfect tense. This is used to express continuity or repetition in the past, often corresponding to *was/were -ing* or *used to ...* . The imperfect tense considers states or events in terms of duration, without specific reference to beginning or end, and is thus the tense of description. Because the simple English past (*did, went, looked*, etc.) can perform both this function and that of expressing a simple completed action, you need to consider which aspect is meant when talking about the past. Often the presence of a particular adverb (or adverbial phrase/clause) will make the distinction very clear; compare **Ho vam fer ahir** *We did it yesterday* or **Ho hem fet aquest matí** *We did it this morning*, with **Ho fèiem sovint quan érem joves** *We did it often when we were young*. When no clues of this kind are given, your choice of tense will be determined by implications of context. A good bit of advice, if you are hesitating between use of the imperfect or perfect/ preterite, is to ask yourself what kind of adverb(ial) could be inserted that would make sense in line with the meaning you wish to convey: **Ho va dir** (e.g. **al començament del discurs**), **però nosaltres no escoltàvem** *He said so, but we weren't listening* compared with **Ho deia** (e.g. **sempre**), **però nosaltres no ho crèiem** *He (always) said so, but we didn't believe it.* Another tip is to think that the imperfect tense often expresses the 'background' (description, states occurring, things going on) to single completed actions:

Brillava el sol i vaig decidir de fer un tomb.	*The sun was shining and I decided to take a stroll.*
Quan vam arribar-hi, en Miquel ja tocava.	*When we arrived Miquel was already playing.*
Jo me n'anava quan va sonar el timbre.	*I was just leaving when the bell rang.*

Now consider how the choice of tense itself conveys the aspect of 'past-ness' intended, by comparing:

Ho va pagar tot amb xecs de viatge.	*He paid for everything with travellers' cheques* (on one particular occasion).
Ho pagava tot ...	*He paid* (i.e. used to pay) ...
Era difícil convènce'l.	*It was hard to convince him* (description of the other's attitude).
Va ser difícil convènce'l.	*It was hard to convince him* (but we did succeed).

Before beginning work in this unit, have a careful look at Grammar A, which explains how the imperfect tense is formed.

---

1 Els mobles eren vells *The furniture was old*

Tim is visiting a relative (**un parent**), who lives in the recently restored family home, an old farmhouse (**una masia**), where he hasn't been for a long time.

Tim	Quin canvi!
Parent	Què, t'agrada? L'any passat vam fer obres i vam canviar moltes coses. Tot era molt vell: les portes i finestres, i també la majoria dels mobles.
Tim	Doncs ara es veu una casa molt moderna. La veritat és que m'agrada molt més que abans.
Parent	Vam decidir arreglar les habitacions de dalt i redistribuir-les. Les parets estaven a punt de caure i el sostre també estava força malament. Ara al terra hi ha parquet i totes les habitacions tenen calefacció.
Tim	I aquell armari tan antic, on és?
Parent	Encara te'n recordes? El vam vendre a un antiquari. L'habitació és completament nova: llit nou, calaixera, butaca, mirall, i fins i tot el matalàs. Què te'n sembla del color de les parets? Ens hi hem gastat un dineral!
Tim	Això rai, tu ja tens calés!
Parent	No em facis pas riure! ... Vine, que t'ensenyaré la terrassa: hi he posat unes escales que donen directament al jardí ...
Tim	Carai, no sabia que tenies tants arbres com la veïna del costat! Abans no es tenia tan bona vista des d'aquí dalt.
Parent	Per cert, et quedes a dinar?
Tim	Prou! Et pensaves que venia només a veure la casa?
Parent	Doncs au, ajuda'm a parar la taula. Posa-hi els gots i els tovallons. Els coberts són al primer calaix.

QUICK VOCAB

l'obra (f.) *building work*
la majoria *majority*
arreglar *to fix, to repair, to sort out*
redistribuir *rearrange*
la paret *wall*
estar a punt de ... *to be about to ...*
el sostre *ceiling*
estar malament *to be in a bad way*
el terra *floor*
la calefacció *heating*
antic/-ga *ancient*
l'antiquari (m.) *antique dealer*

la calaixera chest of drawers
la butaca armchair
el matalàs mattress
un dineral piles of money
això rai! no problem!
els calés money (colloquial)
riure (irregular) to laugh
la terrassa large balcony area
l'escala (f.) staircase, stairs
carai! gosh!
veí/-ïna neighbour(ing)
prou! (here) of course!
au! come on!
parar la taula to lay the table
el got glass
el tovalló serviette, napkin

els coberts cutlery
la forquilla fork
la cullera spoon
el ganivet knife

---

2 No hi estic d'acord *I don't agree*

Over a drink before their meal, they talk about things in general.

Parent	Dijous, quan em va trucar la teva mare, m'explicava que ja has trobat feina.
Tim	Sí, però pis encara no! De moment m'estic a casa d'una amiga.
Parent	Ja t'ho deia jo, que tornaries a Catalunya!
Tim	Sí però no m'esperava trobar els lloguers tan cars. A la ciutat serà difícil quedar-s'hi. Ara estic buscant un estudi o un piset als afores de Barcelona, en algun poble potser. De moment no em vull pas gastar més d'una tercera part del sou en el lloguer.
	(Contd)

CD2, TR 24, 02:47

Parent	No vinguis pas al poble! Des que han decidit construir una nova autovia que passarà just a un quilòmetre d'aquí s'ha disparat l'especulació. Els grups ecologistes ja s'hi han oposat, perquè sembla ser que la carretera travessarà una zona d'interès natural, però el govern diu que endavant. Em sembla una bestiesa, no hi estic gens d'acord, tan tranquils que estàvem abans al poble.
Tim	I en general, la gent del poble, què en pensa?
Parent	Depèn. Els més vells, aquells que han viscut tota la vida aquí, estan en contra de tots aquests canvis recents, no els agraden gens. Els joves i els que fa poc que viuen aquí ho veuen diferent. Els agrada més tenir bones comunicacions i 'qualitat de vida' que no pas viure una mica aïllats però en pau. És com vivíem abans, saps? ... El tema surt sovint als mitjans de comunicació i se'n parla molt, però jo no sé com acabarà ...

QUICK VOCAB

esperar-se *to expect*
el piset *small flat*
els afores *outskirts*
des que ... *since ...*
l'autovia (f.) *dual carriageway*
disparar-se *to rocket* (prices)
oposar-se *to object*
la bestiesa *madness, stupid thing*
estar d'acord *to agree*
estar en contra *to disagree*
*que no pas *than*
aïllat/-da *isolated*
la pau *peace*
el tema *subject*
els mitjans de comunicació *media*

Insight

Notice **no hi estic gens d'acord** *I do not agree at all (with this).* **Estar d'acord amb ...** means *to agree/be in agreement* with (something), while **estar en contra de** ... translates *to be against (something)*. In each case, when what is referred to appears in pronoun form, **hi** is used. This is because **hi**, as well as standing for **a** + pronoun, also represents any other preposition except **de** combined with a pronoun (and **en contra de** here functions as a single, compound preposition). Another example to illustrate this point: **el camí era tan estret que el camió no podia passar-hi** *the track was so narrow that the lorry couldn't get along it*, where **hi** represents **pel camí**.

Exercise 1
Read both dialogues again and act them out, preferably with a partner.

Exercise 2
Answer the following questions.

1 Per què el parent d'en Tim va fer obres a casa seva?
2 Què hi falta en una de les habitacions de la casa?
3 De què se sorprèn en Tim quan veu el jardí?
4 Què és el que, segons en Tim, ha canviat de la vida a Catalunya?
5 Què opina el parent d'en Tim de la construcció de la nova autovia?

Cultural information
The media

Everybody living in the Catalan-speaking areas has access to information provided through media operating in Catalan: the television channels **TV3** and **33**, as well as the international **TV3cat,** are controlled by the autonomous government of Catalonia, **La Generalitat**, as is **Catalunya Ràdio**. These services can be received in the Balearics and the País Valencià, each community also having its own broadcasting institutions with a proportion of programmes in Catalan. The Rosselló has its own **Ràdio Arrels** which broadcasts exclusively in Catalan. There is also a territory-wide press presence, in the shape of the daily *Avui* and the Catalan-language edition of *El Periódico*, both from

(Contd)

Barcelona, and the weekly magazine *El Temps*, from Valencia, together with a new sports paper *El 9*. Other features of this panorama are strong competition from a persuasive and powerful Spanish-language (and, in the Rosselló, French-language) media presence, together with a quite marked regional diversity. There are some important local daily newspapers (*El Punt, Regió 7, Segre, Diari d'Andorra* or *Diari de Balears*). Local press and local radio stations are predominantly in Catalan. There are also some well-established and widely distributed magazines like *Serra d'Or* (culture and ideas), *Sàpiens* (general history), *L'Avenç* (history, politics, culture) and *Cavall Fort* (for children).

Grammar

A The imperfect tense

This tense is formed for the three conjugations as follows:

parl-ar	**perd-re**	**dorm-ir**
parl-ava	perd-ia	dorm-ia
parl-aves	perd-ies	dorm-ies
parl-ava	perd-ia	dorm-ia
parl-àvem	perd-íem	dorm-íem
parl-àveu	perd-íeu	dorm-íeu
parl-aven	perd-ien	dorm-ien

The imperfect of third-conjugation 'inceptive' verbs (like **patir > pateixo**, etc. seen in Unit 5) is formed as for **dormir: patia, paties, patia, patíem, patíeu, patien**.

Relatively few verbs are irregular in the imperfect if you understand that the stem for this tense is the same as that of the first-person plural of the present indicative. Thus **prendre** (**pren-em**) has **pren-ia**, etc; **beure** and **deure** (**bev-em, dev-em**) have **bevia** and **devia**, etc; **escriure** and **viure** (**escriv-im, viv-im**) have **escrivia, vivia**, etc. Tenir, **venir** and anar are quite straightforward (**tenia, venia, anava**).

The general pattern for this tense is for the stress to fall upon the ending in all parts. There are, however, some exceptions which are frequently-used verbs whose imperfect forms have the stress on the irregular stem, as for **dir: deia, deies, deia, dèiem, dèieu, deien.**

caure	>	queia	fer	>	feia	seure	>	seia
creure	>	creia	riure	>	reia	treure	>	treia
dur	>	duia	ser	>	era	veure	>	veia

Note finally how verbs like **conduir** require a diaeresis (ï) in some parts, consistent with the stress on the **i** of the ending: **conduïa, conduïes, conduïa (conduíem, conduíeu) conduïen.**

Insight

Three good tips for proper use of the imperfect tense: when the sense of the verb can be conveyed by English *was...ing or used to...*; when you could insert (if not already present) an adverb like **sempre** *always*, **normalment** *usually*, contrasting with the idea of *on that occasion*; when there is a concept of background (description, states occurring, things going on ...) to a single action completed in the past.

Exercise 3

Josep Mª Mir has been retired since 2005. He explains where he used to live while he was an employee, comparing it with how he lives now. Place a correct verb in each gap (choosing between the imperfect tense and the present).

Quan vaig començar a treballar _____ **1** (tenir) 14 anys i vaig deixar l'escola per entrar d'aprenent de pintor, perquè a casa meva no _____ **2** (haver-hi) diners i _____ **3** (necessitar) menjar. _____ **4** (ser) els anys de la postguerra. La gent _____ **5** (viure) com _____ **6** (poder). Els de la meva generació ara _____ **7** (estar) tots retirats i tenen de tot. De petit, cada Nadal els nostres pares ens _____ **8** (regalar) dues taronges i als 15 anys em vaig comprar la meva primera bicicleta. _____ **9** (ser) groga i els meus germans sempre la _____ **10** (voler) agafar. Jo de jove _____ **11** (treballar) fins a 12 hores diàries i avui dia, en canvi, _____ **12** (passar-se) 12 hores sense fer res.

Exercise 4

Now it is your turn. Write a short paragraph from your own experience on how things used to be when you were younger, comparing the situation then with the present.

Reading

Read this opening extract from a short story by a distinguished contemporary author.

Als límits del fricandó

Va trucar per dir-me que volia parlar amb mi. D'entrada, no em va agradar gens. El dia que van acomiadar-me de l'empresa, el gerent també *volia* parlar amb mi. I quan va morir el pare, el meu oncle *havia* de parlar amb mi. Vaig empassar-me els dubtes, la saliva i la por, i vam quedar de trobar-nos en un d'aquests bars blancs que s'han posat de moda.

Ella va ser estranyament puntual. Duia un vestit de color blau cel i ulleres de sol. Estava nerviosa. Va demanar un entrepà molt estrany de pernil dolç i pinya, i una tònica. No havia dinat. Ho va dir de manera que jo entengués que no havia tingut gana perquè estava inquieta, desesperada o trista. Involuntàriament, vaig vessar la Coca-Cola i li vaig tacar el vestit. Una vella de la taula del costat va comentar-nos que les taques de Coca-Cola no marxaven amb res, però el cambrer ens va assegurar que la vella mentia i que, amb una mica d'aigua, marxarien de seguida.

Sergi Pàmies, *T'hauria de caure la cara de vergonya* (Barcelona: Quaderns Crema, 1986).

Exercise 5

Study carefully the tenses of all the verbs in the text above (**entengués** in the second paragraph is the imperfect subjunctive of **entendre**, meaning *so that I should understand*). List all the verbs in the preterite and imperfect tenses. Translate the text into English. Then, some hours later or next day, translate your version back into Catalan. Don't expect this version of yours to coincide exactly with the Catalan original. You will learn a lot from working 'both ways'.

Exercise 6

For further practice, rewrite the text as though the events in the story occurred *today* (beginning **Ha trucat per dir-me que volia ...**). Pay careful attention to pronouns combining with verbs.

Grammar

Insight

In Grammar section B we consolidate understanding of how **ser** and **estar** express different aspects of *to be*. Even if nuances apply very often, remember these three main areas of meaning where **ser** will occur: identity or belonging, location and time. Where adjectives are involved (especially with personal subjects), the distinction between inherent/permanent states (**ser**) and temporary/changeable ones (**estar**) will be important.

B Review of *ser* and *estar*

Refer back, first, to comments made on these two verbs in Unit 12. What follows is a fuller overview of the topic.

Ser expresses:

1 identity or belonging to an identifiable set:
> **Sóc en Pere. Sóc metge. La camisa és de cotó. Aquesta moto és del veí.**

2 location:
> **El cotxe és al garatge. Banyoles és a prop de Girona.**

3 time:
> **Són les vuit i deu minuts. La reunió serà a les tres en punt.**

A distinction is made between mere location (**ser**) and location extended over time, when **estar** has the implication of *to stay*:

Aviat serem a Blanes: hi estarem dues hores.	*We will soon be in Blanes: we'll be (= stay) there for two hours.*
Estigues a la plaça fins que jo hi sigui.	*Stay in the square until I'm there.*

Remember also **estar-se** meaning *to reside*, as practised in Unit 2.

Estar is used with adverbs or with phrases which do not indicate location (and are not **de** phrases like those in 1 above).

Com estàs? – Estic molt bé.	*How are you? – I am fine.*
Això no està bé.	*This is not right.*
Avui el peix no està a l'abast de tothom	*These days not everybody can afford fish.*
Està en coma a la clínica.	*She is in a coma at the clinic.*
Jo hi estic a favor/en contra.	*I'm for/against it.*

You have looked at different uses of **ser** and **estar** with adjectives in Unit 12. Generally **estar** goes with adjectives denoting temporary or changeable states: as in the Reading passage, **estava nerviosa, estava inquieta** … When the subject is inanimate, however, **ser** is preferred in cases like: **l'aigua és bruta, la sopa era freda, el raïm ja és madur.**

There is some fluctuation in this area among native speakers, and the matter is made more complicated by the fact that it overlaps with 'passive' constructions of the kind: **Va ser educada per una tia seva** *She was brought up by an aunt of hers* (passive equivalent of **La va educar una tia seva**).

In general we can say that, accompanying past participles, **ser** expresses action being done (the passive constructions) while **estar** indicates state resulting from such action.

Exercise 7

Fill in the blanks with a correct conjugated verb, **ser** or **estar**.

1 A l'estiu, a la piscina s'hi _____ més bé.
2 No sé on _____ les sabates.
3 L'arròs _____ massa salat.
4 Ja _____ aquí, ja he arribat!
5 L'enciclopèdia _____ (imperfect) al prestatge.
6 Vam _____ un mes fora de casa.
7 El nou model ja _____ a la venda.

Grammar

C Comparison (2)

You were introduced to basic constructions of comparison in Unit 7 and you should revise that section for work in the present unit. *Than* in comparisons often appears as **que no** or even **que no pas**. The **no** (**pas**) element is optional for introducing simple terms of comparison:

> És millor ara que (no/no pas) abans.
> Aquest cotxe és més ràpid que (no/no pas) el nostre.

D Suffixes

In Dialogue 2 use of the word **piset**, is an example of a very common feature of colloquial Catalan: the use of an ending element (suffix) to modify the meaning of a noun or adjective: see Unit 6, Grammar D. Here we have **pis** *flat*, modified by the diminutive suffix **-et**. As well as denoting smallness of size, this suffix (**-et/-eta** with both adjectives and nouns) also carries a note of intimacy or favourable disposition in the speaker. Here are a couple more examples, where the translation expresses something of the nuances conveyed in Catalan:

Espera't un momentet.	*Wait just a moment.*
una truiteta crueta per dins i ben rosseta per fora	*a little omelette, nice and runny inside and nicely browned on the outside*

Catalan is rich in suffixes of this kind and here we can only mention a few of the most common which you are likely to encounter in everyday situations:

- -ó/-ona (diminutive with favourable note): **un cafetó** *a nice little cup of coffee*;
- -às/-assa (augmentative): **una manassa** *a big, huge hand*;
- -ot/-ta (strongly depreciative): **paraulotes ben fortes** *very strong swear words*.

Insight

This is a good point at which to recall the superlative suffix **-íssim/-a** (with adjectives), introduced in the second insight box of Unit 6.

Exercise 8

Imagine you are visiting a property agency and you want to talk about one of the flats you have just seen. Complete your part in the dialogue.

CD2, TR 25, 00:02

Agent	Bona tarda. Què, va anar a veure el pis del barri Les Forestes.
Tu (1)	*(Say 'yes', and say you were there all afternoon waiting for the owner, (el propietari).)*
Agent	Què li va passar?
Tu (2)	*(Say he didn't remember he had an appointment with you.)*
Agent	I el pis, què li va semblar?
Tu (3)	*(Say this flat is better situated than the house you saw on Monday, but the flat is much older.)*
Agent	I l'interior?
Tu (4)	*(Say some doors didn't close properly and the parquet in the living room was dirty. Add you thought the flat had two bathrooms but you found that it has only one.)*
Agent	La cuina és molt gran i equipada, oi?
Tu (5)	*(Say you agree with that but the window was really small.)*

Agent	Vol veure'n algun altre?
Tu (6)	*(Say yes; you would like to visit a two-room flat, with parking included in the price, with a large terrace and central heating.)*

Exercise 9
🔊 **CD2, TR 25, 02:01**

Listen to a business conversation between Aleix Gasau and Imma Comas. Then, according to what you hear, match the sentences on the right with those on the left:

1 Imma Comas considera que
2 Aleix Gasau proposa

3 Comas diu que
4 Gasau diu que

a aquest no és un bon moment.
b hauran de parlar-ne amb el president.
c d'obrir les vendes a tot el món.
d el negoci anava millor abans.

Exercise 10
Now listen again and tick the phrases you hear.

1 **Asking for opinions**
   a Què en penses ...?
   b Què et sembla ...?
   c Com ho veus ...?
3 **Disagreeing**
   a No hi estic d'acord.

   b Perdona, però no em sembla bé.
   c Hi estic en contra.

2 **Giving opinions**
   a Em sembla que ...
   b Des del meu punt de vista ...
   c Crec que ...
4 **Agreeing**
   a Hi estic completament d'acord.
   b Tens raó.
   c Em fa molt content.

Insight

Refer back to the Insight box at the end of Unit 10. You were told there that progress would be accelerated in the final stage of this course, and you are now in a position to review

(Contd)

the ground covered and what has been achieved. In the last six units you have been working at the 'threshold' level of competence in Catalan. Your ability to understand and respond to linguistic stimuli, both idiomatic and formal, gives you the basis for spontaneous, natural communication with native speakers. Moreover you have covered the fundamental aspects of Catalan grammar, the prerequisite for being able to extend your proficiency further. We hope that you will be encouraged to consolidate and develop the position you have reached, and the section on **Taking it further** is designed to guide you forward. **Bona sort!**

Points to remember

1 **què opina / què pensa de… / què li sembla…?** *what do you think of…?*
2 **no hi estic (gens) d'acord / hi estic en contra** *I don't agree with it (at all) / I am against it*
3 **hi estava a favor** *I was/used to be in favour (of it/that)*; **hi estava d'acord** *I agreed/ used to agree (with it/that)*
4 **vostè creu / pensa que…? jo crec que sí/ que no** *do you believe / think that…? I think so / I don't think so*
5 **depèn / segons… / tens raó** *it depends / according to… / you are right*
6 **abans el poble m'agradava més que (no/no pas) ara.** *I used to like the village before more than I do now*
7 Conjugation patterns of the imperfect tense for regular and irregular verbs.
8 The functions of the imperfect tense, especially when used in conjunction with other verbs expressing actions completed in the past.
9 A final review of **ser** and **estar**.
10 Meanings and nuances conveyed by Catalan suffixes.

Taking it further

Congratulations on completing the course. This section provides some guidance for you to consolidate the linguistic knowledge and competence you have acquired. First, there is a Catalan page on the Teach Yourself website

www.teachyourself.co.uk/tycatalantest.htm

Here you will find 50 multiple-choice questions for revision and self-assessment. Also provided are some introductory articles on aspects of Catalan culture, together with a Language learning section giving on-line and printed resources.

Formal examinations. The Institut Ramon Llull (http://www.llull.cat) organizes examination and certification in Catalan according to the Common European Framework of Reference for Languages. Full details are available via the above web address. Additional useful information on language study, bibliography, etc. can be found at http://www20.gencat.cat/portal/site/llengcat/.

WORKS FOR FURTHER LANGUAGE STUDY
AND REFERENCE

In English
Alexander Ibarz & Toni Ibarz, *Colloquial Catalan. A Complete Course for Beginners* (London, Routledge, 2008)

Alan Yates & Toni Ibarz, *A Catalan Handbook: working with 'Digui, digui'* (Sheffield, Botifarra, 1992, with subsequent edition, Barcelona, Departament de Cultura, 1993), English-language companion to *Curs de català per a estrangers* (Multimedia *Digui, digui* method by Mas et al.).

Max. W. Wheeler, Alan Yates and Nicolau Dols, *Catalan: a Comprehensive Grammar* (London, Routledge, 1999). This is a thorough and detailed reference guide to modern Catalan (covering regional diversity): an accessible and systematic description of the modern language, indispensable for advanced study. The preface provides a brief overview of the history and present-day status of the language.

In Catalan

Bennàssar, C. et al., *Xarxa: llengua catalana 1* (Palma, Moll, 1997). A useful introduction to Balearic usage.

Giner, R. et al., *Reciclatge. Nivells elemental i mitjà* (València, Editorial 3 i 4, 1992). Presenting Valencian usage for intermediate level.

Mas, M. et al., *Veus 3. Curs de català* (Barcelona, Publicacions Abadia de Montserrat, 2008), a course specially created for adult non-Catalan speakers corresponding to the B1 (pre-intermediate) European level.

Alemany, E et al., *Curs de llengua catalana. Nivell intermedi*, 3 vols, (Barcelona, Castellnou, 2004), correponding to the B2 (intermediate) level.

Badia, J. et al., *Nivell B Llengua Catalana* (Barcelona, Castellnou, 2001), manual designed for the Intermediate (B2) certificate level.

Alemany, E. et al., *Curs de llengua catalana. Nivell suficiència*, 3 vols, (Barcelona, Castellnou, 2005), corresponding to the C1 (advanced) level.

On the Internet
http://www.parla.cat
This is is a virtual learning space introduced in different languages that offers all the educational materials for learning Catalan. The course can be done through a (free) self-managed learning method or (for a fee) with a personal tutor. Highly recommended.

http://www.intercat.cat
Resources for university students to learn the language as well as tips for living in Catalonia.

http://ub.edu/sonscatala
Web page entirely in Catalan providing clear illustration of the sounds of Catalan.

Website dictionaries English/Catalan/English:
http://www.catalandictionary.org
http://www.diccionaris.net

Phrasebooks and dictionaries
Faluba, K. and Morvay, K., *Conversation Guide: English–Catalan–Spanish* (Barcelona, Edicions de la Magrana, 1992).

Diccionari Oxford Pocket, català–anglès/anglès–català (Oxford University Press, 1994).

A number of other useful dictionaries are published by Enciclopèdia Catalana SA, details of which can be consulted at http://www.enciclopedia.cat

BACKGROUND READING

On society, culture, etc.
Robert Hughes, *Barcelona* (London, Vintage paperback, 1993).

Colm Tóibín, *Homage to Barcelona* (London, Picador paperback, 2002).

John Payne, *Catalonia: History and Culture* (Nottingham, Five Leaves Publications, 2004).

Michael Eaude, *Catalonia. A Cultural History* (Oxford, University Press, 2008). Highly recommended.

On politics
Albert Balcells, *Catalan Nationalism: Past and Present* (London, Macmillan, 1995).

Montserrat Guibernau, *Catalan Nationalism: Francoism, Transition and Democracy* (London, Routledge, 2004).

There is, unfortunately, no work currently available in English which gives a reliable account of the *Països Catalans* as a distinctive language-community, with its own history, social evolution, culture and literature. Internet searches for this perspective can be productive, e.g. vilaweb: http://www.vilaweb.cat; (see below).

CATALAN PRESS AND SEARCH ENGINES

Daily newspapers: http://www.avui.cat, http://www.elperiodico.cat, http://www.elpunt.cat

http://www.vilaweb.cat – This address provides a major search and directory facility for all Catalan subjects, as well as an independent electronic daily news service.

Catalunya Ràdio on the internet: http://www.catradio.cat
Televisió de Catalunya (TVC) on the internet: http://www.tv3.cat, broadcasting also by satellite via TVC International, 24 hours a day.

Official web sites
http://www.gencat.cat, web page of the Generalitat de Catalunya.
http://www.govern.ad, web page of the Govern del Principat
  d'Andorra.
http://www.caib.es, web page of the Govern de les Illes Balears.
http://www.gva.es, web page of the Generalitat Valenciana.

Reference tables

1 Number and gender (basic scheme* for nouns and adjectives)

N = noun	singular		plural	
A = adjective	masculine	feminine	masculine	feminine
N	senyor	senyora	senyors	senyores
A	molt	molta	molts	moltes
A	simpàtic	simpàtica	simpàtics	simpàtiques
N/A	pobre	pobra	pobres	pobres
N	cosí	cosina	cosins	cosines
A	bo	bona	bons	bones
N	amic	amiga	amics	amigues
A	casat	casada	casats	casades
A	nou	nova	nous	noves

(Contd)

N = noun A = adjective	singular		plural	
	masculine	feminine	masculine	feminine
N/A				
A	anglès	anglesa	anglesos	angleses
A	mateix	mateixa	mateixos	mateixes
N	pis		pisos	
A	gros	grossa	grossos	grosses
N	despatx		despatxos	
N	gust		gustos	
A	trist	trista	tristos	tristes
A	fresc	fresca	frescos	fresques
A	roig	roja	rojos	roges
A	mig	mitja	mitjos	mitges
A	dolç	dolça	dolços	dolces
A	feliç	feliç	feliços	felices
N	dependent	dependenta	dependents	dependentes
A	calent	calenta	calents	calentes
A	vinent	vinent	vinents	vinents
A	important	important	importants	importants
A	agradable	agradable	agradables	agradables
A	lliure	lliure	lliures	lliures

*The groupings indicate the main patterns which nouns and adjectives follow as they change for number and gender.

2 Weak object pronouns: forms and functions

		singular		plural		functions (see opposite)
		before verb	after verb	before verb	after verb	
1st person		em m'	-me 'm	ens	-nos 'ns	1
2nd person		et t'	-te 't	us	-vos -us	2
3rd person	masculine	el l'	-lo 'l	els	-los 'ls	3
	feminine	la l'	-la	les	-les	
	neuter	ho	-ho			4, 5
	indirect object	li	-li	els	-los 'ls	6
	reflexive	es s'	-se 's	es s'	-se 's	7

	before verb	after verb	before verb	after verb	
adverbial	en	n'	-ne	'n	8
	hi	-hi			9

1 Direct and indirect object (including reflexive use)
Em miren. M'han vist. Vull banyar-me. Va escriure'm.
Ens parla. Van trucar-nos. Escolta'ns.

2 Direct and indirect object (including reflexive use)
Et miren. T'acomiades. Pots maquillar-te. Renta't.
Us pentineu. Van abraçar-vos. Vol veure-us.

3 Animate and inanimate direct object
El paga. L'ha reservada. La neteja. Envia'l. Penso portar-lo.
Les deu estimar. Sap escoltar-los. Espera'ls aquí.

4 Neuter direct object, standing for **això**, **allò**, or whole
sentence.
Com ho escrius? Deixa-ho allà. Ho sento. Ha d'ajudar-me
però no ho fa mai.

5 Nominal predicate of **ser, estar, semblar**
No és pas catalana però ho sembla.
És professor? – Sí que ho és.

6 Indirect object (masculine and feminine)
Li duc l'esmorzar. Li he comprat el diari. Explica-li això.
Els volem escriure. Vaig preparar-los un pastís.
Digue'ls la veritat.

7 Reflexive direct or indirect object
Es vesteix. S'empassa el menjar. Volen casar-se.
Posi's l'abric.

8 Standing for **de** + pronoun.
De germans, no en té cap. N'han vist molts, de petits
i de grans. Porteu forquilles de plàstic? – Si, vam
comprar-ne un paquet. A la platja n'hi ha molts. Obre la
nevera i treu-ne els ous.

9 Standing for any preposition except **de** + pronoun
A la reunió, hi aniré amb cotxe. Hi estic d'acord.
Voleu entrar-hi ara?

3 Irregular verbs

Only tenses with irregular parts are listed.

Anar, *to go:* conjugated like **anar-se'n,** without the pronouns: **vaig, vas,** etc.

Anar-se'n, *to go (away)*
    Present: me'n vaig, te'n vas, se'n va, ens n'anem, us n'aneu, se'n van
    Future: me n'aniré, te n'aniràs, se n'anirà, ens n'anirem, us n'anireu, se n'aniran
    Imperative: vés-te'n, vagi-se'n, anem-nos-en, aneu-vos-en, vagin-se'n
    Present subjunctive: me'n vagi, te'n vagis, se'n vagi, ens n'anem, us n'aneu, se'n vagin

Aprendre, *to learn*
    Gerund: **aprenent**
    Past participle: **après**
    Present: **aprenc, aprens, aprèn, aprenem, apreneu, aprenen**
    Imperfect: **aprenia, aprenies, aprenia, apreníem, apreníeu, aprenien**
    Imperative: **aprèn, aprengui, aprenguem, apreneu, aprenguin**
    Present subjunctive: **aprengui, aprenguis, aprengui, aprenguem, aprengueu, aprenguin**

Beure, *to drink*
    Gerund: **bevent**
    Past participle: **begut**
    Present: **bec, beus, beu, bevem, beveu, beuen**
    Imperfect: **bevia, bevies, bevia, bevíem, bevíeu, bevien**
    Imperative: **beu, begui, beguem, beveu, beguin**
    Present subjunctive: **begui, beguis, begui, beguem, begueu, beguin**

Caldre, *to be necessary*
    Gerund: **calent**
    Past participle: **calgut**

Present: cal, calen
Imperfect: calia, calien
Present subjunctive: calgui, calguin

Caure, *to fall*
Gerund: caient
Past participle: caigut
Present: caic, caus, cau, caiem, caieu, cauen
Imperfect: queia, queies, queia, quèiem, quèieu, queien
Imperative: cau, caigui, caiguem, caieu, caiguin
Present subjunctive: caigui, caiguis, caigui, caiguem, caigueu,
  caiguin

Conèixer, *to know*
Gerund: coneixent
Past participle: conegut
Present: conec, coneixes, coneix, coneixem, coneixeu, coneixen
Future: coneixeré, coneixeràs, coneixerà, coneixerem,
  coneixereu, coneixeran
Imperative: coneix, conegui, coneguem, coneixeu, coneguin
Present subjunctive: conegui, coneguis, conegui, coneguem,
  conegueu, coneguin

Córrer, *to run*
Gerund: corrent
Past participle: corregut
Present: corro, corres, corre, correm, correu, corren
Future: correré, correràs, correrà, correrem, correreu, correran
Imperative: corre, corri, correguem (correm), correu, corrin
Present subjunctive: corri, corris, corri, correguem, corregueu,
  corrin

Creure, *to believe*
Gerund: creient
Past participle: cregut
Present: crec, creus, creu, creiem, creieu, creuen
Imperfect: creia, creies, creia, crèiem, crèieu, creien
Imperative: creu, cregui, creguem, creieu, creguin

Present subjunctive: **cregui, creguis, cregui, creguem, cregueu, creguin**

Deure, *to owe, must*: conjugated like **beure.**

Dir, *to say, to tell*
  Gerund: **dient**
  Past participle: **dit**
  Present: **dic, dius, diu, diem, dieu, diuen**
  Imperfect: **deia, deies, deia, dèiem, dèieu, deien**
  Imperative: **digues, digui, diguem, digueu, diguin**
  Present subjunctive: **digui, diguis, digui, diguem, digueu, diguin**

Dur, *to carry, to take, to wear*
  Gerund: **duent**
  Past participle: **dut**
  Present: **duc, duus (dus), duu (du), duem, dueu, duen**
  Future: **duré, duràs, durà, durem, dureu, duran**
  Imperfect: **duia, duies, duia, dúiem, dúieu, duien**
  Imperative: **duu (du), dugui, duguem, dueu, duguin**
  Present subjunctive: **dugui, duguis, dugui, duguem, dugueu, duguin**

Encendre, *to light* and **entendre,** *to understand*: conjugated like **aprendre,** but with acute accent in the third person singular: **encén** and **entén** and also **tu** form imperative.

Endur-se, *to take away*: conjugated like **dur.**

Escriure, *to write*
  Gerund: **escrivint**
  Past participle: **escrit**
  Present: **escric, escrius, escriu, escrivim, escriviu, escriuen**
  Imperfect: **escrivia, escrivies, escrivia, escrivíem, escrivíeu, escrivien**
  Imperative: **escriu, escrigui, escriguem, escriviu, escriguin**
  Present subjunctive: **escrigui, escriguis, escrigui, escriguem, escrigueu, escriguin**

Estar, *to be*
  Present: estic, estàs, està, estem, esteu, estan
  Imperative: estigues, estigui, estiguem, estigueu, estiguin
  Present subjunctive: estigui, estiguis, estigui, estiguem, estigueu,
    estiguin

Fer, *to do, to make*
  Gerund: fent
  Past participle: fet
  Present: faig, fas, fa, fem, feu, fan
  Future: faré, faràs, farà, farem, fareu, faran
  Imperfect: feia, feies, feia, fèiem, fèieu, feien
  Imperative: fes, faci, fem, feu, facin
  Present subjunctive: faci, facis, faci, fem, feu, facin

Haver, *to have* (auxiliary verb)
  Past participle: hagut
  Present: he, has, ha, hem, heu, han
  Future: hauré, hauràs, haurà, haurem, haureu, hauran
  Present subjunctive: hagi, hagis, hagi, hàgim, hàgiu, hagin

Néixer, *to be born*
  Gerund: naixent
  Past participle: nascut
  Present: neixo, neixes, neix, naixem, naixeu, neixen
  Future: naixeré, naixeràs, naixerà, naixerem, naixereu, naixeran
  Imperfect: naixia, naixies, naixia, naixíem, naixíeu, naixien
  Present subjunctive: neixi, neixis, neixi, naixem, naixeu, neixin

Obrir, *to open*
  Past participle: obert
  Present: obro, obres, obre, obrim, obriu, obren
  Imperative: obre, obri, obrim, obriu, obrin

Ploure, *to rain*
  Gerund: plovent
  Past participle: plogut

Present: **plou**
Imperfect: **plovia**
Present subjunctive: **plogui**

Poder, *to be able, can*
Past participle: **pogut**
Present: **puc, pots, pot, podem, podeu, poden**
Future: **podré, podràs, podrà, podrem, podreu, podran**
Present subjunctive: **pugui, puguis, pugui, puguem, pugueu, puguin**

Prendre, *to take*: conjugated like **aprendre,** but without a written accent in the following parts:
Past participle: **pres**
Present (3rd person singular): **pren**
Imperative (2nd person singular): **pren**

Riure, *to laugh*
Gerund: **rient**
Past participle: **rigut**
Present: **ric, rius, riu, riem, rieu, riuen**
Imperfect: **reia, reies, reia, rèiem, rèieu, reien**
Imperative: **riu, rigui, riguem, rieu, riguin**
Present subjunctive: **rigui, riguis, rigui, riguem, rigueu, riguin**

Saber, *to know*
Present: **sé, saps, sap, sabem, sabeu, saben**
Future: **sabré, sabràs, sabrà, sabrem, sabreu, sabran**
Imperative: **sàpigues, sàpiga, sapiguem, sapigueu, sàpiguen**
Present subjunctive: **sàpiga, sàpigues, sàpiga, sapiguem, sapigueu, sàpiguen**

Ser, *to be*
Gerund: **essent / sent**
Past participle: **estat** (colloquial **sigut**)
Present: **sóc, ets, és, som, sou, són**
Future: **seré, seràs, serà, serem, sereu, seran**

Imperfect: era, eres, era, érem, éreu, eren
Imperative: sigues, sigui, siguem, sigueu, siguin
Present subjunctive: sigui, siguis, sigui, siguem, sigueu, siguin

Seure, *to sit down*: conjugated like **creure**.

Sortir, *to go out, to leave*
Present: surto, surts, surt, sortim, sortiu, surten
Imperative: surt, surti, sortim, sortiu, surtin
Present subjuntive: surti, surtis, surti, sortim, sortiu, surtin

Tenir, *to have*
Past participle: tingut
Present: tinc, tens, té, tenim, teniu, tenen
Future: tindré, tindràs, tindrà, tindrem, tindreu, tindran
Imperative: té, tingui, tinguem, teniu (tingueu), tinguin
Present subjunctive: tingui, tinguis, tingui, tinguem, tingueu, tinguin

Treure, *to remove, to take out/off*
Gerund: traient
Past participle: tret
Present: trec, treus, treu, traiem, traieu, treuen
Future: trauré, trauràs, traurà, traurem, traureu, trauran
Imperfect: treia, treies, treia, trèiem, trèieu, treien
Imperative: treu, tregui, traguem, traieu, treguin
Present subjunctive: tregui, treguis, tregui, traguem, tragueu, treguin

Valer, *to be worth*
Past participle: valgut
Present: valc, vals, val, valem, valeu, valen
Future: valdré, valdràs, valdrà, valdrem, valdreu, valdran
Imperative: val, valgui, valguem, valeu, valguin
Present subjunctive: valgui, valguis, valgui, valguem, valgueu, valguin

Vendre, *to sell*: conjugated like **prendre** except:
Past participle: **venut**

Venir, *to come*
Past participle: **vingut**
Present: **vinc, véns, ve, venim, veniu, vénen**
Future: **vindré, vindràs, vindrà, vindrem, vindreu, vindran**
Imperative: **vine, vingui, vinguem, veniu, vinguin**
Present subjunctive: **vingui, vinguis, vingui, vinguem, vingueu, vinguin**

Veure, *to see*
Gerund: **veient**
Past participle: **vist**
Present: **veig, veus, veu, veiem, veieu, veuen**
Imperfect: **veia, veies, veia, vèiem, vèieu, veien**
Imperative: **veges, vegi, vegem, vegeu (veieu), vegin**
Present subjunctive: **vegi, vegis, vegi, vegem, vegeu, vegin**

Viure, *to live*
Gerund: **vivint**
Past participle: **viscut**
Present: **visc, vius, viu, vivim, viviu, viuen**
Imperfect: **vivia, vivies, vivia, vivíem, vivíeu, vivien**
Imperative: **viu, visqui, visquem, viviu, visquin**
Present subjunctive: **visqui, visquis, visqui, visquem, visqueu, visquin**

Voler, *to wish, to want, to like*
Past participle: **volgut**
Present: **vull, vols, vol, volem, voleu, volen**
Future: **voldré, voldràs, voldrà, voldrem, voldreu, voldran**
Imperative: **vulgues, vulgui, vulguem, vulgueu, vulguin**
Present subjunctive: **vulgui, vulguis, vulgui, vulguem, vulgueu, vulguin**

Key to the exercises

The symbol * means that the answer provided is a suggestion or a possible response, and that alternatives may be equally acceptable.

Unit 1

3 1 començar **2** informe **3** companys **4** pastissos **5** bufanda **6** ganxo **4** Hola, és (vostè) el senyor Reig? / Sí, i vostè com es diu? / Jo sóc en Pere Marquès, de Lleida. I vostè, d'on és? / Sóc de Lleida també, com vostè! **5 1b, 2c, 3d, 4a 6 1** l'Imma **2** en/el Tomàs **3** l'Hortènsia **4** en/el Jordi **5** la Carme **6** l'Enric **7 1** es diu **2** és **3** ets **4** sóc **5** són **6** ens diem **8 1** escocès **2** irlandès **3** anglesa **4** italiana **5** andalús **6** espanyola **7** francès **8** japonesa **9 1** No, jo sóc en/el (name) **2** D'on ets? **3** Adéu, (que vagi bé)!

Unit 2

1 1 false **2** false **3** true **4** true **3 1** stressed **2** unstressed **3** stressed **4** unstressed **5** stressed **6** stressed **7** unstressed **8** unstressed **4 1** Antoni **2** Mir Rissec **3** Carrer Major, n° 17 **4** 17800 **5** Vilanova **6** 77.91.54.23 **7** 38 anys **8** casat **5 a** sala d'estar **b** menjador **c** cuina **d** bany **e** habitació **f** entrada/rebedor **6 1a** teus/vostres **2a** Les teves/Les vostres **1b** seus/seus **2b** Les seves/Les seves **1c** seus/seus **2c** Les seves/Les seves **1d** nostres **2d** Les nostres **1e** seus **2e** Les seves **7** *Em dic Cristina i tinc dinou anys. Sóc de Sabadell però visc a Barcelona. Sóc/Estic soltera. El meu germà es diu Esteve i té 23 anys. El meu pare és d'Andorra (andorrà) i la meva mare d'Itàlia (italiana). **8 1** casada **2** fill **3** germana **4** pares **5** cosí **6** Marta **7** el pare **8** oncle **9 1** una cosina alemanya **2** un senyor espanyol/francès **3** uns nois catalans **4** les amigues angleses **5** l'amic francès/espanyol **10** 1a 2b 3b 4c

Unit 3

1 1 true **2** false **3** false **4** false **2 1** unstressed **2** close **3** unstressed **4** open **5** close **6** close **7** close **8** unstressed **9** close **10** open **3 1** correct **2** (93 285 31 88) **3** (973 21 68 45) **4** correct **5** (629 46

28 17) **6** (971 87 74 12) **4 1d 2c 3b 4f 5a 6e 5 1** Són tres quarts de
nou/Són les nou menys quart **2** Són dos quarts de set/Són les sis i
mitja **3** És un quart de sis/Són les cinc i quart **4** És un quart i cinc
(minuts) de dotze/Són les onze i vint (minuts) **5** Són tres quarts i
cinc (minuts) de quatre/Són les quatre menys deu (minuts) **6 1** No,
no hi és (ara). **2** un moment/que hi és **3** Perdoni/Em sap greu/Ho
sento. **4** moment, sisplau **5** (ara) no hi és **6** de part de qui/amb qui
parlo **7 1** Sí, n'hi ha un al final (de tot) d'aquest/del carrer. **2** Sí,
n'hi ha una a la primera cantonada a mà dreta. **3** Sí, n'hi ha un a la
segona cantonada a l'esquerra. **4** Sí, n'hi ha una al final del carrer/
a la tercera cantonada a mà dreta. **8** 4, 3, 2, 6, 1, 5 **9 1** Surt a les
deu i deu minuts (del matí). **2** Surt a les onze i vint-i-cinc minuts
(un quart i deu minuts de dotze). **3** Surt a les dues i cinc minuts.
4 Arriba a tres quarts de nou (les nou menys quart). **5** Arriba a dos
quarts i cinc de sis (les cinc i trenta-cinc minuts).

Unit 4

2 1 unstressed **2** unstressed **3** open **4** open **5** close **6** close
7 open **8** open **9** close **10** unstressed **3** 1e, 2c, 3a, 4b, 5f, 6d
4 1 El restaurant obre a la una del migdia i a dos quarts de nou
del vespre. **2** Al supermercat fan horari intensiu. Obren a les deu
del matí i tanquen a les nou del vespre. **3** Sí, obren a les cinc (de
la tarda). **4** A l'ajuntament obren a les nou (del matí) i tanquen a
les tres (de la tarda). **5** A correus tanquen a les dues. **5 1** (1.153€,
mil cent cinquanta-tres euros) **2** (21€65, vint-i-un euros i seixanta-
cinc cèntims) **3** (217€, dos-cents disset euros) **4** (38€19, trenta-
vuit euros amb dinou cèntims) **5** (74€40, setanta-quatre euros i
quaranta cèntims) **6 1** (mel, galeta, pernil, vi, sucre) **2** (porc, pernil)
3 (coca, pa) **4** (gamba, lluç) **5** (all, tomàquet, patata) **6** (segell,
tabac) **7** (coca, pastís de poma) **7 1** A qui toca? **2** Voldria patates/
peres/taronges …(f.pl.) **3** les vol **4** les vull (més aviat) **5** Alguna cosa
més?/Res més? **6** vull (any product like préssecs, alls …) **7** en tinc/
tenim **8** Quant és/quant val? **9** Són/Val **10** euros **11** cèntims **8 1** els
2 la **3** les **4** en **5** -la **6** El **7** en **8** -lo **9 1** Pots/venen **2** sé/puc/Saps/fan
3 Pots/tinc/tinc **4** saben/valen **5** Fem **10 1** pastanaga-pastanagues
2 patata-patates **3** tomata-tomates **4** all-alls **5** taronja-taronges
6 pera-peres **7** raïm-raïms **8** maduixa-maduixes

Unit 5

1 1 false **2** false **3** true **4** false **3 1** like cat **2** like cat (x 2) **3** like cent **4** like cat **5** like cent **6** like cat **4 1** false **2** false **3** true **4** true **5** false **6** false **5 1** llegim **2** dedueixes **3** construeixen **4** dirigiu **5** descobreixo **6 1** plega **2** està treballant **3** Està preparant **4** mira **5** està esperant **6** van **7** vens **8** baixo **9** espera **10** es maquilla **11** es pentina **12** pateix **13** s'adona **14** està **8 a** En Quim es desperta a dos quarts de set/les sis i mitja del matí. **b** Es lleva/s'aixeca a les set. **c** Es renta la cara. **d** Esmorza a les vuit. **e** Llegeix el diari. **f** Entra/ comença a la feina a les vuit i mitja/dos quarts de nou. **g** Plega/surt de la feina a les sis de la tarda. **h** Sopa a les vuit del vespre. **i** Mira la televisió. **j** Va a dormir a les onze de la nit. // **a** Em desperto a les sis i mitja/dos quarts de set. **b** Em llevo/m'aixeco a les set. **c** Em rento la cara. **d** Esmorzo a les vuit. **e** Llegeixo el diari. **f** Començo/ entro a la feina a les vuit i mitja/dos quarts de nou. **g** Surto/plego de la feina a les sis. **h** Sopo a les vuit. **i** Miro la televisió. **j** Vaig a dormir a les onze. **9* 1** Vas al (cinema, teatre …) avui? **2** Quan vas al (gimnàs …)? **3** A quina hora esmorzes? **4** Quan vas a (Mataró, al dentista …)? **5** A quina hora surt (el tren, de treballar …)? **6** Què fas (diumenge …)? **10 1** Because he is saving money to buy a flat. / Perquè està estalviant diners per pagar l'entrada d'un pis. **2** The property prices in Barcelona are very high / Els preus de l'habitatge a Barcelona són molt alts. **3** Watching a film or reading science-fiction books / Mirar alguna pel·lícula o llegir llibres de ciència-ficció. **4** Yes, he does fitness training and plays tennis with a friend / Sí, fa gimnàstica i juga a tennis amb un amic. **5** Saturday afternoons / Els dissabtes a la tarda.

Unit 6

1 1 false **2** true **3** true **4** false **3 1** not sounded **2** not sounded **3** sounded **4** sounded **5** not sounded **6** not sounded **7** sounded **8** not sounded **4 1 c 2 a** and **c 3 b** and **c 4 d 5 a** and **b 6 d 5** A (Esqueixada, bistec amb patates, aigua, vi negre) B (sopa de verdures, lluç a la planxa, cervesa) **6 1b 2c 3a 4e 5d 7 1** cap **2** no en queda/no n'hi ha gens **3** gens de **4** cap **5** cap **6** té gens **7** queda/ hi ha cap **8 1** li agrada **2** es gasta **3** li **4** li **5** m'escolta **6** vénen **7** toquen **8** ens molesta **9** Els **10** ens **11** em sembla **9 A** esquiar i baixar per les pistes, passejar pel poble, anar/estar-se al bar, anar al restaurant, la cuina elaborada **B** fer cua per a pujar les pistes, llevar-se aviat, la pizzeria Don Antonio

Unit 7

1 1 veritat **2** fals **3** veritat **4** fals **3 1** like see **2** like s̱ee **3** like s̱ee **4** like s̱ee **5** like nos̱e **6** like s̱ee **7** like nos̱e **4 1** avió **2** vaixell **3** tren **4** barca **5** autocar **6** cotxe **7** moto **8** bicicleta **5** 1c, 2a, 3c, 4b, 5b, 6a **6 1** ningú **2** cap **3** gens **4** res **5** algú **7 1** El dia 10 de setembre. **2** Al vespre. **3** Dura quaranta-cinc minuts/tres quarts d'hora. **4** 103€ **5** Pensa que està molt bé de preu **8 1 A** és tan alt com **B. 2 A** és més feliç que **B. 3 A** és més ràpida que **B. 4 A** és menys jove que **B. 5 A** és tan gros com **B. 6 A** és més modern que **B. 9 1** iguals **2** ampla **3** superior **4** amable / avorrida **5** útil **6** bona **10** Across: **1** fleca **2** casat **3** zero **4** migdia **5** rento **6** val Down: **1** carrer **2** adéu **3** esmorzar **4** morena **5** oncle **6** vull

Unit 8

1 1 v **2** f **3** f **4** v **3 1** like give **2** give **3** meas̱ure **4** give **5** give **6** give **7** meas̱ure **8** meas̱ure **4** 10, 4, 1, 2, 8, 3, 5, 9, 6, 7 **5 1** el llum **2** les finestres **3** recepció **4** el telèfon **5** tovalloles **6** sabó **7** l'ascensor **8** habitació **9** clau **6 A** Bany complet, quatre nits, llit doble i esmorzar, dinar i sopar **B** Dutxa, dues nits, llit doble i esmorzar **C** Bany complet, cinc nits, dos llits i esmorzar i sopar **D** Dutxa, una nit, dos llits i esmorzar **7 1 a 2** right **3** en **4** right **5 a 6** right **7** right **8 a 9** de **10 A 11** right **12** right **13** d' **14** fins **8 1** És una casa rural, agroturisme, turisme rural **2** Obren tot l'any però tanquen per vacances a l'abril i a l'octubre **3** Sí **4** No, n'hi ha quatre que tenen bany i dues que tenen dutxa. **5** Possibilitats de fer excursions guiades, esquiar, relaxar-se i gaudir de l'alta muntanya.

Unit 9

2 a4, b2, c1, d5, e6, f3 **3 a 1** final **2** final **3** next to last **4** final **5** two before last **6** next to last **7** final **4 1** l'esquerra / a sota **2** lluny **3** la dreta **4** dins / a sobre **5** a dalt **5 1** La finestra que és a la dreta està tancada. **2** El cotxe que és de la família d'aquí davant té set anys. **3** El museu que volem visitar és molt interessant. **4** El noi que viu al pis de dalt treballa a l'estació. **5** El tren que surt a dos quarts de sis porta retard. **6 1** Museu Tèxtil (C) **2** Museu d'Art (B) **3** Museu

d'Història (D) **4** Museu de la Indústria (A) **7 1** unta'l **2** barreja
3 afegeix-hi **4** Treballa **5** posa-la **6** Col.loca/Posa **7** espera **8** posa
9 retira **10** afegeix **11** tira **12** posa-la

Unit 10
1 1 f **2** f **3** f **4** v **3 1** single **2** silent **3** double **4** double; single **5** silent
6 single **7** single **8** single **5 1a, 2c, 3b, 4c, 5b 6** *Marta*: **a** mig any
després **b** va tenir **c** vam marxar **d** Ens vam instal.lar **e** va començar
f em va agradar **g** vaig abandonar **h** Fa deu anys *Miquel*: **a** vaig
decidir anar **b** l'any abans **c** vaig conèixer **d** vaig trobar **e** vaig
comprar **f** Des de fa *Pilar*: **a** de petita **b** Tot va començar **c** em va
portar **d** vam anar a **e** em va convidar **f** Vaig agafar **g** vaig voler
7 va desaparèixer – van tenir lloc – entraren – va durar – tardà –
van poder desconnectar ... i entrar – va arribar – va poder – mostrà
8* 1 El robatori va tenir lloc ahir, al voltant de les onze de la nit.
2 La policia va tardar/tardà 15 minuts a arribar-hi. **3** Llibres
de gran valor. **4** Els lladres van sortir per la part de darrere de
la biblioteca. **5** El director va mostrar sorpresa i ràbia davant
l'incident.

Unit 11
2 *As* in taxi: excursió, màxim / *As* in xavi: mateix, baixar, xai,
peix, marxar / *As in* examen: exercici, exacte, exemple / As in
cotxe: dutxa **3** 1j, 2g, 3e, 4k, 5l, 6f, 7a, 8c, 9d, 10b, 11h, 12i **4**
1 Unes jaquetes cares, curtes i blanques. **2** Una beguda fresca,
vermella i ben bona. **3** Uns cafès descafeïnats, negres i congelats.
4 Uns dies grisos, llargs i ben avorrits. **5** Unes galetes marró,
salades i barates. **6** Una bicicleta nova, groga i moderna. **7** Uns
animals salvatges, grossos i lliures. **8** Unes camises blau fosc,
econòmiques i ben elegants. **5 1** No, també ven bosses i cinturons.
2 A finals de l'hivern, principis de la primavera. **3** Tenen dues
botigues, una a Tortosa i l'altra a Amposta. **4** Un cinturó de pell.
6 1 v 2 v 3 v 4 f **7** 1 aquest llibre **2** calent **3** el disc compacte
4 el jersei de llana **5** que fumar és dolent **6** alt i ros **7** que aquest
és el seu cotxe **8** és teu això d'aquí? **8 1** Fa un metre i seixanta
centímetres aproximadament. **2** Té els cabells foscos, llargs i
estirats. **3** (No acostuma a) maquillar-se. **4** Vesteix/porta/duu roba
d'esport: texans i samarretes. **5** Sovint duu ulleres i porta una cua

als cabells. **10** 1d, 2e, 3b, 4f, 6c **11 1** maca **2** cercar **3** semblant
4 agradable **5** dinàmic **6** seriós/-osa

Unit 12

2 1 aigua **2** guia **3** guitarra **4** pingüí **5** vegada **6** cargol **7** lloguer
8 següent **9** gust **10** botiguera **11** segon **3 1** v **2** v **3** f **4** f **4 1** han
decidit **2** ha passat / va passar **3** ha acceptat **4** va entrar **5** va
proclamar-se/es va proclamar **6** ha parat **7** ha participat **8** va
quedar 9 van tenir lloc **5 1** Benvolgut senyor / Benvolguda senyora
2 L'ajuntament es complau a … **3** Esperem la seva assistència a
l'acte **4** Molt atentament **5** Preguem confirmació **6** P.D. **6 1** és,
està **2** és, és **3** És, està **4** és, està **5** Estan **6** És, està **7 A** Terrassa
B Tàrrega **C** Maldà **D** Sabadell **8*** L'Andreu avui s'ha llevat a les
nou del matí, ha llegit el diari i després ha acompanyat la filla a la
ciutat. Tot seguit ha vist un client i ha jugat un partit d'esquaix que
ha guanyat. Immediatament s'ha dutxat i ha fet el dinar. Després
ha recollit la nena, ha treballat a l'ordinador i s'ha connectat a
Internet. Finalment ha anat a una festa on ha ballat i ha begut
cervesa. **9*** Ahir l'Andreu es va llevar/va llevar-se a les nou del
matí, va llegir el diari i després va acompanyar la filla a la ciutat.
Tot seguit va veure un client i va jugar un partit d'esquaix que
va guanyar. Immediatament es va dutxar/va dutxar-se i va fer el
dinar. Després va recollir la nena, va treballar a l'ordinador i es va
connectar/va connectar-se a Internet. Finalment va anar a una festa
on va ballar i va beure cervesa.

Unit 13

1 1 f 2 v 3 f 4 v 3 1d, 2a, 3b, 4h, 5f, 6e, 7c, 8g **4*** **1** No, vol
ingressar diners al seu compte. **2** No, en Tim li dóna la llibreta.
3 No, val menys. Val 1,15 dòlars. **4** No, estaran disponibles en
dos/un parell de dies feiners. **5 a 1** one **2** two **3** one **4** two **5** one
6 one **7** two **8** one **9** one **10** two **b 1** parlarà, vindran, cançó,
cargol, bonic, aniré, donem **2** parla, arriba, plàtan, donen, ràpid,
sabates, règim **3** església, secretària, música, pàgina **6 1** ha arribat,
arribarà **2** s'ha distribuït, es distribuirà **3** s'ha publicat, es publicarà
4 s'ha posat a la venda, es posarà a la venda/s'hi posarà **7 1** La
Dolors els hi col.loca. **2** No va poder comprar-me-la./No me la va
poder comprar. **3** Els meus amics ens hi convidaran. **4** Els ho diré.

5 Te les tornem. **6** Els en porto. **7** Ens n'ha repartit. **8 1** Diumenge, dinou de maig **2** 9H. del matí **3** Davant de l'Estació **4** Plaça de l'Ajuntament **5** Oficina de Turisme. Fins el quinze de maig **6** Un viatge per a dues persones a Londres **7** Una bicicleta **8** Un lot de llibres per un valor de 150€ **9 1** Em sap molt de greu/Ho sento però no podré venir. **2** Me'n vaig a Andorra a visitar un/el meu cosí que és a l'hospital. **3** M'hi estaré un parell de dies. **4** Sí, ja et trucaré. **10 1** haurà **2** pluja **3** baixaran **4** s'iniciarà **5** dominarà **6** temperatures **7** arribaran **8** bufarà **9** boira **10** farà **11** núvol **12** estarà **13** es mantindran

Unit 14

2* 1 És una empresa privada gran, filial d'una marca internacional. **2** Es dedica a la producció de productes nutricionals per a animals. **3** Ser llicenciat en químiques i tenir experiència en laboratori. **4** Dominar/Conèixer l'alemany escrit i parlat. **4 1 a** em pot posar/ puc parlar **b** Ho sento/Em sap greu **c** parlant per una altra línia **d** tornar **a** trucar **2 a** Puc parlar/Em pot posar **b** sisplau **c** part de qui **d** pengi **3 a** Digui? **b** Sí senyor. **c** hi és/hi ha d s'hi posa **5* 1** Quan hauré de començar?/Quan començo? **2** Quants treballadors té l'empresa? **3** El sou és negociable?/Es podrà discutir el sou? **4** S'ha de tenir experiència en el sector? **5** Quants dies de vacances tindré? **6** Pots/Pot tornar a trucar (més tard)? **6 1** S'ha d'utilitzar **2** S'ha de respectar **3** S'han de tirar **4** S'ha de reciclar **5** S'han de preferir **6** S'han de conduir **7** S'ha d'evitar **7** 1c, 2d, 3a, 4f, 5b, 6e **8 1** Cada dia l'hi paga **2** L'Antoni les hi posa **3** Ens la recomana **4** La hi/L'hi ensenya **5** Us els hem de deixar/Hem de deixar-vos-els **9** 1e, 2c, 3g, 4b, 5d, 6f, 7a **10 1** engega els ordinadors; etiqueta els nous exemplars; truca a la distribuïdora; encarrega les obres; connecta la caixa **2** abans de, primer de tot, llavors, tot seguit, finalment **11*** Primer/En primer lloc heu de corregir els exercicis de la setmana passada. Després agafeu el llibre de Ciències i obriu-lo a la pàgina 125. Llavors heu de copiar els dos primers paràgrafs i heu de respondre a les preguntes. Tot seguit aneu al laboratori i acabeu l'experiment. Immediatament heu d'escriure els resultats a la llibreta. Finalment deixeu les llibretes al meu despatx. **12* 1** La finalització de la temporada turística i el termini de la majoria de contractes laborals per a la recollida de fruita. **2** En primer lloc, els serveis i en segon lloc, el sector agrícola. **3** El govern ha decidit aplicar un pla (que permetrà als aturats trobar feina per a la tardor-hivern). **4** El pla consisteix en uns cursos formatius orientats a la preservació del medi ambient i de la natura (a la costa i a l'interior de Catalunya). **5** Diu que el pla li permetrà treballar tot l'any i no haver de marxar lluny a buscar feina. **6** L'atur baixarà en un 2,8 %.

Unit 15
1 1 f **2** v **3** v **4** v **4 1** el cap **2** l'esquena **3** el braç **4** el colze **5** la mà **6** el ventre **7** el dit **8** el pit **9** el genoll **10** la cama **11** el peu **12** el nas **13** l'ull **14** l'orella **15** la boca **16** el coll **5 1** deixaria **2** podria **3** canviarien **4** tindria **5** faríem **6** duraria **6 2 a** Tinc fred **b** em posaria un jersei **3 a** Tinc gana **b** menjaria alguna cosa **4 a** Tinc son **b** aniria al llit/a dormir **5 a** Estic nerviós **b** em relaxaria **6 a** Tinc set **b** beuria aigua **7 1** No aprenguis anglès. **2** No tanquis la finestra. **3** No condueixis tan ràpid. **4** No escriguis tan a poc a poc. **5** No truquis al metge. **6** No prenguis aquest medicament. **8 1**b, **2**a, **3**a, **4**b, **5**a **9 1** b and c **2** f and h **3** a, e and g **4** cuidar la (seva) salut

Unit 16
2* 1 Perquè la casa era molt vella. **2** Un armari molt antic. **3** Dels arbres que hi ha: n'hi ha tants com al jardí de la veïna del costat. **4** Els preus dels lloguers (de l'habitatge). **5** Creu que és una bestiesa, no hi està gens d'acord (abans estaven molt tranquils). **3 1** tenia **2** hi havia **3** necessitàvem **4** Eren **5** vivia **6** podia **7** estan **8** regalaven **9** Era **10** volien **11** treballava **12** em passo **5** *Preterite:* va trucar, em va agradar, van acomiadar-me, va morir, vaig empassar-me, vam quedar, va ser, va demanar, va dir, vaig vessar, vaig tacar, va comentar-nos, ens va assegurar. *Imperfect:* volia (2), havia, duia, estava, marxaven, mentia. *Translation*:* She called to tell me she wanted to talk to me. At first, I was not at all pleased. The day I got the sack, the manager also *wanted* to talk to me. And when my father died, my uncle *had to* talk to me. I swallowed doubts, saliva and fear and we agreed to meet in one of those white bars that have become fashionable. She was strangely on time. She was wearing a sky-blue dress and sunglasses. She was nervous. She ordered a very strange sandwich of boiled ham and pineapple,

and a tonic water. She had not had lunch. She said this in a way to make me understand she hadn't been hungry because she was worried, desperate or sad. Accidentally, I spilt my Coca-Cola, and stained her dress. An old woman at the next table commented that nothing would get rid of Coca-Cola stains, but the waiter assured us that the old woman was lying and, with a little bit of water, they would disappear straight away. **6** *Ha trucat* per dir-me que volia parlar amb mi. D'entrada, no *m'ha agradat* gens. El dia que van acomiadar-me de l'empresa, el gerent també *volia* parlar amb mi. I quan va morir el pare, el meu oncle *havia de* parlar amb mi. M'he empassat els dubtes, la saliva i la por, i hem quedat de trobar-nos en un d'aquests bars blancs que s'han posat de moda. Ella *ha estat* estranyament puntual. Duia un vestit de color blau cel i ulleres de sol. Estava nerviosa. *Ha demanat* un entrepà molt estrany de pernil dolç i pinya, i una tònica. No havia dinat. Ho *ha dit* de manera que jo entengués que no havia tingut gana perquè estava inquieta, desesperada o trista. Involuntàriament, *he vessat* la Coca-Cola i li he tacat el vestit. Una vella de la taula del costat ens *ha comentat* que les taques de Coca-Cola no marxaven amb res, però el cambrer ens *ha assegurat* que la vella mentia i que, amb una mica d'aigua, marxarien de seguida. **7 1** està **2** són **3** és/està **4** sóc **5** era **6** estar **7** està/és **8* 1** Sí, i vaig estar allà tota la tarda, esperant el propietari. **2** No recordava que tenia una cita amb mi. **3** Aquest pis està millor/més ben situat que la casa que vaig veure dilluns, però el pis és molt més vell. **4** Algunes portes no tancaven bé i el parquet de la sala d'estar era brut. A més, jo pensava/creia que el pis tenia dos banys però vaig trobar que només en té un. **5** Sí, hi estic d'acord, però la finestra era molt petita/petitíssima. **6** Sí. M'agradaria visitar un pis de dues habitacions, amb pàrquing inclòs al preu, amb una gran terrassa i calefacció central. **9 1d, 2c, 3a, 4b 10 1c, 2a, 3c, 4b.**

Catalan–English vocabulary

This wordlist is not intended to be exhaustive, and it will have limited use except as a complement to the course itself. It does not include articles (Units 1, 2, 6), numbers (Units 1, 2, 3), possessives (Unit 2), subject and object pronouns (Units 1, 4, 6), days, months or seasons (Units 5, 7). Adverbs in **-ment** (Unit 8) are given only in special cases. Also excluded are words whose form and meaning is identical or very close to English. The conjugation of verbs marked with an asterisk is given in the **Reference tables**. The symbol > indicates a change of construction. Numbers in brackets refer to units.

a *to, at, in, on*
a part *except for, apart from*
abandonar *to leave, to give up*
abans (de) *before*
abans-d'ahir *day before yesterday*
abraçada *(f.) embrace*
abrigar-se *to put on warm clothes, to keep warm*
acabar *to end, to finish;* **acabar de ...,** *to have just ...*
acomiadar *to see off, to dismiss;* **acomiadar-se** *to say good-bye*
acompanyar *to accompany, to give a lift*
aconsellar *to advise, to recommend*
acord *(m.) agreement;* **d'acord** *fine, agreed;* **estar* d'acord** *to agree*
acostar-se *to approach, to go/ come near*
acostumar a *to do usually; to be in the habit of*

acte *(m.) event, ceremony*
actualment *now, at present*
adéu *goodbye*
adonar-se *to realize*
adreça *(f.) address*
adrogueria *(f.) hardware shop*
advocat *(m.) lawyer*
afaitar-se *to shave*
afavorir *to favour*
afeccionar-se *to grow fond of*
afegir *to add*
afores *(m. pl.) outskirts*
agafar *to take;* **agafar a pit** *to take to heart*
agradable *pleasant, nice*
agradar *to appeal, to be pleasing;* > *to like (U6)*
agroturisme *(m.) farm house accommodation*
ahir *yesterday*
aigua *(f.) water;* **aigua amb gas/ sense gas** *fizzy/still mineral water*

aïllat/-da isolated
aire condicionat (m.) air conditioning
així thus, so, like this/that; **així que** so, as soon as; **així com** and also
això this, that; **això rai** no problem!
ajuda (f.) help
ajudar to help
ajuntament (m.) town hall
alberg de joventut (m.) youth hostel
alcalde (m.) mayor
alçada (f.) height
alegre/-a cheerful
alemany/-a German
aleshores then
algú someone, somebody
algun/-a any, some
alimentació (f.) food
all (m.) garlic
allà there
allioli (m.) garlic and oil paste
allò that
allotjament (m.) accommodation
alt/-a high, tall
altre/-a other
alumne/-a (m./f.) pupil, student
amable kind, nice
amanida (f.) salad
amant (m./f.) **(de)** lover, fond of
amb with, in; by (transport)
ambdós/-dues both
amic/amiga (m./f.) friend
amistat (f.) friendship
amor (m.) love
amplada (f.) width

ample/-a wide, large, full
ampli/àmplia wide
ampolla (f.) bottle
amunt up(wards), high
anada (f.) outward journey
anar* to go; **anar bé** to be fine/all right
anar-se'n* to go (away)
andalús/-usa Andalusian
ànec (m.) duck
anglès/-esa English
aniversari (m.) birthday
anterior preceding, earlier
antic/-ga old, ancient
antipàtic/-a unlikeable, unfriendly
antiquari (m.) antique dealer
anunci (m.) advertisement
anxova (f.) anchovy
any (m.) year; **fer* anys** to have one's birthday; **per molts anys!** happy birthday!
apa! come on!
aparcar to park
aparellador/-a (m/f.) master builder
apartar to move away, to separate
àpat (m.) meal
aprendre* to learn
aprenent (m.) apprentice, learner
aprimar-se to slim, to lose weight
aprofitar to take advantage
apropar-se to approach, to go/come near
apuntar-se to enrol, to sign up
aquarel·la (f.) watercolour

aquí *here;* **aquí mateix** *right here;* **d'aquí a ...,** *in ... (from now)*
ara *now;* **ara mateix** *right now*
arbre *(m.) tree*
armari *(m.) cupboard, wardrobe*
arquitecte/-a *(m./f.) architect*
arran de *level with; immediately after, as a result of*
arreglar *to fix, to repair, to sort out*
arreu *everywhere*
arribada *(f.) arrival*
arribar *to arrive*
arrissat/-da *curly-haired*
ascensor *(m.) lift*
assegurança *(f.) insurance*
assegurar *to assure, to insure*
assistència *(f.) attendance, presence*
assortit *(m.) selection, range*
atent/-a *polite, attentive*
atentament *sincerely, faithfully*
atracament *(m.) hold-up*
atractiu/-iva *attractive*
atur *(m.) unemployment*
aturat/-da *unemployed*
au! *come on!*
autobús *(m.) bus*
autocar *(m.) coach*
autovia *(f.) dual carriageway*
avall *down(wards)*
avi/àvia *(m./f.) grandfather/ mother*
aviat *soon, early;* **més aviat** *rather*
avinguda *(f.) avenue*
avió *(m.) aeroplane*
avorrit/-da *boring, bored*
avui *today;* **avui dia,** *these days*

bacallà *(m.) cod*
badia *(f.) bay*
baix *(m.) bass*
baix/-a *small, short, low*
(a) baix *down, below*
baixada *(f.) fall, decrease*
baixar *to go/come down, to take down; to get out of (vehicle)*
ball *(m.) dance, dancing*
ballar *to dance*
banc *(m.) bank*
bany *(m.) bathroom, toilet*
banyar-se *to bathe, to take a bath*
barat/-a *cheap*
barca *(f.) (small) boat*
barra *(f.) baguette; bar, counter*
barrejar *to mix*
barri *(m.) neighbourhood, district*
bateria *(f.) drum-kit, drums*
bé *well, fine*
beguda *(f.) drink*
ben *very, really*
benefici *(m.) profit*
benvolgut/-da *dear*
berenar *(m.) afternoon light meal*
bessó/-ona *(m./f.) twin*
bestiesa *(f.) madness, stupid thing*
beure* *to drink*
biblioteca *(f.) library*
bicicleta *(f.) bicycle*
bistec *(m.) steak*
bitllet *(m.) ticket; banknote*
blanc/-a *white*
blau/-va *blue*
bo (bon)/bona *good (U4)*
boca *(f.) mouth*

boig/boja *mad*
boira *(f.) fog*
bol *(m.) bowl*
bolet *(m.) mushroom*
bonic/-a *nice, pretty, attractive*
bosc *(m.) forest, wood*
bossa *(f.) bag, handbag*
botifarra *(f.) Catalan sausage*
botiga *(f.) shop*
botiguer/-a *(m./f.) shopkeeper*
botó *(m.) button*
braç *(m.) arm*
a la brasa *charcoal-grilled*
breu *short, brief*
brusa *(f.) blouse*
brut/-a *dirty; gross, before tax*
bufar *to blow*
bullir *to boil*
buscar *to look for*
bústia *(f.) mailbox*
butaca *(f.) armchair*

ca *house, home (U6)*
cabell *(m.) hair*
cabina telefònica *(f.) telephone box*
cada *each, every*
cadira *(f.) chair*
cafè *(m.) coffee*
caixa *(f.) savings bank; checkout, till*
caixer automàtic *(m.) cash machine*
calaix *(m.) drawer*
calaixera *(f.) chest of drawers*
calamar *(m.) squid*
calamarsa *(f.) hail*
calçat *(m.) footwear*

caldre* *to be necessary, must (U15)*
calefacció *(f.) heating*
calent/-a *hot*
calés *(m. pl.) money (colloquial)*
callar *to be quiet*
calor *(f.) hot;* **tenir* calor** *to be/ feel hot*
cama *(f.) leg*
cambrer/-a *(m./f.) waiter*
camí *(m.) track, way*
caminar *to walk*
camió *(m.) lorry*
camisa *(f.) shirt*
camp *(m.) field, country*
campanya *(f.) campaign*
càmping *(m.) camp site*
campió/-ona *(m./f.) champion*
campionat *(m.) championship*
can/cal/ca l' *(see* **ca***)*
cançó *(f.) song*
cansat/-da *tiring, tired*
cantonada *(f.) corner*
canvi *(m.) change, exchange;* **en canvi** *on the other hand*
canviar *to change*
cap *(m.) head, end*
cap *any; none, not one (U6)*
cap a *towards*
capa *(f.) layer*
capaç *able, capable*
capdamunt *(m.) top*
capdavall *(m.) bottom*
car/-a *expensive, dear*
cara *(f.) face*
carai! *gosh!*
cargol *(m.) snail*
carn *(f.) meat*

carnet (m.) **carnet de conduir** driving licence; **carnet d'identitat**, identity card
carnisseria (f.) butcher's (shop)
càrrec (m.) load, weight; charge, duty; **a càrrec de** chargeable to
carrer (m.) street
carrera (f.) university studies; career
carretera (f.) (main) road
carta (f.) letter; playing card; menu
carter/-a (m./f.) postman/woman
cartera (f.) wallet
cartró (m.) cardboard
casa (f.) house, home; **casa de pagès** farmhouse
casar-se to get married
casat/-da married
castell (m.) castle
castellà/-ana Castilian
caure* to fall (down); **caure malament** > to dislike
cava (m.) cava, Catalan sparkling wine
cavall (f.) horse
ceba (f.) onion
cel (m.) sky
cèntim (m.) cent
centre comercial (m.) shopping centre
cercar to look for
cert/-a certain, sure; **per cert** by the way
cervesa (f.) beer
científic/-a scientist, scientific
cine/cinema (m.) cinema
cintura (f.) waist

cinturó (m.) belt
cita (f.) appointment
ciutat (f.) city, town
clar/-a clear, light, light-coloured; **és clar** of course, obviously
classe (f.) class, lesson; classroom
clau (f.) key
client/-a (m./f.) customer
cobert/-a covered, overcast
coberts (m. pl.) cutlery
coca (f.) flat cake
codi (m.) code
cognom (m.) surname
col (f.) cabbage
col.locar to place, to insert
coll (m.) neck, throat
colze (m.) elbow
com how, as, like; **com que as**, since; **com va això?** how are you?
comarca (f.) district, region
comarcal local
començar to start, to begin
comentar to comment/remark on
comissaria (f.) police station
còmode/-a comfortable
compartir to share
complaure's to be pleased
comportament (m.) behaviour
comprar to buy
compte (m.) bill, account
conduir to drive
conèixer* to know, to meet
congelat/-da frozen
conill (m.) rabbit
conjunt (m.) combination; **de conjunt** matching
connectar to plug in
consulta (f.) surgery

content/-a *pleased, happy*
contestador *(m.) answering machine*
contra *against;* **estar* en contra** *to disagree*
contractar *to hire, to engage*
contracte *(m.) contract*
convidar *to invite*
convidat/-da *(m./f.) guest*
cop *(m.) blow, knock; time;* **cop d'ull** *glance, quick look*
copa *(f.) glass (with stem)*
corbata *(f.) tie*
corregir *to correct*
córrer* *to run*
correu *(m.) mail*
correus *(m. pl.) post office*
cortina *(f.) curtain*
cos *(m.) body*
cosa *(f.) thing*
cosí/-ina *(m./f.) cousin*
cost *(m.) cost, price*
costa *(f.) coast*
costar *to cost; to be hard*
costat *(m.) side;* **al costat de** *next to*
cotxe *(m.) car*
coure *to cook*
crear *to create, to make*
cregut/-da *conceited, big headed*
crema *(f.) cream, sun-cream*
crema catalana *(f.) crème brulée*
creuer *(m.) cruise*
creure* *to believe, to think*
cru/-a *raw*
cua *(f.) tail, queue*
cuidar *to look after, to take care of*

cuina *(f.) kitchen, cuisine*
cuit/-a *cooked, stewed*
cullera *(f.) spoon*
cunyat/-da *(m./f.) brother-/sister-in-law*
curs *(m.) course*
cursa *(f.) race*
curt/-a *short*

dades *(f. pl.) data*
dalt *above, upstairs*
damunt (de) *on (top of), over*
danès/-esa *Danish*
darrer/-a *last, latest*
darrere (de) *behind*
davant (de) *in front (of)*
de *of, from*
de debò *real, really, for sure*
dèbil *weak*
decidir *to decide*
dedicar *to dedicate; to spend (time);* **dedicar-se (a)** *to work (as)*
deixalla *(f.) rubbish*
deixar *to leave, to lend/loan; to let/allow;* **deixar de** *to stop*
demà *tomorrow;* **demà passat** *the day after tomorrow*
demanar *to ask for*
demanda *(f.) request, demand*
dent *(f.) tooth*
dependre *to depend*
des de *since*
desanimat/-da *discouraged, downhearted*
desaparegut/-da *missing*
desaparèixer *disappear*
descafeïnat *decaffeinated*

descans (m.) rest, break
descansar to rest
descobrir to discover, to find out
desconnectar to switch off
desconegut/-da unknown
desesperat/-da desperate
desitjar to want
desmotivat/-da dispirited, listless
despatx (m.) office
despertar-se to wake up
despesa (f.) expense, expenditure
després after (wards)
destacar to (make) stand out,
  to highlight
Déu n'hi do! [emphatic
  affirmation or agreement]
deure* to owe; must = to be likely
  (U9)
dia (m.) day; **bon dia** good day/
  morning
diari/-ària daily; **diari** (m.)
  newspaper
dinar to have lunch; **dinar** (m.)
  lunch, midday meal
diner(s) (m.) money
dineral (m.) piles of money
(a) dins de inside, in
dipòsit (m.) tank, deposit
dir* to say, to tell; **dir-se** to be
  called (U1)
direcció prohibida (f.) one way
  (traffic)
dirigir to direct
disc (m.) disc, record
discurs (m.) speech
discutir to discuss
disparar to fire, to launch;
  disparar-se, to rocket (prices)

disponible available
a disposar you are welcome!
dissenyador/-a (m./f.) designer
distribuir to deliver
dit (m.) finger
divertir-se to enjoy oneself, to
  have fun
divertit/-da amusing
doble double
dolent/-a bad
dolor (m.) pain
domini (m.) command
dona (f.) wife, woman
donar to give, **donar a** to look
  out on, to face towards
doncs well, so, then
dormir to sleep
dret (m.) right, entitlement
dret/-a right, straight; **tot dret**
  straight ahead
dreta (f.) right-hand side
dubte (m.) doubt
dur* to carry, to wear
durant during, for
durar to last
dutxa (f.) shower
dutxar-se to take a shower

econòmic/-a cheap, economical
edat (f.) age
edifici (m.) building
editorial (f.) publishing house
educat/-da good mannered,
  polite
efectiu cash; **en efectiu** in cash
ei hey!
eixida (f.) exit, way out; departure
elaborar to prepare, to make

elaborat/-da refined
elegant elegant
elevat/-da high
embaràs (m.) pregnancy
embotit (m.) cured meat, salami
empassar-se to swallow
empleat/-da (m./f.) employee, clerk
empresa (f.) enterprise, business
emprovador (m.) fitting room
emprovar-se to try on
en in, at, on
encantat/-da charmed, nice to meet you
encara still; **encara no** not yet; **encara que** although
encarregar to order; **encarregar-se (de)** to be in charge of
encendre* to switch on, to light
enciam (m.) lettuce
endarrere back(wards)
endavant ahead, forward
endur-se* to take away
enfadar-se to get angry
enfadat/-da angry
enfeinat/-da busy
enganyar to deceive
engegar to switch on, to start, to set in motion
enginyer/-a (m./f.) engineer
enguany this year
enhorabona! congratulations
ennuvolat/-da cloudy
ensenyar to show, to teach
entendre* to understand; **entesos** OK, fine
entrada (f.) entrance; ticket (for entry); down payment; **d'entrada** first(ly), at first
entrar to enter, to come/go in

entre between, among
entrecot (m.) steak
entrenar-se to train
entrepà (m.) sandwich
entrevista (f.) interview
enviar to send
equipar to fit out
equipatge (m.) luggage
equivocar-se to be wrong
error (m.) mistake
escacs (m. pl.) chess
escala (f.) staircase, stairs
escalar to climb
escalivada (f.) chargrilled vegetables
escenari (m.) stage, set
escocès/-esa Scottish
escola (f.) school
escollir to choose
escoltar to listen (to)
escriure* to write
escudella (i carn d'olla) (f.) traditional stew
església (f.) church
esmorzar to have breakfast, (m.) breakfast
espantat/-da frightened
espanyol/-a Spanish
espardenya (f.) espadrille, trainer
espàrrec (m.) asparagus
especialitat (f.) speciality
espera (f.) waiting
esperar to wait (for), to hope, to expect
espès/-essa thick
esport (m.) sport
esprai (m.) spray
esquaix (m.) squash (sport)

esqueixada (f.) dried cod, shredded and dressed
esquena (f.) back
esquerra (f.) left-hand side
esquiar to ski
est (m.) east
estació (f.) station
estacionament (m.) parking
estacionar to park
estalvis (m. pl.) savings
estalviar to save
estanc (m.) tobacconist's (shop)
estar* to be; **estar a punt de** to be about to; **estar d'acord** to agree; **estar en contra**, to disagree; **estar-se** to live, to stay (U2)
estat civil (m.) marital status
estel (m.) star
estimar to love, to be fond of; **estimar-se més** to prefer
estirat/-da straight
estómac (m.) stomach
estona (f.) (short) time
estranger/-a, foreign(er); **a l'estranger** abroad
estrany/-a strange
estret/-a tight, narrow
estudiant (m./f.) student
estudiar to study
estufa (f.) heater, stove
etapa (f.) period, stage
etiquetar to label
evitar to avoid
exacte/-a exact; that's right, right
excursió (f.) trip, outing
exemplar (m.) copy (of book)
èxit (m.) success

experiència (f.) experience
explicar to explain
exposició (f.) exhibition
extravagant eccentric, outlandish

fa ago (U10)
fabricar to manufacture
fàcil easy
facultat (f.) faculty
faldilla (f.) skirt
faltar to be missing/lacking
família (f.) family
farina (f.) flour
farmàcia (f.) chemist's (shop)
fart/-a fed up
fat/-da tasteless
fatal not (at all) good, rubbish
favor (m.) favour; **a favor (de)** for, in favour (of); **per favor** please
feble weak
febre (f.) fever, temperature
feina (f.) work, job
feiner, dia working day
feliç happy
felicitats! congratulations!, happy birthday!
fer* to do, to make (and numerous idioms): **fer bondat** to behave oneself; **fer cas (de)** to pay attention (to); **fer córrer** to draw (curtains); **fer cua** to queue; **fer de** to work/have a job as; **fer falta** to be necessary; **fer fora** to get rid of; **fer llit** to stay in bed; **fer mal** to hurt; **fer res** > to mind (U8); **fer-s'ho** to manage
ferit/-da wounded, injured
festa (f.) party, festival

fet (m.) fact, event
fet/-a done, cooked
ficar to put in
fill/-a (m./f.) son/daughter
final (m.) end; **al final de tot (de)** at the very top/end (of)
finestra (f.) window
fins (a) until, up to, as far as; **fins que** until; **fins i tot** even; **fins després** see you later
fira (f.) market
fitxa (f.) filing card
flam (m.) crème caramel
fleca (f.) baker's (shop)
flor (f.) flower
foc (m.) fire, burner, ring
fonda (f.) inn
fons bottom, end; background; stock; **al fons** at the bottom/end
(a) fora out, outside
força very, quite a lot (of)
formació (f.) training
formar part to take part
formatge (m.) cheese
forn (m.) oven; **al forn** baked; **forn de pa** (m.) baker's (shop)
forquilla (f.) fork
fort/-a strong, heavy, powerful
fosc/-a dark; **a les fosques** in the dark
fotut/-da in a (bloody) bad way (colloquial)
francès/-esa French
fred (m.) cold(ness); **tenir* fred** to be/feel cold
fregir to fry
fresc/-a fresh, cool
fruit (m.) fruit; **fruit sec** dried fruit

fruita (f.) (fresh) fruit
fruiteria (f.) green grocer's (shop)
fumador/-a (m./f.) smoker
fumar to smoke
funcionar to work
fuster (m.) carpenter, joiner

(no) gaire (not) very, (not) very much; (pl) (not) very many
gairebé nearly, almost
galeta (f.) biscuit
gamba (f.) prawn
gana (f.) hunger; **tenir* gana** to be/feel hungry; **tenir* ganes de** to be keen to
ganivet (m.) knife
gasolina (f.) petrol
gastar(-se) to spend
gaudir (de) to enjoy
gelat (m.) ice cream
genoll (m.) knee
(no) gens (not) any (U6); not at all
gent (f.) people
gerent (m.) manager
germà/-na (m./f.) brother/sister
gimnàs (m.) gym(nasium)
girar to turn
gos (m.) dog
got (m.) glass
govern (m.) government
gràcies thanks/thank you
gran big; elder
gras/-sa fat
gratinar to brown under grill
gratuït/-a free
grau (m.) degree
greu serious; **saber* greu >** to be sorry

grip *(f.) influenza*
gris/-a *grey*
groc/-ga *yellow*
gros/-sa *big*
gual *(m.) ford; entrance* (no parking)
guant *(m.) glove*
guanyar *to win*
guarnició *(f.) garnish*
guia *(m./f.) guide; (f.) guide book*
guitarra *(f.) guitar*
gust *taste, pleasure;* **molt de gust** *pleased to meet you;* **pel meu gust** *to/for my taste;* **venir* de gust** *to appeal > to feel like*

habitació *(f.) room, bedroom*
habitatge *(m.) housing*
haver* *to have (auxiliary: U12);* **haver de** *to have to, must (U14)*
hi ha *there is, there are*
història *(f.) history, story*
hola *hello*
home *(m.) man*
home! *well (exclamation)*
hora *(f.) hour; time (U3)*
horari *(m.) timetable, opening hours;* **horari intensiu,** *continuous working day without lunchtime break*
hostal *(m.) budget hotel*
hostaler/a *(m./f.) hotel owner*
humor *(m.) mood*

i *and*
igual *equal, (the) same;* **igualment** *me too, likewise*

il·limitat/-da *unlimited*
importar *to import; to matter, to be important*
imprescindible *essential*
inauguració *(f.) opening*
incendi *(m.) fire*
inclòs/-osa *included; including*
independitzar-se *to become self-sufficient*
indicació *(f.) sign*
individual *individual, single (room)*
infància *(f.) childhood*
infermer/-a *(m./f.) nurse*
influir *to influence, to affect*
infusió *(f.) infusion, herbal tea*
ingressar *to pay in; to admit (to hospital)*
iniciar *to start, to begin*
inquiet/-a *anxious, worried*
instal.lació *(f.) fittings, equipment; facility*
intel.ligent *intelligent, clever*
interessant *interesting*
involuntari/-ària *accidental, not deliberate*
irlandès/-esa *Irish*
italià/-ana *Italian*

ja *already, yet, (by) now (U7);* **ja no** *no longer*
japonès/-esa *Japanese*
jaqueta *(f.) jacket*
jardí *(m.) garden*
jersei *(m.) jersey, jumper*
joc *(m.) game;* **a joc** *matching*
joieria *(f.) jeweller's (shop)*
jove *young*

jovent (m.) young people
jugar to play
just/-a right; **justament** as it
  happens

laborable working
lamentar to be sorry
lampista (m./f.) plumber
lavabo (m.) toilet, WC; washbasin
licor (m.) spirit
línia (f.) line
lot (m.) batch, portion
lladre (m./f.) thief
llana (f.) wool
llarg/-a long
llargada (f.) length
llàstima (f.) pity
llauna (f.) tin, can
llavors then, next
llegir to read
llei (f.) law
llençol (m.) sheet (for bed)
llengua (f.) language; tongue
llenguado (m.) sole
llest/-a clever, bright
llet (f.) milk
lletrejar to spell
llevar-se to get up
llevat (m.) yeast
llibre (m.) book
llibreta (f.) notebook, exercise
  book; passbook
llicenciat/-da (m./f.) graduate
lliçó (f.) lesson
llimona (f.) lemon
llit (m.) bed
lliura esterlina (f.) pound
  (sterling)

lliure free
lloc (m.) place; **tenir* lloc** to take
  place
llogar to hire, to rent
lloguer (m.) rent, hire charge
lluç (m.) hake
llum (f.) light; (m.) lamp, lighting
lluny far

mà (f.) hand
maco/-a nice, attractive
maduixa (f.) strawberry
madur/-a ripe
(no) mai (not) ever, never
major bigger, biggest; main
majoria (f.) majority
mal (m.) harm, badness, pain;
  mal de cap (m.) headache;
  fer* mal to hurt
mal/-a bad; **malament** in a bad
  way, badly
malaltia (f.) illness
maleta (f.) suitcase
mandra (f.) lethargy, laziness
manera (f.) manner, way;
  de manera que so, so that
mantega (f.) butter
mantenir to maintain
mapa (m.) map
maquillar-se to put on make up
mar (m./f.) sea
marca (f.) (trade) mark, brand
mare (f.) mother
marejar-se to be/feel (travel) sick
marejat/-da feeling sick
mariner/-a marine
marit (m.) husband
marró brown

marxar *to leave, to go away*
masia *(f.) farmhouse, farmstead*
massa *(f.) dough*
massa *too much*
matalàs *(m.) mattress*
mateix/-a *same, self;* **ahir mateix** *just yesterday*
matí *(m.) morning*
matinada *(f.) early morning*
mató *(m.) cottage cheese, curds*
mecànic *(m.) mechanic*
medi ambient *(m.) environment*
medicament *(m.) medicine, medication*
meitat *(f.) half, middle*
mel *(f.) honey*
melmelada *(f.) jam*
meló *(m.) melon*
menjador *(m.) dining room*
menjar *to eat; to have lunch; (m.) food*
menor *smaller, smallest*
mensual *monthly*
mentida *(f.) lie*
mentir *to lie*
mentre *while*
menú *(m.) (set) menu, table d'hôte*
menys *less, least*
mercat *(m.) market*
mes *(m.) month*
més *more, most, else;* **més aviat** *rather, tending to be;* **a més** *as well, moreover*
mescla *(f.) mixture*
mestre/-a *(m./f.) school teacher*
mestressa de casa *(f.) housewife*
mesura *(f.) measure*

metge/-ssa *(m./f.) doctor;* **metge de capçalera** *GP, family doctor*
metro *(m.) underground*
mica *(f.) (little) bit*
mida *(f.) measurement;* **anar* a la mida** *to fit*
mig *(m.) middle*
mig/-tja *half*
migdia *(m.) noon, midday*
millor *better, best*
mínim/-a *minimum, least;* **com a mínim** *at least*
minut *(m.) minute*
mirall *(m.) mirror*
mirar *to watch, to look (at)*
missatge *(m.) message*
mitjà *(m.) means, way;* **mitjans de comunicació** *media*
mitjó *(m.) sock*
moble *(m.) item of furniture*
moda *(f.) fashion*
molestar *to annoy*
moll/-a *wet*
molt *very*
molt/-a *much, a lot; (pl), many*
moment *(m.) moment;* **de moment** *at present, for the time being*
món *(m.) world*
moneda *(f.) coin, currency*
mongeta *(f.) bean*
morè/-ena *dark-haired/skinned*
morir *to die*
moro/-a *Moorish*
mostrar *to show, to display*
moto *(f.) motorbike*
mullar *to soak;* **mullar-se** *to get wet*

mundial *worldwide*
munt *(m.) heap, lot*
muntanya *(f.) mountain*
muntar *to assemble, to set up*
música *(f.) music*

naixement *(m.) birth*
nap *(m.) turnip*
nas *(m.) nose*
nata *(f.) cream*
nebot/-da *(m./f.) nephew/niece*
necessitar *to need*
nedar *to swim*
negoci *(m.) business*
negre/-a *black, red* (wine)
nen/-a *(m./f.) (young) child,*
  boy/girl
néixer* *to be born*
nerviós/-osa *nervous*
net/-a *clean; after tax*
netejar *to clean*
neu *(f.) snow*
nevada *(f.) snow fall*
nevar *to snow*
nevera *(f.) fridge*
ni *neither, nor; not even*
ningú *nobody*
nit *(f.) night;* **bona nit** *good night*
nivell *(m.) level*
no *no, not;* **no ... pas**
  (emphatically) *not*
noi/-a *(m./f.) boy/girl*
nom *(m.) name, first name*
només *only*
nord *(m.) north*
notar *to (take) note, to notice*
nou/-va *new*

número *(m.) number*
núvol *(m.) cloud;* (adj.) *cloudy*

o *or*
obert/-a *open*
oblidar *to forget*
obligatori/-òria *mandatory*
obra *(f.) play, drama, work*
obrir* *to open*
ocupat/-da *busy*
oest *(m.) west*
oferir *to offer*
oferta *(f.) offer*
oficina *(f.) office*
oh i tant! *of course!*
oi? *isn't that so? (U10)*
oli *(m.) oil*
oliva *(f.) olive*
olla *(f.) cooking pot*
on *where*
oncle *(m.) uncle*
opció *(f.) option*
opinar *to have an opinion, to think*
oposar-se *to object*
ordenar *to put in order,*
  to arrange
ordinador *(m.) computer*
orella *(f.) ear*
orgullós/-osa *proud*
ostres! *gosh!*
ou *(m.) egg*

pa *(m.) bread*
pagar *to pay (for)*
pagès/-esa *(m./f.) country*
  person
pàgina *(f.) page*

país (m.) country
paisatge (m.) landscape, scenery
paleta (m./f.) bricklayer, builder
pantalons (m. pl.) trousers
paperera (f.) waste-paper basket
paquet (m.) packet, parcel
parada (f.) stop
parar to stop; **parar la taula** to lay the table; **parar el sol** to sit out in the sun
paraula (f.) word
pare father; (pl.) parents
parell (m.) pair, couple
parella (f.) couple (people)
paret (f.) wall
parlar to talk, to speak
parquímetre (m.) parking meter
pàrquing (m.) car park
part (f.) part, side; a part, separately; **de part de qui?** who is calling?
partit (m.) game, match
passadís (m.) corridor
passaport (m.) passport
passar to pass; to cross; to call in; to happen; to put on (telephone); to spend (time)
passar-s'ho bé to have a good time; **passi-ho-bé** goodbye (formal)
passar a + inf. to go/come and …
passat/-da last
passeig (m.) promenade
passejar to go for a walk
pasta (f.) pastry, cake, bun
pastanaga (f.) carrot
pastilla (f.) tablet, pill

pastís (m.) cake, pie
pastisseria (f.) cake shop
patata (f.) potato
patinatge (m.) skating
patir to suffer, to bear
pau (f.) peace
pebrot (m.) pepper
peça (f.) piece
peix (m.) fish
peixateria (f.) fish shop
pel.lícula (f.) film, movie
pell (f.) skin, leather
pèl-roig/roja red haired
penjar to hang (up)
pensar to think; (+ inf.) to intend
pensió (f.) guest house; **pensió completa** full board; **mitja pensió** half board
pentinar(-se) to comb (one's hair)
pentinat (m.) hairstyle
per by, through, for, along; (+ inf.) in order to (U9); **per a** for (U9)
per què? why?
pera (f.) pear
perdonar to forgive, to excuse
perdre to lose
perfeccionament (m.) improvement
perfecte/-a perfect, all right
periodista (m./f.) journalist
perjudicat/-da damaged
pernil (m.) ham; **pernil dolç/ salat** boiled/cured ham
però but, however
perquè because; in order that (U9)
perruquer/-a (m./f.) hairdresser

persona (f.) person
personal (m.) staff
pes (m.) weight
pesar to weigh
pescar to fish
petit/-a small; **de petit/-a** when I was young
petó (m.) kiss
peu (m.) foot; **a peu** on foot, walking
pintor/-a (m./f.) painter
pintura (f.) painting
pinya (f.) pineapple
pis (m.) floor; apartment, flat
piscina (f.) swimming pool
pista (f.) track, court; ski run
pit (m.) chest, breast
pitjor worse
plaça (f.) square; seat, place, position
planxa (f.) grill
planxar to iron
plat (m.) dish, plate, course (of meal)
plàtan (m.) banana
platja (f.) beach
ple/-na full
plegar to finish (work)
plom (m.) lead
ploure* to rain
pluja (f.) rain
població (f.) town, city, village; population
poble (m.) village, town
pobre/-a poor
poc (m.) a little
poc/-a little, small; not much, (pl.) not many; **a poc a poc** slowly, gradually

poder* to be able, can
policia (f.) police (force)
pollastre (m.) chicken
poma (f.) apple
pont (m.) bridge
por (f.) fear; **fer* por** to frighten; **tenir* por** to be afraid
porc (m.) pig, pork
porro (m.) leek
porta (f.) door
portal (m.) access, doorway
portar to carry, to bring, to take, to wear, to drive
portuguès/-esa Portuguese
posar to put, to put on; **posar-se** to become; **posar-se al telèfon** to come to/answer the phone
postal (f.) postcard
postguerra (f.) postwar period
postres (f. pl.) dessert; **per postres** on top (of all that)
pot (m.) can, tin
potser perhaps, maybe
preciós/-osa lovely, beautiful
preferir to prefer
pregar to pray; to ask (for), to beg
pregunta (f.) question
preguntar to ask
prémer to press
premi (m.) prize, award
prendre* to take
preocupat/-da worried
preparar to prepare, to get ready
presentar to present, to introduce
préssec (m.) peach
prestatge (m.) shelf
preu (m.) price
preveure to foresee

prim/-a *slim, thin*
primer/-a *first*
principi *(m.) beginning; principle*
privat/-da *private*
professor/-a *teacher* (secondary),
  lecturer (university)
programa *(m.) programme*
prohibit/-da *forbidden*
prometre *to promise*
pronosticar *to predict, to forecast*
(a) prop (de) *near (to), close (to)*
proper/-a *next*
propi/-òpia *own*
propina *(f.) tip*
proposar *to propose*
proposta *(f.) proposal*
prou *enough, sufficient(ly);*
  definitely, of course
prova *(f.) test, proof*
provar *to try, to taste, to test*
publicar *to publish*
pujada *(f.) rise*
pujar *to go/come up; to take/*
  carry up
pulmó *(m.) lung*
punt *(m.) point, dot;* **en punt**,
  exactly (time); **estar* a punt de**
  to be about/ready to
puntual *punctual, on time*

quadre *(m.) picture*
quan *when*
quant/-a *how much; (pl.) how*
  many
quantitat *(f.) quantity, amount*
quart *(m.) quarter*
que *which, who (U9); that; than;*
  because (U13); **que** + *adj.*
  how ...!

què? *what?*
quedar *to be left, to remain;*
  > to have left (U6); to be
  situated; to suit; to agree (on
  an arrangement); **quedar-se** *to*
  stay
queixal *(m.) (back) tooth*
queviures *(m. pl.) groceries*
qui *who*
quilo *(m.) kilo(gram)*
quilometratge *(m.) mileage*
  (in km)
química *(f.) chemistry*
quin/-a? *which?, what?*

ràbia *(f.) rage, anger*
ràdio *(f.) radio*
raïm *(m.) grape(s)*
raó *(f.) reason;* **tenir* raó** *to be*
  right
rap *(m.) monkfish*
ràpid/-a *quick, fast*
rebedor *(m.) entrance, hall*
rebre *to receive*
recepció *(f.) reception*
recepta *(f.) recipe, prescription*
receptar *to prescribe*
recipient *(m.) receptacle*
recollida *(f.) collection, gathering*
recollir *to collect, to pick (up)*
recomanar *to recommend*
recordar *to remember,*
  to remind
recorregut *(m.) route*
recuit *(m.) curds, cottage cheese*
redistribuir *to rearrange*
reduir *to reduce*
reemborsable *refundable*
refredar-se *to have/catch a cold*

refredat (m.) (head) cold
refresc (m.) soft drink
refugi (m.) shelter, lodge
regalar to give (as a present)
règim (m.) diet
rei (m.) king
rellotge (m.) watch, clock
renovació (f.) renewal
rentar to wash, to clean
repartir to distribute, to deliver
repetir to repeat
repòs (m.) rest
representació (f.) performance
requerir to ask (for), to request, to require
(no) res (not) anything, nothing; **de res** don't mention it; **no hi fa res** don't worry about it/that; **res més** nothing else
requisit (m.) requirement
reserva (f.) booking, reservation
reservar to book
resoldre to solve, to resolve
respondre to respond, to reply
resposta (f.) answer
retard (m.) delay
retirar to remove
retirat/-da retired
reunió (f.) meeting
revista (f.) magazine
riu (m.) river
riure* to laugh
roba (f.) clothes
robar to steal, to commit burglary
robatori (m.) robbery, burglary
roig/-ja red
romà/-ana Roman
ros/-sa fair haired, fair skinned

rosa pink
rosat rosé (wine)
rostir to roast
rotonda (f.) roundabout

sabata (f.) shoe
saber* to know; **saber greu** > to be sorry
sabó (m.) soap
sal (f.) salt
sala (f.) room; **sala d'estar** living room
salat/-da salty
saltar to jump; **saltar-se** to miss, to get round
salut (f.) health
salvatge wild
samarreta (f.) vest, T-shirt
sandàlies (f. pl.) sandals
secretari/-ària (m./f.) secretary
segell (m.) (postage) stamp
segle (m.) century
segon/-a second
segons according to, depending on
següent following
seguir to follow; to continue, to go on
seguit (m.) series, sequence or **(seguit/-da) de seguida** immediately, straight away; **tot seguit** then, next see **sigui** below
segur/-a safe, sure
seguretat (f.) safety, security
seleccionar to select
semàfor (m.) traffic lights
semblant similar, like, alike

semblar to seem; > to think (U6)
sempre always; **com sempre** as usual
senglar (m.) wild boar
sens dubte definitely
sense without
sentir to feel; to hear; to be sorry; **ho sento** I'm sorry
senyal (m.) signal, tone
senyor/-a (m./f.) gentleman/lady; sir/madam
senzill/-a simple, natural, straightforward
ser* to be (U1); **som-hi** let's go
seriós/-osa serious
servei (m.) service
servir to serve
set (f.) thirst; **tenir* set** to be thirsty
seure* to sit (down), to be seated
setmana (f.) week; **cap de setmana** (m.) weekend
si if
sí yes
sigui: o sigui that is (to say)
simpàtic/-a nice
sisplau/si us plau please
situar to place
sobre on, upon, over; about; **a sobre** above
sobre (m.) envelope
sobretot above all
societat (f.) society
sol (m.) sun
sol/-a alone
solter/-a single, unmarried
somni (m.) dream

son (f.) sleep, sleepiness; **tenir* son** to be/feel sleepy
sopa (f.) soup
sopar to have dinner/evening meal; (m.) dinner, evening meal
soroll (m.) noise
sorprendre to surprise
sorprès/-esa surprised
sorpresa (f.) surprise
sort (f.) (good) luck; **per sort** luckily
sortida (f.) way out, exit, departure
sortir* to leave, to go out, to appear
sostre (m.) ceiling
(a) sota beneath, below; **a sota (de)** underneath, under
sou (m.) salary, wage
sovint often
suc (m.) juice
sucre (m.) sugar
sud (m.) south
suís/-ïssa Swiss
superior higher, superior, better
supermercat (m.) supermarket

tabac (m.) tobacco
taca (f.) stain
tacar to stain
tall (m.) slice, piece
talla (f.) size
tallat (m.) coffee with a dash of milk
taller (m.) workshop
també also, as well, too
tampoc neither
tan so, as (U7)
tancar to close

tancat/-da closed

tant/-a so much (U15); (pl.), so many; **de tant en tant** every now and then; **i tant!** definitely!

tard late

tarda (f.) afternoon

tardar to delay, to take time

targeta (f.) card

tarifa (f.) tariff

taronja (f.) orange

taula (f.) table

taulell (m.) counter

tauleta (f.) bedside table

te (m.) tea

teatre (m.) theatre, drama

tema (m.) subject

tempesta (f.) storm

temporada (f.) season

temps (m.) time; weather

tenir* to have; **tenir … anys** to be … (years old); **tenir lloc** to happen, to take place

tenyit/-da dyed

termini (m.) end, term, time limit

terra (m.) floor

terra (f.) earth, land

terrassa (f.) large balcony area, open veranda

texans (m. pl.) jeans

tia (f.) aunt

tímid/-a shy, timid

tipus (m.) type, kind

tiquet (m.) ticket

tirar to throw; to shoot; to pull; to push; **tirar fotos** to take photos

tocar to touch; to be one's turn; to play (instrument)

tomàquet (m.)/**tomata** (f.) tomato

tombar to turn

tònica (f.) tonic (water)

tonyina (f.) tuna

tornada (f.) return, journey back

tornar to return, to come back; to give back; **tornar a** + inf. to … again

torrada (f.) toast

tot/-a all

tot everything; completely; **tot i que** although; **tot plegat** all together; **tot seguit** next, immediately afterwards; **i tot** even

tothom everybody

tots dos/totes dues both

tovalló (m.) serviette, napkin

tovallola (f.) towel

tractar-se to be about, to involve

tramuntana (f.) northerly wind

tramvia (m.) tram

tranquil·litzar-se to calm down

transferència (f.) transfer

trànsit (m.) traffic

travessar to cross

treball (m.) work

treballador/-a (m./f.) worker

treballar to work; to knead

tren (m.) train

trencar to break

treure* to remove, to take off, to take out

trimestre (m.) term

trist/-a sad

trobada (f.) meeting

trobar to find
trobar-se to meet; to feel, to be
trompeta (f.) trumpet
tronar to thunder
trucar to call, to knock; to telephone
truita (f.) omelette

ui! oh!
ull (m.) eye
ulleres (f. pl.) glasses
últim/-a last
untar to spread
útil useful, usable
utilitzar to use

vaca (f.) cow
vacances (f. pl.) holidays
vainilla (f.) vanilla
vaixell (m.) ship
valent/-a brave
valer* to be worth, to cost
valor (m.) value
valorar to value
valuós/-osa valuable
vedella (f.) calf, veal, beef
vegada (f.) time; **una vegada** once
veí/-ïna (m./f.) neighbour
vell/-a old
venda (f.) sale, selling
vendre* to sell
venir* to come; **venir de gust** to appeal > to feel like, to fancy; **l'any que ve** next year
vent (m.) wind
ventre (m.) stomach
verd/-a green, unripe

verdureria (f.) greengrocer's (shop)
verdures (f. pl.) (green) vegetables
veritat (f.) truth
vermell/-a red
vespre (m.) evening
vessar to spill
vestir to dress; **vestir-se** to dress, to get dressed
vestit (m.) dress
veure* to see; **a veure** let's see
vi (m.) wine
via (f.) line, way
vianant (m./f.) pedestrian
viatge (m.) journey, trip
viatjar to travel
vida (f.) life
vidre (m.) (pane of) glass, window
vinagre (m.) vinegar
vinent next
visita (f.) visit
vista (f.) view
viure* to live
voler* to want; **voler dir** to mean
volt (m.) walk, ride
volta (f.) stroll
(al) voltant (de) around
voltar to go around
(a la) vora (de) nearby, near (to), close (to)

xai (m.) lamb
xerrar to chat
xicot/-a (m./f.) boy/girl; boyfriend/girlfriend
xocolata (f.) chocolate

English–Catalan vocabulary

This list is devised as a selective, ready means of access, via English, to the basic vocabulary related to the topic areas of the course. It will not serve as a substitute for a dictionary or even for a reliable phrase-book: see **Taking it further**. See also the preliminary remarks to the Catalan–English vocabulary.

a, an **un/una**
(to be) able to **poder***
(to be) about to **estar* a punt de**
above **sobre, damunt (de)**
abroad **a l'estranger** *(m.)*
to accompany **acompanyar**
according to **segons**
account **compte** *(m.)*
across **a través de**
address **adreça** *(f.)*
advice **consell** *(m.)*
(to be) afraid (of) **tenir* por (de)**
after **després de**
afternoon **tarda** *(f.)*
afterwards **després, llavors**
again **de nou, un altre cop;**
  > **tornar a**; *never again* **mai més**
age **edat** *(f.)*
ago **fa** *(U10)*
to agree **estar* d'acord**; *agreed* **d'acord, entesos**
airport **aeroport** *(m.)*
all **tot/-a**
to allow **permetre, deixar**
almost **gairebé**
alone **sol/-a**

along **per, al llarg de**
already **ja**
also **també**
although **encara que**
always **sempre**
among **entre**
amount **quantitat** *(f.)*
amusing **divertit/-da**
and **i**
angry **enfadat/-da**
another **un/-a altre/-a**
answer **resposta** *(f.); to answer* **respondre, contestar**
any **algun/-a;** (question or negative), **gens (de), cap** *(U6)*
anyone **algú;** (after negative) **ningú**
apartment **apartament** *(m.),* **pis** *(m.)*
appointment **cita** *(f.)*
arm **braç** *(m.)*
arrival **arribada** *(f.)*
as **com; tan;** *as far as* **fins a;** *as much ... as* **tant/-a ... com;** *as soon as* **així que**
to ask **preguntar;** *to ask for,* **demanar**

at **a**; at all (with negative) **gens**
at least **almenys**
to attend **assistir**
aunt **tia** (f.)
away **(a) fora**; to go away
  marxar, anar-se'n*

back **esquena** (f.)
bad **dolent/-a, mal/-a**
bag **bossa** (f.)
baker **forner** (m.)
bank **banc** (m.)
bathroom **bany** (m.)
to be **ser***, **estar*** (U5, 12, 16)
beach **platja** (f.)
because **perquè**
bed **llit** (m.)
beer **cervesa** (f.)
before **abans; abans de/que**
to begin **començar**
behind **darrere (de)**
to believe **creure***
better, best **millor**
between **entre**
big **gran; gros/-sa**
bill **compte** (m.), **factura** (f.)
birthday **aniversari** (m.)
(a) bit **una mica**
black **negre/-a**
blouse **brusa** (f.)
blue **blau/-va**
boat **barca** (f.), **vaixell** (m.)
body **cos** (m.)
to boil **bullir**
book **llibre** (m.)
to book **reservar**
to be born **néixer***
both **ambdós/dues**

bottle **ampolla** (f.)
bottom **fons** (m.)
box **caixa** (f.), **capsa** (f.)
boy **noi** (m.); little boy **nen** (m.)
bread **pa** (m.)
to break **trencar**
breakfast **esmorzar** (m.)
bricklayer **paleta** (m./f.)
bridge **pont** (m.)
to bring **portar, dur***
brother **germà** (m.)
brother-in-law **cunyat** (m.)
brown **marró**
to build **construir**
building **edifici** (m.)
bus **autobús** (m.)
business **comerç** (m.), **negoci** (m.)
but **però**
butcher **carnisser/-a** (m./f.)
to buy **comprar**
by **per, de; amb** (transport)

café **cafeteria** (f.)
to call **cridar**; to be called **dir-se***
camera **màquina (fotogràfica)**
  (f.)
can (to be able) **poder***
capital (city) **capital** (f.)
car **cotxe** (m.)
car park **aparcament** (m.),
  pàrquing (m.)
card **carnet** (m.), **targeta** (f.)
to carry **portar, dur***; to carry on
  seguir
castle **castell** (m.)
to catch **agafar**
cathedral **catedral** (f.)
ceiling **sostre** (m.)

cent **cèntim** (m.)
chair **cadira** (f.)
champagne **xampany** (m.)
change **canvi** (m.)
to change **canviar**
to charge **cobrar**
to chat **xerrar**
cheap **barat/-a, econòmic/-a**
cheerful **alegre/-a**
chemist's shop **farmàcia** (f.)
cheque **taló** (m.)
chicken **pollastre** (m.)
children **nens** (m. pl.); (sons and
  daughters) **fills** (m. pl.)
to choose **escollir, triar**
Christmas **Nadal** (m.)
church **església** (f.)
cinema **cine(ma)** (m.)
city **ciutat** (f.)
class, classroom **classe** (f.)
clean **net/-a**
to clean **netejar**
clear **clar/-a**
clerk **empleat/-da** (m./f.),
  dependent/-a (m./f.)
climate **clima** (m.)
clock **rellotge** (m.)
to close **tancar**
clothes **roba** (f.)
cloud **núvol** (m.)
coast **costa** (f.)
coffee **cafè** (m.)
cold **fred/-a**; to be/feel cold **tenir***
  fred; (weather), **fer*** fred
to come **venir***; to come in
  entrar; to come out, **sortir***
computer **ordinador** (m.)
to continue **seguir, continuar**

cool **fresc/-a**
(street) corner **cantonada** (f.)
to cost **valer*, costar**
cotton **cotó** (m.)
to count **comptar**
country **país** (m.)
couple (things) **parell** (m.);
  (people) **parella** (f.)
cousin **cosí/-na** (m./f.)
to cross **travessar**
cup **tassa** (f.)
cupboard **armari** (m.)
curtain **cortina** (f.)
customer **client/-a** (m./f.)
to cut **tallar**

dangerous **perillós/-osa**
dark **fosc/-a**; (hair/skin) **morè/**
  -ena
date **data** (f.)
day **dia** (m.); next day
  endemà (m.)
to decide **decidir**
delay **retard** (m.)
to be delighted **alegrar-se**
to deliver **distribuir**
to deny **negar**
to depart **partir, marxar,**
  anar-se'n*
departure **sortida** (f.)
to depend (on) **dependre (de)**
to deposit **dipositar**
detail **detall** (m.)
to die **morir**
difficult **difícil**
to dine **dinar**
dining room **menjador** (m.)
direction **direcció** (f.)

dirty **brut/-a**
disagreeable **antipàtic/-a**
discount **descompte** (m.)
to discuss **discutir, debatre**
dish **plat** (m.)
district **barri** (m.)
to do **fer***
doctor **metge/-essa** (m./f.)
dog **gos** (m.)
door **porta** (f.)
double **doble**
doubt **dubte** (m.); no doubt **sens dubte**
down **avall**
dozen **dotzena** (f.)
drawer **calaix** (m.)
to dress **vestir**; to get dressed **vestir-se**
drink **beguda** (f.)
to drink **beure***
dry **sec/-a**
to dry **eixugar; assecar**
during **durant**

each **cada**
ear **orella** (f.)
early **aviat, d'hora**
to earn **guanyar, cobrar**
easy **fàcil**
to eat **menjar**
egg **ou** (m.)
empty **buit/-da**
end **fi** (f.), **final** (m.), **cap** (m.)
to enjoy oneself **divertir-se**
enough **prou, bastant**
to enter **entrar** (a)
entrance **entrada** (f.)
envelope **sobre** (m.)

even **fins i tot**
evening **vespre** (m.)
ever **mai, alguna vegada**
every **cada; tots/-es**
everybody/everyone **tothom**
everything **tot, tot el que**
exactly (time) **en punt**
to exchange **canviar**
to excuse **perdonar**
exercise **exercici** (m.)
exhibition **exposició** (f.)
expense **despesa** (f.)
expensive **car/-a**
to explain **explicar**
eye **ull** (m.)

fact **fet** (m.); in fact, **de fet**
factory **fàbrica** (f.)
fair **just/-a**; (hair, etc.) **ros/-sa**
to fall **caure***
family **família** (f.)
famous **famós/-osa**
far, far away **lluny**; as far as **fins a**
farm(house) **mas** (m.), **masia** (f.), **casa de pagès** (f.)
farmer **pagès** (m.), **agricultor** (m.)
fast **ràpid/-a**
fat **gras/-sa**
father **pare** (m.)
to fear **tenir* por de**
festival **festa** (f.)
to fetch **anar* a buscar**
fever **febre** (f.)
few **pocs/-ques**; a few **uns/-es quants/-es**
fiancé/e **promès/-esa** (m./f.)
field **camp** (m.); **prat** (m.)

finally **per fi**
to find **trobar**
finger **dit** (m.)
to finish **acabar; enllestir;** (work)
  plegar
firm **ferm/-a;** (company)
  empresa (f.)
first **primer/-a**
fish **peix** (m.)
flavour **gust** (m.)
floor **terra** (m.)
flu **grip** (f.)
fog **boira** (f.)
to follow **seguir**
food **menjar** (m.)
foot **peu** (m.)
football **futbol** (m.); football
  ground **camp** (m.) **de futbol**
for **per, per a** (U9)
foreign(er) **estranger/-a**
to forget **oblidar, descuidar-se**
  (de)
fork **forquilla** (f.)
fortnight **quinzena** (f.)
free **lliure;** (no charge) **gratuït/-a**
French **francès/-esa**
fresh **fresc/-a; natural**
friend **amic/-ga** (m./f.)
from **de, des de**
in front (of) **davant (de)**
frontier **frontera** (f.)
fruit **fruita** (f.)
full **ple/-na**
fun(ny) **divertit/-da**
furniture **mobles** (m. pl.)

game **joc** (m.), **partit** (m.)
garage **garatge** (m.)
garden **jardí** (m.)

gentleman **senyor** (m.)
to get off/out of (vehicle) **baixar**
  de; to get on (vehicle), **pujar a;**
  to get up **llevar-se, aixecar-se**
girl **noia** (f.); little girl **nena** (f.)
to give **donar;** (as present),
  regalar; to give back **tornar**
glass (material) **vidre** (m.); **got**
  (m.), **vas** (m.); (with stem)
  copa (f.); (spectacles) **ulleres**
  (f. pl.)
to go **anar*;** to go away/off
  anar-se'n*; to go back **tornar;**
  to go down **baixar;** to go in(to)
  entrar a; to go out **sortir*;** to go
  up **pujar;** to go up to (approach)
  acostar-se a
gold **or** (m.)
good **bo(n)/-a** (U4); good
  morning **bon dia**
goodbye **adéu;** to say goodbye to
  acomiadar-se de
government **govern** (m.)
grandfather/mother **avi/àvia**
  (m./f.)
grandson/daughter **nét/-a** (m./f.)
to be grateful for **agrair**
great **gran**
green **verd/-a**
to greet **saludar**
grey **gris/-a**
ground **terra** (m.)
to grow **créixer**
guide **guia** (m./f.)
guidebook **guia** (f.)

hair **cabell** (m.), **pèl** (m.)
half **meitat** (f.); **mig/-tja**
ham **pernil** (m.)

hammer **martell** *(m.)*
hand **mà** *(f.), by hand* **a mà**
to hang **penjar**
happy **content/-a; feliç**
hard **dur/-a; difícil**
to harm **perjudicar**
hat **barret** *(m.)*
to have **tenir***; *(auxiliary)* **haver***;
  to have just **acabar de**; *to have*
  left > **quedar** *(U6); to have to,*
  must, **haver* de** *(U14)*
head **cap** *(m.)*
headache **mal de cap** *(m.)*
health **salut** *(f.)*
to hear **sentir**
heart **cor** *(m.)*
heat **calor** *(f.)*
to heat (up) **escalfar**
heating **calefacció** *(f.)*
height **alçada** *(f.)*
hello **hola**; *(on phone)* **digui?**
help **ajuda** *(f.)*
to help **ajudar**
here **aquí**; *here is* **aquí tens**; *here*
  (you are) **té, tingui**
to hide **amagar**
high **alt/-a**
hire charge **lloguer** *(m.)*
to hire **llogar**
history **història** *(f.)*
to hit **pegar**
to (take) hold (of) **agafar**; *to hold*
  (party, etc.) **celebrar**
hole **forat** *(m.)*
holidays **vacances** *(f. pl.)*
home **casa** *(f.); at home* **a casa**
hot **calent/-a**; *to be/ feel hot;*
  tenir* calor; *to be hot (weather),*
  fer* calor

hour **hora** *(f.)*
house **casa** *(f.)*
how **com**; *how ...!* **que ...!**; *how*
  much **quant/-a**; *how many,*
  quants/-es
however **però**
hunger **gana** *(f.)*
to be hungry **tenir* gana**
hurry **pressa** *(f.); to be in a hurry,*
  tenir*/portar pressa; *hurry up!*
  apa!, au!, corre!, afanya't
husband **marit** *(m.)*

ice cream **gelat** *(m.)*
if **si**
ill **malalt/-a**
immediately **de seguida, tot**
  seguit
to improve **millorar**
in **a, en**; *(transport),* **amb**
in front of **(al) davant (de)**
in this/that way **així**
to injure **ferir**
inside **(a) dins/dintre (de)**; *inside*
  out **al revés**
instead of **en comptes de**
to introduce (people) **presentar**
to invite **invitar, convidar**
iron **ferro** *(m.); (smoothing)*
  planxa *(f.)*
to iron **planxar**

jacket **jaqueta** *(f.),* **americana** *(f.)*
jeans **texans** *(m. pl.)*
journey **viatge** *(m.)*
juice **suc** *(m.)*
to jump **saltar**
just (only) **només**; *to have just*
  acabar de

to keep **guardar; quedar-se;** *to
keep quiet* **callar;** *to keep
…-ing,* **anar*/seguir/continuar** +
gerund (U5)

key **clau** *(f.)*
to kill **matar**
kilo(gram) **quilo(gram)** *(m.)*
kilometre **quilòmetre** *(m.)*
kind (sort/type) **mena** *(f.),*
tipus *(m.)*
kind **amable**
king **rei** *(m.)*
kitchen **cuina** *(f.)*
knife **ganivet** *(m.)*
to know **saber*, conèixer***

lady **senyora** *(f.)*
language **llengua** *(f.),*
idioma *(m.)*
last **últim/-a, darrer/-a**
to last **durar**
late **tard; tardà/-ana;** … *later al
cap de* …; *to be late* **fer* tard,
arribar amb retard**
latest **últim/-a, darrer/-a**
lavatory **WC** *(m.),* **lavabo** *(m.)*
to lead **conduir, portar**
leaf **fulla** *(f.); (paper)* **full** *(m.)*
to learn **aprendre***
leather **pell** *(f.),* **cuir** *(m.)*
to leave **partir, sortir*, marxar,
anar-se'n*; deixar**
left **esquerre/-a;** *on the left* **a
l'esquerra/ a mà esquerra**
to have left > **quedar** *(U6); to be
left over* **sobrar**
leg **cama** *(f.)*

to lend **deixar**
less **menys;** *less than* **menys de**
lesson **lliçó** *(f.),* **classe** *(f.)*
to let (allow) **deixar, permetre**
letter **carta** *(f.)*
library **biblioteca** *(f.)*
lift **ascensor** *(m.)*
light **llum** *(f.); (lamp)* **llum** *(m.)*
light **lleuger/-a**
like **com;** *like this/that* **així**
to like > **agradar** *(U6)*
likeable **simpàtic/-a**
line **línia** *(f.)*
to listen (to) **escoltar**
little **petit/-a;** *(quantity)* **poc/-a;**
a little **una mica**
to live **viure***
lively **viu/-va, animat/-da**
long **llarg/-a**
to look (at) **mirar;** *to look for*
buscar; *to look like* **semblar**
to lose **perdre**
a lot **molt; molt/-a** *(de)*
to love **estimar**
luck **sort** *(f.)*
luggage **equipatge** *(m.)*
lunch **dinar** *(m.); to have lunch*
dinar

machine **màquina** *(f.)*
magazine **revista** *(f.)*
majority **majoria** *(f.)*
to make **fer***
man **home** *(m.)*
manager **director** *(m.),*
gerent *(m.)*
many **molts/-es**
market **mercat** *(m.)*

married **casat/-da**
match **partit** *(m.)*; (ignition)
  llumí *(m.)*
matter **qüestió** *(f.),*
  assumpte *(m.)*
to matter **importar, tenir***
  importància; *it doesn't matter*
  no importa, no hi fa res
mayor **alcalde** *(m.)*
meal **àpat** *(m.)*
to mean **voler* dir**; *(intend)*
  voler*, pensar
means **mitjà** *(m.)*
meat **carn** *(f.)*
to meet **trobar, trobar-se; reunir-**
  se; conèixer*
meeting **reunió** *(f.)*
to mend **arreglar, adobar**
midday **migdia** *(m.)*
middle **mig** *(m.),* **centre** *(m.)*
mile **milla** *(f.)*
minute **minut** *(m.)*
mirror **mirall** *(m.)*
Miss **senyoreta** *(f.)*
to miss **perdre**
mist **boira** *(f.)*
to mix **barrejar**
money **diners** *(m. pl.)*
month **mes** *(m.)*
mood **humor** *(m.),* good/bad
  mood **bon/mal humor**
more **més**
morning **matí** *(m.);* early morning
  matinada *(f.);* good morning
  bon dia
most **més;** **majoria** *(f.),* **gairebé**
  tots/-es; > **-íssim/-a** (suffix) (U6)
mother **mare** *(f.)*

motorbike **moto** *(f.)*
motorway **autopista** *(f.)*
mountain **muntanya** *(f.)*
mouth **boca** *(f.)*
to move **moure**
much **molt/-a**
museum **museu** *(m.)*
mushroom **bolet** *(m.)*
must **haver* de** (U14);
  (probability), **deure*** (U9)

name **nom** *(m.);* (family) **cognom**
  (m.)
narrow **estret/-a**
near (to) **(a) prop (de), (a la)**
  vora (de)
neck **coll** *(m.)*
to need **necessitar;** > **caldre***
  (U15); **fer* falta**
neighbour **veí/-ïna** *(m./f.)*
neighbourhood **barri** *(m.)*
neither **tampoc; ni**
nephew **nebot** *(m.)*
nervous **nerviós/-osa**
never **(no) ... mai**
new **nou/-va**
news **notícies** *(f. pl.)*
newspaper **diari** *(m.)*
next **després, llavors;**
  proper/-a, pròxim/-a;
  entrant, vinent
next day **endemà** *(m.)*
nice **simpàtic/-a, amable,**
  agradable; bonic/-a, maco/-a
niece **neboda** *(f.)*
night **nit** *(f.)*
nil **zero**
no **no**

nobody/no one **ningú**

noise **soroll** (m.)

none (at all) **no ... gens; no ... cap**
(U6)

nose **nas** (m.)

not **no**; *not at all* **no ... gens**; *not very (much)* **no ... gaire**

notebook **llibreta** (f.)

nothing **(no) ... res**

notice **avís** (m.)

to notice **fixar-se en**

to notify **avisar**

now **ara**; *right now* **ara mateix**

number **número** (m.); *(quantity)*
nombre (m.)

occasionally **de tant en tant**

of **de**

offer **oferir**

office **despatx** (m.), **oficina** (f.)

often **sovint**

oil **oli** (m.)

old **vell/-a; antic/-ga;** *to be ...
years old* **tenir*... anys**

on **a, en; sobre, damunt;**
on(wards) **endavant;** *on the
other hand* **en canvi;** *on the
contrary* **al contrari**

once **una vegada, un cop**

onion **ceba** (f.)

only **només, únic/-a**

open **obert/-a**

to open **obrir***

opposite **contrari/-ària;** *(just)*
davant de

or **o**

order **ordre** (m.); *in order to* **per +
infinitive**

to order **demanar, encarregar;
manar**

to organize **organitzar, muntar;
arreglar**

other **altre/-a**

ought (to) **haver* de** (U14)

out(side) **(a) fora (de)**

over **(per) damunt (de);**
(quantity) **més de**

overcoat **abric** (m.)

own **propi/-òpia**

to own **posseir**

owner **propietari/-ària** (m./f.)

to pack (bag, case) **fer* la maleta**

packet **paquet** (m.)

to paint **pintar**

painting **pintura** (f.)

paper **paper** (m.)

parcel **paquet** (m.)

parents **pares** (m. pl)

to park **aparcar, estacionar**

party **festa** (f.)

to pass **passar;** *(exam)* **aprovar**

passport **passaport** (m.)

path **camí** (m.)

to pay (for) **pagar;** *to be paid*
cobrar

peaceful **tranquil/-l.la**

peach **préssec** (m.)

(ball-point) pen **bolígraf** (m.),
boli (m.)

pencil **llapis** (m.)

people **gent** (f.), **persones** (f.pl.)

perhaps **potser**

permission **permís** (m.)

person **persona** (f.)

petrol **benzina** (f.), **gasolina** (f.)

photo(graph) **foto(grafia)** *(f.)*
picture **quadro** *(m.),* **quadre** *(m.)*
pie **pastís** *(m.)*
piece **tros** *(m.);* **peça** *(f.)*
pity **llàstima** *(f.)*
place **lloc** *(m.)*
plan **projecte** *(m.)*
to play **jugar**; *(instrument)* **tocar**
pleasant **agradable**
please **si us plau/sisplau, per
favor**
pleased **content/-a**
pleasure **gust** *(m.),* **plaer** *(m.)*
pocket **butxaca** *(f.)*
police **policia** *(f.); policeman/
woman* **policia** *(m./f.); police
station* **comissaria** *(f.)*
poor **pobre/-a**
post **correu** *(m.); post box* **bústia**
(f.); post office **(oficina de)
correus**
to post **portar a correus, tirar a
la bústia**
postcard **postal** *(f.)*
potato **patata** *(f.)*
pound (sterling) **lliura** *(f.)* **esterlina**
to prefer **estimar-se més, preferir**
present **regal** *(m.)*
pretty **bonic/-a**
price **preu** *(m.)*
prize **premi** *(m.)*
pullover **jersei** *(m.)*
pupil **alumne/-a** *(m./f.)*
to push **empènyer**
to put **posar**; *to put on* *(light)*
encendre; *(clothes)* **posar-se**; *to
put back* **tornar**; *to put in* **tirar,
ficar**

quarter **quart** *(m.)*
question **pregunta** *(f.); (matter,
point),* **qüestió** *(f.)*
quick **ràpid/-a**
*quiet to be(come) quiet, to keep
quiet* **callar**

railway **ferrocarril** *(m.)*
rain **pluja** *(f.)*
to rain **ploure***
rather **més aviat**
to reach (arrive) **arribar**
to read **llegir**
ready **llest/-a, preparat/-da**
to realize **adonar-se (de)**
really **de debò**
reason **raó** *(f.);* **motiu** *(m.)*
to receive **rebre**
to recognize **conèixer***,
reconèixer
record **disc** *(m.)*
red **vermell/-a, roig/-ja**; *(wine)*
negre/-a
to refuse to **negar-se a**
relative **parent/-a** *(m./f.)*
to remember **recordar(-se de)**
to remind **recordar**
reply **resposta** *(f.)*
to reply **respondre, contestar**
to rest **descansar**
result **resultat** *(m.)*
to return **tornar**
rice **arròs** *(m.)*
rich **ric/-a**
right **dret** *(m.);* **dret/-a**; *on the
right(-hand side)* **a la/mà dreta**;
to be (all) right **estar*** **bé**; *to be
right* **tenir*** **raó**

road **carretera** *(f.)*
room **habitació** *(f.)*, **sala** *(f.)*
rubbish **escombraries** *(f. pl.)*
to run **córrer***

sad **trist/-a**
salary **sou** *(m.)*
same **mateix/-a; igual**
sandwich **entrepà** *(m.)*
to save **salvar; estalviar**
savings bank **caixa** *(f.)* **d'estalvis**
to say **dir***
school **escola** *(f.)*, **col·legi** *(m.)*
sea **mar** *(m./f.)*
seaside **platja** *(f.)*
secretary **secretari/-ària** *(m./f.)*
to see **veure***
to seem **semblar**
to sell **vendre***
to send **enviar, trametre**
serious **greu; seriós/-osa**
several **diversos/-es; uns/-es quants/-es**
shade **ombra** *(f.)*
to shave **afaitar(-se)**
sheet **llençol** *(m.)*
to shine **brillar**
ship **vaixell** *(m.)*
shirt **camisa** *(f.)*
shoe **sabata** *(f.)*
shop **botiga** *(f.)*
shopping **compra** *(f.)*; to go shopping **anar* a comprar**
short **curt/-a**
to show **ensenyar**
to shut **tancar**; to shut up **callar**
silk **seda** *(f.)*
silly **ximple/-a**

simple **senzill/-a**
since (reason) **com que, ja que**; (time) **des de/que**
to sing **cantar**
single **sol/-a**; (unmarried) **solter/-a**
to sit (down) **seure***
sitting (seated) **assegut/-da**
size **mida** *(f.)*, **talla** *(f.)*
skin **pell** *(f.)*
skirt **faldilla** *(f.)*
to sleep **dormir**
to be/feel sleepy **tenir* son**
slow **lent/-a**
small **petit/-a; baix/-a**
to smile **somriure**
to smoke **fumar**
(afternoon) snack **berenar** *(m.)*
snow **neu** *(f.)*
to snow **nevar**
so **així; tan**; so much **tant/-a**; so many **tants/-es**
soap **sabó** *(m.)*
sock **mitjó** *(m.)*
some **uns/-es; alguns/-es**
somebody, someone **algú**
something **(alg)una cosa**
sometimes **a/de vegades**
son **fill** *(m.)*
song **cançó** *(f.)*
soon **aviat**
to be sorry **sentir; > saber* greu**
sort **mena** *(f.)*
soup **sopa** *(f.)*
to speak **parlar**
to spend **despendre, gastar(-se)**; (time) **passar**
spoon **cullera** *(f.)*

square **plaça** *(f.)*
stairs **escala** *(f.)*
stamp **segell** *(m.)*
station **estació** *(f.)*
to stay **estar(-se)*, quedar(-se)**
still **encara**
stocking **mitja** *(f.)*
stone **pedra** *(f.)*
stop **parada** *(f.)*
to stop **parar**
storey **pis** *(m.),* **planta** *(f.)*
straight **dret/-a, recte/-a**; *straight away* **de seguida**
strange **estrany/-a**
stranger **foraster/-a** *(m./f.)*
street **carrer** *(m.)*
to stroll **passejar(-se)**
strong **fort/-a**
to study **estudiar**
to succeed **tenir* èxit**
to suffer **patir**
suitcase **maleta** *(f.)*
sun **sol** *(m.);* *to be sunny* **fer* sol**
supermarket **supermercat** *(m.)*
supper **sopar** *(m.)*
sure **segur/-a**
surname **cognom** *(m.)*
surprise **sorpresa** *(f.);* *to surprise* **sorprendre**
sweater **suèter** *(m.),* **jersei** *(m.)*
to sweep **escombrar**
sweet **dolç/-a**; *(dessert)* **postres** *(f. pl.)*

table **taula** *(f.)*
tablet **pastilla** *(f.)*
to take **prendre*, agafar; portar**

to take away **endur-se*, emportar-se**; *to take back* **tornar**; *to take off* (clothes) **treure's***; *to take out* (off, from, etc.: to remove) **treure***
to talk **parlar**
tank **dipòsit** *(m.)*
to taste **tastar**
tax **impost** *(m.)*
tea **te** *(m.)*
teacher **professor/-a** *(m./f.)*
telephone **telèfon** *(m.)*
to (tele)phone **telefonar, trucar**
thank you, thanks **gràcies**
to thank **agrair**
that (conjunction) **que;** (pronoun) **això, allò**
theatre **teatre** *(m.)*
then **aleshores, llavors; doncs**
there **allí;** *there is/are* **hi ha**
thick **espès/-essa, gruixut/-da**
thief **lladre** *(m./f.)*
thin **prim/-a**
thing **cosa** *(f.)*
to think **pensar; creure*; > semblar** *(U6)*
to be thirsty **tenir* set**
this (pronoun) **això**
throat **coll** *(m.)*
through **per, a través de**
to throw **tirar, llançar;** *to throw away* **llençar**
ticket **bitllet** *(m.);* *(admission)* **entrada** *(f.)*
time **temps** *(m.);* **vegada** *(f.),* **cop** *(m.);* **hora** *(f.);* *what time is it?* **quina hora és?** *(U3)*
tip **propina** *(f.)*

tired **cansat/-da**
to **a, cap a**
tobacco **tabac** *(m.)*
tobacconist's (shop) **estanc** *(m.)*
today **avui**
together **junt/-a**
tomato **tomàquet** *(m.)*, **tomata**
  (f.)
tomorrow **demà**; *day after*
  tomorrow **demà passat**
too (also) **també**; *too (much)/too*
  many **massa**
tool **eina** *(f.)*
tooth **dent** *(f.)*, *(molar)*, **queixal**
  (m.)
top **capdamunt** *(m.)*; *on top of*
  damunt (de); *at the top* **a dalt**
to touch **tocar**
tourist **turista** *(m./f.)*
towards **cap a**
towel **tovallola** *(f.)*
tower **torre** *(f.)*
town **ciutat** *(f.)*, *(small)* **poble** *(m.)*
town hall **ajuntament** *(m.)*
traffic lights **semàfor** *(m.)*
train **tren** *(m.)*
to travel **viatjar**
tree **arbre** *(m.)*
trousers **pantalons** *(m. pl.)*
true **cert/-a**; *(és)* **veritat**
to trust **fiar-se (de)**
truth **veritat** *(f.)*
to try **provar**; *to try to* **provar**
  de, intentar de; *to try on*
  emprovar-se
to turn **tombar, girar**
twice **dos cops, dues vegades**

ugly **lleig/-tja**
umbrella **paraigua** *(m.)*
uncle **oncle** *(m.)*
under (a) **sota (de), davall (de)**
underground **metro** *(m.)*
to understand **comprendre,**
  entendre
unless **si no**
until **fins (a), fins que**
up **amunt**
to use **emprar, utilitzar, fer***
  servir
useful **útil**

very **molt**; > **-íssim/-a** *(suffix)*;
  not very **no ... gaire**
view **vista** *(f.)*
village **poble** *(m.)*
visit **visita** *(f.)*
to visit **visitar**
voice **veu** *(f.)*

to wait (for) **esperar**
waiter **cambrer/-a** *(m./f.)*
to wake up **despertar-se**
to walk **caminar, anar* a peu**
wall **paret** *(f.)*
wallet **cartera** *(f.)*
to want **voler***; **tenir ganes de**
to wash **rentar(-se)**
washing machine **rentadora** *(f.)*
watch **rellotge** *(m.)*
to watch **mirar**
water **aigua** *(f.)*
way **camí** *(m.)*; *(manner)*
  manera *(f.)*
weak **dèbil**; **fluix/-a**

to wear **portar, dur***
weather **temps** *(m.)*
week **setmana** *(f.)*
weekend **cap de setmana** *(m.)*
to weigh **pesar**
weight **pes** *(m.)*
well **bé; doncs**
wet **mullat/-da**
what? **què?; quin/-a; el que**
wheel **roda** *(f.)*
when **quan**
where **on, a on**
whether **si**
which **que**; *which?* **quin/-a?**
while **mentre**
white **blanc/-a**
who? **qui?**
whole **tot/-a; sencer/-a**
why? **perquè?**
wide **ample/-a**
widow **vidu/vídua** *(m./f.)*
wife **dona** *(f.)*, **esposa** *(f.)*,
  muller *(f.)*
to win **guanyar**
wind **vent** *(m.)*
window **finestra** *(f.)*
wine **vi** *(m.)*
with **amb**
within **(a) dins (de)**
without **sense**
woman **dona** *(f.)*

to wonder **preguntar-se**
wood **fusta** *(f.)*; (forest) **bosc** *(m.)*
wool **llana** *(f.)*
word **paraula** *(f.)*
work **feina** *(f.)*, **treball** *(m.)*;
  obra *(f.)*
to work **treballar; funcionar**
workshop **taller** *(m.)*
world **món** *(m.)*
worried **preocupat/-da**
to worry **preocupar,**
  preocupar-se
worse **pitjor**
to be worth **valer***; *to be*
  worthwhile **valer* la pena**
to wrap (up) **embolicar**
to write **escriure***
to be wrong **equivocar-se**; *what*
  is wrong? **què passa?**

year **any** *(m.)*
yellow **groc/-ga**
yes **sí**
yesterday **ahir**; *day before*
  yesterday **abans-d'ahir**
yet **encara; ja** *(U7)*
young **jove**; *young lady*
  senyoreta *(f.)*; *young people*
  joventut *(f.)*, **joves** *(m. pl.)*;
  younger/youngest (brother/
  sister) **(més) petit/-a**

Index

Numbers refer to units (e.g. 13 = Unit 13); letters or symbols refer to Grammar or other sections (e.g. 9B = Unit 9, Grammar section B); RT = Reference tables.